Nc ild

Susan Hendrix

Table of Contents

In The Loving Memory of

Keith Hendrix

Introduction

Opening up is hard.

Especially for those who have dealt with nothing but toxicity in their early lives, opening up might usually seem like a trap. It becomes something you cannot believe in because you see so many people do it, only to regret it every time much further down the line of their lives.

Survivors learn to therapy themselves, talk themselves into calmer, more reasonable states of mind. Still, when it comes to narrating or what is their issue, they close off. It is as if by simply wanting to know more about them, the other individual is being too invasive and threatening.

Social life, social norms and relationships are very hard for abuse survivors, along with several many other things that someone who grew up in or was born in a relatively protected environment would find it hard to relate to. For the children who have learned to protect themselves from the very people who were supposed to do the protecting and efficient raising, develop a storyline that is worthy of knowing.

It is, in fact, quite important to know an abuse victim's story for many reasons. Firstly. The most obvious reason is, this kind of literature, regardless of the form of media, takes to the cautious reach to its audience, for example, discussion videos, skit videos, podcasts, books or blogs, help other abuse victims and survivors through their own lives.

Survivors continue to live certain parts of their life exactly as if they are still stuck in a circle of abuse. This is an odd characteristic survivors have despite the human capabilities of simply breaking a cycle of habit and, logically speaking, not being stuck in trauma-reliving activities or engagements anymore.

Not only does talking about, discussing and possibly even humorously but respectfully mocking one's abuse period in front of an audience gives one the courage to finally deal with or unpack their past, it enables the survivor themselves to help still existing victims in several ways.

My name is Susan Hendrix, and I am a survivor.

I bring to you this book, in the form of my autobiography for current victims and other survivors like me to help unpack our lives, step by step, event by event. We will do so not to merely and superficially narrate the story, but to process it slowly in our brains and put these painful and triggering memories, habits and coping mechanisms to rest.

I am a survivor of child abuse, which unfortunately included every form of abuse possible.

It is to be noted that this book may contain words that could trigger certain people, but are essential to the story itself since it all sadly makes up a large chunk of my story.

Despite the storyline peppered throughout with physical, sexual and emotional abuse, hopelessness and earth-shattering realisations, I stand here today, grateful and emotional over how far I have come today on my own.

I want others to learn from my life. Even though talking and writing about several aspects of my life was triggering, sad and brought about many undesired emotions that I felt like I could not narrate or even properly explain to anyone, I have pushed on trying to get every detail as accurate to my then-and-now state as possible.

Abuse is a fraudulent usage and exploitation of power that is intended to manipulate, hurt, harm or control another person or people. The mistreatment and exploitation can be emotional, verbal, physical, and sexual. Every type of abuse can cause the victim or survivor pain and psychological distress that may last up to several years, even sometimes entire lifetimes.

Abuse can leave mental wounds that are harder to heal and far more stubborn, long-lasting and affecting than bodily injuries, sometimes even ones caused during the abuse itself. Survivors of abuse may have extremely negative thoughts, feelings and outlooks on themselves, other people who might even mean good and their lives, even long after the abuse has ended. Some are psychologically conditioned to stay in a state of hurt and harm. In this case, survivors may continue to harm themselves to keep themselves in touch with the only familiar feeling that they have known their entire life; pain. This may continue to happen even many years after the abuse may have ended.

Survivors quite often experience anxiety, flashbacks, delusional thoughts, and trust issues. The traits of overthinking, self-reliance, introvertedness, and certain fears such as agoraphobia or necrophobia are common in people who have experienced abuse. In fact, they may continue to intensify to a crippling extent where such people need help with many everyday life things and issues. Abuse impacts a survivor's ability to find people to connect to, form healthy or standard relationships and find love, joy and happiness. Such people are reclusive, restless, very busy as if it were a means to stay away from disturbing memories or thoughts and are also very private.

However, these crippling effects during or after abuse do not have to be permanent.

Types of Abuse

There are many types of abuse. Forms of abuse include:

- Physical Abuse: When someone intentionally causes physical harm to another. This type could include patterns of behaviour. It also includes actions that are very specific, like poisoning that can cause illness or disability.

- Sexual Abuse: This form of abuse includes any form of sexual contact or advances made without consent. It may evolve into acts of sexual violence and can hence also leave physical harm and injuries that could last a very long time.
- Emotional/Psychological Abuse: This form of abuse includes a chronic pattern of manipulation to control another person. Forms of emotional abuse may include verbal attacks, humiliation, isolation, or threats. The abuser may tend to also use psychologically altering tactics. Such as gaslighting to make the victim doubt their sanity, memories and emotions.
- Financial Abuse: It is when someone uses their or the victim's financial assets to gain control over

them. They may take over one's bank account, assets or pretend to be the victim by stealing their identity to rack up debt to keep them bound to them forever. Giving away or taking one's property without permission and full manipulation also counts as abuse.

Abuse can occur within any kind of relationship, whether romantic, sexual, professional, familial, or merely social. It is also possible to occur between strangers, and sometimes unknowingly. However, this pattern of manipulation, verbal degradation and attempts at financial abuse tends to be rarer since people who once would have been considered easy targets are a lot more cautious and careful today. There are also many other people who may witness the attempts at abuse who would step in and confront the abuser before they got away with hurting and harming the victim.

Many current day survivors have been known to communicate the happenings and events during the abuse-dominated years of their lives. They do it to help them receive closure, which also helps them relieve themselves of coping mechanisms they may have developed to keep themselves away from pain, hurt and suffering they would experience they would be left with if they were to fully unpack the physical, emotional and psychological damage that took place over the years.

So, by opening up about their abuse, and their life story in general. Not only do victims help get the burden of their story off their chests and stop succumbing to hurtful mechanisms, but they also get to teach the world a valuable lesson.

These lessons of experience may be triggering, but are especially valuable to those similar to themselves; other abuse victims or survivors. The survivors can take away many lessons and better ideas, or simply relatability and the feeling of "not being alone" from these stories if not anything else. Meanwhile, current victims can get ideas or ways to either deal with the abuse and abuser or find ideas to run away from it and seek help.

The purpose of me narrating my story from the start is my acknowledgement of how many unfortunate people out there in the world may have similar lives to mine. Although I present no groundbreaking tactics on how to escape the pain, I hope my story lives on to inspire someone, give them hope and give them the courage to deal with what they are or have dealt with without breaking under the pain and damage.

In my story, I would also like to talk about a big chunk of first world countries' society that is seldom talked about enough. It is the prime product of capitalism, one aspect of society I had never seen before despite my hard life from the start, but ended up eventually witnessing for a short period that shook me up to the core.

And that is homelessness.

I got to experience temporary homelessness, and in those few days saw unspeaking things that have traumatised me probably as much as my years growing up in an abusive household did. The realisation of the extreme unfairness that is capitalist society stunned me.

I have also spent many youthful years in immense luxury. To me, those years of my youth seemed like all that I deserved after growing up in such a traumatic household that was my parents' house. I travelled frequently, owned several businesses, had the material luxury to the maximum and took several vacations a year. All without batting a lash at how many people in major cities such as San Diego, U.S. do not even have a roof to shelter them, or walls to separate them from the danger and harm of the outside world. It made me feel as if the homeless are left with no rights to exist as respectable, individual human beings. They are treated as livestock or worse.

And so, those few extremely traumatic and dense days weighed upon me even more than my painful upbringing did.

I am putting out my story in the form of my autobiography to raise awareness for victims and survivors of abuse, survivors of life-threatening diseases and the homeless who, unlike me, have no one to bail them off the streets and look after them.

I hope my story leaves a message for everyone to understand and see this pain and suffering through my eyes and perspective as I once did and continue to do every day of my life.

Chapter 1: Childhood Home and Early Life

We were one of the first families to move into the new neighbourhoods that comprised my childhood home. The estate that we moved on to was still in the progression of being built. The project was a big one.

I was four years old at the time, wide-eyed and naive to the world. The new estate excited little me as it looked big, grand, and above us. Now I suppose I barely even remember what could be a motion picture of that time. The house seemed so big. We were also excited. There were a lot of things for us to see. There were field farms or marshland all around us. We soon settled into the new house, completely unaware of the life on which we would embark.

Since I was one of many children, my memories have been haphazard and not appropriately sequenced.

The moving, the cold, the freezing weather, the outbursts of excitement among us children, and watching my parents busy a lot of the time paints a picture of a seemingly happy childhood. I suppose that would be a great place to start.

Much like the popular novel series, "A Series of Unfortunate Events" by Lemony Snicket, this storyline would only get about as much better as the Baudelaire childrens' lives did for almost all of my childhood.

I promise you the basic lessons and eye-opening witnessings come after, along with a period of luxurious indulgence that seldom occurs to people who have lived at such an extreme low among society's social strata. That period contrasting my obnoxiously traumatic childhood is the reason you, dear reader, are holding this book in your hands. The lesson too is yours to take.

Soon enough, we settled into the new estate. New neighbours streamed into the estate every few weeks until we had quite the lively neighbourhood as the months went by. There were families just like ours, with children around the ages as us.

We met Mrs Ricehouse and Mrs Hughes. They had children, so we would all play with them. My mum would soon become friends with the neighbours. We spent most of our time on the field nearby, playing with the other children in the neighbourhood. While at home, we were meek little creatures, shying away around the corners and constantly hiding from our parents. We were complete opposites on the streets. My siblings and I were very competitive with or against each other, and the neighbourhood children found us to be a delight.

We were all frightened of my dad. And the mum had no time for us because she was looking after so many. My father would pick on my eldest brother, Frankie; he was the one that got most of the hidings and beatings.

The rest of us were treated differently among ourselves. Frankie and I were the most unfortunate ones.

The house was cold. We would have to sleep through the bedframes, wrapped in our coats, as the bedsprings would cut into us at night. We had to wear the same furs that kept us warm at night during the day.

Franklin and George got into a lot of trouble. The farmer constantly chased them because they would try to steal potatoes and vegetables to bring home so that the family could have a hot meal every night. Our parents did barely anything to ensure we had food on the table at least once a day. My siblings and I grew up extremely familiar with hunger strikes from a young age. We would often have to go to bed very hungry. Despite this, my mum and dad always had enough money for the pub and cigarettes. Thank God we had meals in school because we would have been starving.

My mum would always be screaming at some child or the other, at least one of us, at any given time. Our dad would come home from work, and she would tell him if we had been in any trouble. It wouldn't take him minutes before he would start beating us up. It was hard growing up in a house that had eight children. We just played with each other and argued with each other. And you guarantee one of us would end up being beaten by my dad every day; however, it was usually either Frankie or me.

There's one distinct holiday season I remember. It was the first year of living in the new house. Christmas was fast approaching, and we were all excited to spend it in the new home. It was one of the best Christmases I can remember. We got some new clothes and would always only get new clothes on Christmas. We would have to wear whatever we could find and whatever would fit us.

The first Christmas was pretty magical. We sat down together and sang around the Christmas tree. And we were all excited, wondering what we would get for Christmas. We would get some presents from our parents, but the social services would drop off good gifts nine times out of ten.

I started school a little later and can remember my first day at school. I simply just cried and kept saying I didn't want to go, but my mum left me there. And by the end of a nice fulfilling day, I was pretty happy to go home. We would be in bed on school nights by seven o'clock. And if there were any noise from upstairs, my dad would come up angrily and tell us all to be quiet, which is very difficult when you had three kids in a bed. Each one tossed and turned and complained. Again, a little more than a few shrieks and squeaks, and someone would yet again end up getting a hiding.

I liked school a lot growing up, and I remember my first nativity play. I played a donkey's part and was simply overjoyed at my selection despite not getting a more significant role. I was so excited and happy with what I had just secured, but my mum could not be bothered, so no one noticed my excitement or happiness. I just went home once the play was over and told them what kind of play it was and how I had performed. Even then, no one took any notice of what had already happened.

One particular night, not long after Christmas, I had gotten a new little tea set for a present. I had been playing with it in the bedroom. A little while later, as any child are might, I spilt a little water from my teapot on the ground. After seven o'clock, my dad came up and screamed at me for the spilt water. I had hidden from him on top of the bed under the covers. My father came upstairs to get me, dragged me off the bed, and beat me so hard around the back of my head. He told me to get downstairs and find a cloth to wipe up the water. I remember getting to the top of the staircase. And I remember nothing else. Someone must have picked me up while I was unconscious. My top lip had gone through my teeth. Hence I had a gaping wound smack in the middle of my face.

And I had bruises all over me. I wasn't allowed to go to school until the bruises on my lip had gone down. We never spoke to anybody in school about our issues at home. We never thought anyone would understand. We did not have much of an idea where the house money went specifically every time, but we knew our parents spent everything generously on the pub, alcohol and cigarettes. But there was not enough food on the table, and we would go to bed hungry.

It was hard. My oldest brother, Frankie, would be on whom my dad would initially take out all his anger. But then he started channelling his anger towards me. And I never understood why back then, and to this day, I cannot make much sense of why he specifically hated two of his children the most. Even more heartbreaking was that my six other brothers and sisters were part of this toxic culture. There were times when they would tattle on Frankie and me, simply to shift the blame off themselves when they were in trouble, and hence they made things quite hard for us. I became a very nervous child in the house because I was the main target most of the time, besides Frankie. For some reason Frankie and I were specifically the punching bags my dad would use as stress relief.

Some of my brothers and sisters were heartless because they were treated utterly differently from Frankie, and he and I were held accountable. They would get away with a lot of stuff. But if I did something wrong, they would go to my mum to complain.

Sometimes they went to tattle without knowing that I could simply hide. Sometimes I think some of them enjoy watching me scream and cry.

It was not long until we discovered that my mum was pregnant again. We were all excited, thinking about the new baby. We mostly fantasised about how our lives might change once the latest addition to the family was here. We felt that a new baby might soften our parents' hearts and make them more compassionate towards us. We know that our mother or father would never have time for us and would never have time for the newborn, but maybe things around the house might change.

Soon enough, Rose was born. Mum just carried on doing what she was doing with the kids. There still was no love in the family. There was no attention from either my mother or my father. It just continuously got worse, even much more than we had anticipated.

When Rose was only about two weeks old, we got up one morning, only to find our dad covered in cuts and bruises. He did not explain much, and we didn't understand why. Later that morning, Mrs Rittenhouse knocked on our door to get Rose and look after us. My dad had told her that both he and our mother had been in a terrible car accident the night before on their way home. My mum was seriously injured. Mrs Rittenhouse would take care of baby Rose while we went to school, and when we would get home, my sister Laurie, who was only nine at the time, had to cook and clean and take care of us. Mrs Rittenhouse would bring the baby home, and then I would have to care for the little one.

This period of our mother being in the hospital for several months was challenging. We didn't have much of a home, and we never had any love and affection from both our parents. The violence and aggression came very quickly to my dad. Often, we would be woken many times during the night out of our sleep because of our parents fighting and yelling at each other. The arguments would result in my father hitting my mother. She would end up having black eyes.

Both my two older brothers were just out all the time during the day, trying to find food and getting into all sorts of trouble with the farmer for stealing off their land.

We would all get up early in the morning. And all of us would be fighting for clothes. Some of us had clothes on that were too big, some too small. And shoes, we squeezed our feet into shoes that didn't fit us. And we would go to school with our toes swollen.

Despite being a nervous and anxious child, I blossomed differently in school. A completely different side of me came out in school. Because I knew I was safe. And I did not have to hide for something I did not do or something I got the blame for unjustly. I met Julie, Julie and I became inseparable.

Julie was an only child, had the most fantastic bedroom, and had the most unique, amazing parents. Her parents would treat me like they treated her, no differently. And I never got tired of of living in that family home with Julie. Unfortunately, my own life at home was completely different to hers. I would make stories up and tell people that my home life was perfect. I had everything that I could want. If only that were true; the fights at home continued. My mum and dad would fight every time they came home from the pub. We were scared, but we had to get on with it.

My mum had spent eight months in the hospital after a car accident. And when she got home, she had a permanent limp. And she was in a lot of pain. I would often sneak out and run round to Julie's just to feel safe.

Frankie would sometimes climb out the toilet window just to go out and steal vegetables and potatoes from the farmer. It was quiet on one occasion. Frankie was climbing back in through the toilet window, which was small. My father was waiting for him to return. When he did, my dad gave Frankie such a black eye. All because he was arranging for food to feed us.

I began to spend more time around Julie's house. Her parents were so loving and so full of fun. And that's all I ever dreamed of having. I dreamt of having a happy home full of love and no worries of being beaten. My mum and dad will be in the pub every single night. They would smoke cigarettes, come in drunk and cause mayhem in the house. The fights and chaos would always wake us up in the middle of the night.

Julie's mum and dad both worked. So when Julie finished school, she would go home to an empty house. So Julie and I would leave school and go straight to her place, sometimes without even telling my mother. I sometimes used to think my other brothers and sisters got a little jealous of the relationship Julie and I had because we were so close and her parents treated me like one of thcm.

We would all go to school covered in bruises, and no one would ask about them. If someone did ask, I would tell them that we play rough with the rest of my brothers and sisters. We often went to school with blue bruising on our legs due to the bedsprings sticking out of corners at night. And my feet would be hurting from the undersized shoes too. I could barely walk around the school, and I never took my shoes off.

Back at home, while my parents were away wasting our money in pubs and bar fights, if there were ever a thunderstorm at night in the house, we would all get scared and huddle together. Mrs Rittenhouse would call on us to ensure that we were okay and that the young ones weren't too scared of the thunder and lightning. She was lovely, Mrs Rittenhouse. If she ever cooked something nice for her children while we were out playing together, she would give us some of the cooked food as well. We would be delighted to get a hot meal.

During the summer holidays, we would have playschemes organised by the school committee to educate and entertain children like us from nine o'clock in the morning to four o'clock in the afternoon. And we would still get free school meals during that time. So at least we got fed at school and during the playscheme.

I was making myfirst Holy Communion, I didn't know how my dress would be arranged. But my mum surprised me. She made me this beautiful white dress for my communion. And my uncle, my dad's brother, uncle Tony, lent me his wife's tiara. I looked like a princess and felt like one too. I didn't want the day to end. As we walked home, people stopped to stare, saying how beautiful I looked. I just felt so happy for the rest of the day and prayed it would never end. But unfortunately, it did. And things just went straight back to normal the next day. I would often cry myself to sleep at night. I was wondering why my dad especially was so hard on me. He still always seemed to pick me besides Frankie to reprimand. The rest of my brothers and sisters were left alone.

More and more people were moving into our neighbourhood, and there were more kids, so we just all spent our time together during the summer holidays. We would be busy with the playscheme playing with each other outdoors and getting screamed back to go home. The rest of the children would all go home to their beautiful homes and hot dinners while we went home to be screamed and shouted at, eating whatever was on the table.

Franklin and George spend most of their time on go-karts, running all over the hills and off to the marshes to play. The girls would play hopscotch, T balls, anything that we could find to entertain us. I used to love summers because it was warm. And we would be out all day having fun. It would be cold at home in the winter. We will be huddled in bed or blankets or the coats, trying to keep ourselves warm.

Rose was growing a bit older now and she was learning to walk. So we have to be very careful around her.

On Sundays, we'd go to church, and we would go to Sunday school, which was a lot of fun. One particular year, the head of our Sunday school approached one of my sisters and told her that the Sunday school was making a camping trip for a family who needed it. Our names were put forward. So we all went home from Sunday school so excited, thinking that we would go away on camp for a week. We were so happy to go away to camp for a week.

We all met outside the Sunday school. All of the parents would be with the kids to say goodbye to them, except ours. They allegedly had better things to do. My mum was home looking after the baby, and my dad was at work.

All of us spent a fantastic week at camp. We were fed three fulfilling, hot meals a day, and we were treated equally like every other child. It was amazing. The week went by quickly. Saturday came, and the bus rolled up. Parents were lined up to pick their children from summer camp. After picking them up, they asked them about it, and the children would gush about what a wonderful time they had had. We waited for our parents to show up. And we waited a long time, hoping for something that never happened.

Eventually, the Sunday School teacher put our suitcases in her car and drove out to our house. At the house, we went knocking on the door, but there was no answer. We continued to knock until finally, our mother opened the door. Our parents had a party in the house the night before, and they forgot that we were coming home from camp. It was awful. To think that your parents would forget that all the children were coming home from camp.

I still have great memories of that camp. It was just the most amazing thing that any child could have ever have wanted. But coming back home was like a hard crash back to reality.

Chapter 2: Snow White and the Seven Siblings

One of the books I can relate my experiences with is Franz Kafka's *Letter to His Father*. He set off to hold his father responsible for the psychological abuse, double standards, and consistent disapprobation that marked his childhood — a deliberate yet furious outburst of agony and frustration that built up for thirty long years.

One of the excerpts from his book goes like this:

"Dearest Father,

You asked me recently why I maintain that I am afraid of you. As usual, I was unable to think of any answer to your question, partly for the very reason that I am afraid of you and partly because an explanation of the grounds for this fear would mean going into far more details than I could even approximately keep in mind while talking. And if I now try to give you an answer in writing, it will still be incomplete because, even in writing, this fear and its consequences hamper me in relation to you and because the magnitude of the subject goes far beyond the scope of my memory and power of reasoning."

AND I COULDN'T AGREE MORE!

After I read it, I had this wild urge to reach out to the author and let him know its incredible impact on me. Whenever I read memoirs and books by the people who have been abused, disregarded, or potentially harassed, I think, *YES. Much thanks to you. I know exactly what it feels like.* I feel less sad, less blameworthy and less embarrassed. Indeed, even today, a long time since I left my childhood home, I long for freedom I may never genuinely have.

But I suppose I'm getting ahead of myself and need to get back to my story. I was sixth in line among my siblings; I had five older siblings and four younger ones. We were seven sisters and three brothers.

Anyhow, days went by like how they used to be. We only got to have a bath on Sundays, and even then had to share the water with all of my siblings. I still remember that after a certain age, we would also have to wash our own clothes, and many a time, we went to school with our clothes still wet.

Considering how financially tight our situation was, my mum used to make food for all of us with whatever she could find, to be honest. Sometimes, we had a table of food, but other days, there was nothing to eat.

She used to cook roast potatoes for us. Some days, we ate the leftovers. Sometimes, we had meat, and sometimes nothing at all. In short, we ate whatever we got and whatever my mum made for us.

It was pretty difficult trying to feed twelve mouths, especially at the time when my dad lost his job.

However, even after my dad got the job, nothing seemed to change financially.

We had six rooms at our house. Three siblings would share one bed. Our house was pretty cold all year because we couldn't afford a heater.

It was that horrible, horrible winter, and it felt like we were freezing to death. On our way back home from school, we noticed a poster. The poster said "Talent Contest." We wanted to go and watch it. So the night it was on, we left our home at about 5:30. Our parents didn't even ask where we were going. When we got to the talent contest hall, we found out that we had to pay the entrance fee. Of course, we had no money, but the guy at the door said that we wouldn't have to pay if we were participating in the competition. So we all looked at each other, and the decision was made in a moment. We told the guy, "Okay, we'll all sing together."

Anyway, it was our turn for the talent competition, and despite having no rehearsals, we sang the song. People applauded heartily, and the guy who was the competition's organiser had to turn out the audience. The only reason we were singing in the contest was that we didn't have any money to get in. Everybody laughed at us. I stood there in clothes that were too big for my size and shoes that were too small.

After we left, we looked at each other. We were quite embarrassed about the fact that we didn't even have money to go in and made everyone laugh at us. We walked home, and we never said a word to each other. We knew that we had exceeded our curfew limit of seven o'clock and that when we reached home, our dad would be waiting for us at the door. It would often happen, and although it was hard to handle, we weren't unfamiliar with the situation. We got home and were surprised that today we got away with just my dad screaming at us. After that, we all went straight up to our room.

A couple of days later, we found out that my mum was pregnant again, which meant there was to be another mouth to feed. Rose was barely walking. Each day, there wasn't enough food to last until the night. So what were we going to do? I had no idea what was going to happen. Anyway, months went by, and mum gave birth to the golden child - a boy who came along after seven girls. My dad was almost jumping with joy. We were happy with that too because our mum and dad were happy. He was ecstatic because he had a boy now. When our mum came out of the hospital, we ate cake and sandwiches to celebrate.

Harry was a spoiled brat. After he was born, everything that was done was done for him. When my mum went shopping, she would actually buy food solely for him, and we weren't allowed to touch it. We would often go hungry, watching him eat all the food. Life was getting more difficult for us, especially for me and my oldest brother, Frankie. Frankie was coming to the age where he could earn a really good wage. My dad used to send him out doing odd jobs for everyone so he could bring something at home. Sometimes, I had a feeling that he was detached from all of us because of how Mum and Dad took their anger and frustration out on him and me. I think detaching helped him to stay in the relationship while not losing his sense of self. It was more like setting boundaries within a dysfunctional family.

Even though it was Frankie and me who suffered a lot, I never really had a strong bond with Frankie. I do not have any memories of my brother, maybe because I was given away when I was only 11. To be honest, I didn't have much bonding with my siblings during my childhood, except for perhaps Dori. I do have a few things in common with her. And I believe it might be because we both spent some time together. Also, as of now, neither of us has any kids too.

However, I used to enjoy it sometimes, before I left home. We had our fair share of doing crazy stuff together. For example, at the time of Halloween, we always replaced the slice of apple with a soap bar and then offered it to other people to eat. And then we also had Bonfire Nights – without the fireworks and stuff, of course, but it was a pretty good experience.

A couple of weeks later, England was in some sort of crisis. I didn't understand back then what kind of crisis it was, but we were all sent home from school one day while having no idea why. Apparently, there was going to be a blackout. Nobody understood what that meant until we went home. The house was in complete darkness, and the only light was that from a candle. We would have to eat our supper by candlelight and go straight to bed. There were only three light bulbs in our house anyway – one in the living room, one in the kitchen, and one in my mum and dad's room.

The blackout started to happen every single day. People began losing their job, and dad was one of them. Some people worked three days a week while others wouldn't find work at all. My mum would have to go shopping by gas lamp, which was unbelievable because it was just pitch black. This continued for quite some time.

Things were only that harder now – 12 mouths to feed! Rose was walking all over the place, bumping into everything. Harry cried all the time, but my parents still went to the pub every night despite the crisis. Ask me how they did it, and I don't know. They would still sit almost all night in the pub and come back home very late. Some nights were quiet, while other nights, they'd be fighting loud. So things never really changed.

My dad was out looking for work every day, but he couldn't find any. So, whatever money that was coming in was never enough. I didn't know it at the time, but I found out that it came from the government as I got older. There was no heater in the house. There was only one room that was heated, and that was the living room. By this point, the house was getting really overcrowded now. Ten kids and my mum and dad – 12 people lived in a small house. It was tough.

Frankie was doing what he could and bringing in what little money he could get, but that wasn't enough for my dad. He started on George, but he really didn't know what to do or how to earn any money. So he followed the coal wagons and picked up some coal and sold it. He used to get what they call the ramen-bowl-man that used to come around, and he would give some shabby old clothes that he had so he could get a balloon off him.

In the midst of all the chaos and struggles, there are some memories that stuck with me. The same happened to me when it was the summer and the strike was over. The blackouts lasted for about three months, and it was coming towards the summer. One summer afternoon, Harry and Rose were both in a pram, and we were all playing outside. Some boys passed by us, screaming and shouting. We had no idea what they were screaming and shouting about. Then all of a sudden, a man came with the same kids running with him as fast as they could. We were wondering what was going on. About 5-10 minutes later, the man emerged with the boys behind him, carrying his son. One of the boys had been playing in the marshlands and had a sudden fall into the water. The unfortunate child got tangled up and drowned. The man was carrying his son's body through the streets. That was one of the saddest days that I will never forget.

As a whole, all of us fought for attention from my mum while she was too busy dealing with other things and the younger kids. When I reflect back, I think she had a pretty hard time managing a lot of kids too. It isn't easy to manage a family, let alone with so many kids and so little money or help. To be fair, she herself was burdened with a lot of responsibilities. If someone will ever ask me if I would ever forgive my parents or my family, I would just say that there is nothing to forgive about. I never really knew my mum and my mum never really knew me. I became thick-headed because of how they treated me.

As we all grew up, we all didn't have much interaction to know each other well, and this is the case, even to this day. I was seven at the time, and I could very well understand how pathetically messed up was our dynamics and situation in the house.

I am 57 now, and I can clearly recall everything I experienced during my childhood. Some memories are engraved in your mind like complicated patterns carved into wooden furniture, and even time can't do much to change them or undo them for good.

However, it is really up to a person how they take it and what they can learn from it. I believe, at one point, it is in our control how to grow ourselves into and what kind of a person we want to turn into. I know it can be hard at times, but that is what life is. It isn't easy for everyone.

For me, I have made peace with my life now. However, I kind of created an emotional detachment toward my family. It was the result of traumatic events like childhood abuse and neglect. It is common among children who are mentally or physically abused or neglected by their parents as a means of survival. They tend to shut the world out and build their own happy place in their heads as a counter mechanism. I, too, in more ways than I can ever put into words, had learned to disconnect from my trauma.

Chapter 3: Life Developments of a Young Survivor

As a child living in an abusive household, my life at home was like a ticking time bomb.

There were many instances of abuse that I had faced as a young survivor in an abusive household. One day, I was walking home across the field, and you could see our house straight across the field. I was walking over, and I noticed a man crouching down by Mrs Hughes's house. It was doing something on the gate. There were sparks flying all over the place. So I knew I'd have to be on one side of the street while walking, which I did. So now the sparks wouldn't hit me.

I was just about to knock on the door when my dad opened it. He dragged me in and hit me so hard. It was about to knock me over. He punched me a few times and yelled at me to get up the stairs. I was upstairs thinking, *"What on earth did I do to just deserve that?"* I was past crying anymore. I was numb to all the abuse of him.

My mum called me downstairs and I asked her what did I get hit for she told me I got to near the sparks I just look at her knowing I didn't.

When you are used to getting this kind of negativity from your parents, you have to try and survive in your own way. However, when you're young, you just wonder why. Why does it happen to me? What did I even do to deserve this? Am I a burden on them? Why don't my parents love me? Why do they always want to scream at me and hit me? You just keep trying to piece it together in your own head, thinking you are the problem. You would never understand these things until later in life.

Another thing is, if you don't get your fair share of love from our home, you try to find it from other places and from other people. I did the same. For me, it was from Julie and his parents.

A few days went by, and Julie, my friend from school, was at her house, and her mum and dad were going away for the holidays to the caravans in Wales. Julie's mum asked me if I would like to go. I jumped, and the answer was, "Yes, absolutely." She went down to speak to my mum, and my mum was fine with it. So I went with Julie and her parents to the caravan in Wales. It was a beautiful place. There were sandhills, fairgrounds, and arcades; it was just amazing. Julie's mum treated me exactly like her. They took me out one day. I got this ice cream sundae; that was so big that I had to stand up to eat it. And I thought, *"Oh my god, that is the best thing in the world that I've ever tasted."* Julie and I went to the arcade I won a lot of prizes I pick the crockery so I could take them home to my mum Julie was so mad because I won and she didn't. The way of journey was drawn to an end very soon, and then I had to go home. And I thought, *"Now that I am going home, so what am I going to face?"* We got in the car, and we started our journey home.

I sat in the backseat with an ache and pain in my belly. I felt sick, and I just didn't want to go home. The journey was about a couple of hours, and I just sat there in silence. The trip felt like a dream. The dream I didn't want to end at all. We pulled up outside Julie's house, and her dad said, "I'll take you around to your mum's." So he did, and he opened the boot and took out all the prizes that I had won. So I carried these prizes into the house, and I said, "Look, mum, what I won while I was away." She didn't even look up at me. Nobody spoke to me; I was basically invisible. I just looked around and went outside and sat on the floor, thinking this was just horrible. I don't want to be in this family.

At one event, Julie and I played netball for our school, and we actually got to the finals. We were playing in the finals that day, and we were three quarters away through the game. I noticed my mother and father standing there. I became very nervous. I don't know why, but I was really nervous.

I dropped the ball. And we ended up losing by one point. Eventually, we went home, and as we entered, my dad said, "You lost it. You lost because you dropped the ball." I looked at him, and I could feel the tears welling up; I had this lump in my throat. And I thought, *"I will not let you see me cry anymore. I will never shed another tear in front of you."* I just looked at them and walked away. I went upstairs, and I just sat on the bed. I must have sat there for two to three hours. Eventually, I came down; we had nothing to eat. I went back to bed up to the bedroom. And I was laying in bed praying, *"Lord, please take me away from this family. I don't want to be here."* I was even thinking about ways of going away. So they would never find me. But that was just in my imagination. Where would I go? I was only ten years of age.

Julie and I went to school the next day, and the whole school congratulated us. We didn't win, but we came second. We were all called out one by one at the assembly to pick up medals. Everybody who came first got a gold medal, but w got the silver one instead. And I was so delighted. The first thing I had ever won. And I ran to show my mum the medal for coming second. She just looked at me and said, "Oh, nice," and walked away. My mum's patience with all of us was almost near to none as we grew up. We were trying to find our own way where we fit in the family or family dynamics. But really, it was just a hit and miss. Either they loved us, or they hated us.

I want everyone who is reading this to know that you will eventually get through this. My time went too. As I survived, I want you to know that it was not your fault. You are not the problem. They were adults, they were supposed to protect you, and they failed you; you did not fail them in any way. They failed to fulfil their responsibility. You have to repeat it again and again in your head that it wasn't you. And you'll learn to piece your life back together. It is like a jigsaw puzzle. You have to find the pieces, which you will for sure, as you go on in life. We will all make bad decisions, and likewise, we will all make good decisions in life too. We will gain a lot from it.

Maria was 11 months older then me she was my dad's blue eye even though he had 7 daughters Maria would get her own a lot with my dad I was so jealous all I ever won't was to feel love I still long for that today even though both of my parents are deceased.

Things were a little bit better at home. My dad managed to get a job with Frankie alongside him in the local glass factory. One night I was asked to go to the fish and chips shop, which was very, very rare. I got some pie chips and brought them home. There were 10 of us. We all got a quarter of a pie each. The pies were only small. Frankie got half of the pie, and he was complaining about having half a pie because he gave his wages over to my mum. My mum was so angry and mad that she picked the pie up and smashed it right in his face. I looked up at Frankie, and I thought, "OH MY GOD!" I could see the look on his face. He just glared at me. He got up, went to the bathroom and washed his face.

I was becoming very defiant where my parents were concerned. I had no love or respect for them. They did not even try to maintain that kind of bond with their children.

One day, I came home from school. My mum told me I had to do the dishes and clean the kitchen. I told her I wasn't feeling well. So that night, when I refused to do the dishes, my mum flew into a rage. She pinned me upside the door, and she was screaming at me and telling me how much she hated me. She had hands around my throat and told me to cry. The more I wouldn't cry, the tighter her hands were around my throat. I just glared. And I didn't even blink. She was screaming at me to cry out, I wouldn't. In the end, my dad had to drag her off me. I just stood there and looked up at both of them with total resentment on my face. I just walked away and didn't say anything else.

Anybody that has ever been abused and doesn't know how to move on, write it down. Write how you intend to survive your next day. I can assure you that whatever you will write down will surprise you because, before that, you didn't know that you had that in you until you'll actually physically see it on a piece of paper. That is what I did too, and I want all of you to at least try it once.

Moving forward with the story, we had a phone box at the end of our road. And one day, the phone rang. I picked that up. And it was my aunty Jane who wanted one of us to babysit. So I said, "I'll babysit." She said, "Okay. Can you come down Friday? And if you want, you can stay the weekend." She had one child only. And that was Andrew.

So I went back and told my mother that aunty Jane had called and that I was going to babysit that weekend. I went; I didn't know what to expect, but I had my own room. The room was lovely, but I couldn't believe it. So I babysat the Friday night. And the Saturday night. And Sunday, it was time for me to come home. I'd had a great weekend, and I'd have been fed three meals. And I wasn't hungry at all. Auntie Jane gave me some money for babysitting and said thanks. She said, "Would you like to babysit again?" I jumped at the idea. So from then on, I used to go down at weekends to babysit. And I would go home with the money in my pocket. I wouldn't say anything to my mum or dad that I had any kind of money.

One weekend my auntie Jean, me, and her son went to London to visit her sister. Whilst I was there, she took me shopping for new clothes. I couldn't wait to show my mum how beautiful the clothes were but instead of saying they were nice, she just looked at me and told me I was getting fatter and fatter. Those words cut so deep it still haunt me to this day.

One day, I was walking home from school. I saw this beautiful doll, and it was for a raffle. So with some money that I had from babysitting, I actually went in, and I bought a raffle ticket. A couple of weeks later, the raffle was done, and I actually won. I went to him, and

I picked up this beautiful doll. And I was so excited and so happy.

Things went by. I continued with the babysitting. I used to pack my bags and go away over the weekend. Meanwhile, Frankie started dating a girl. And he was very, very keen on her. They dated for about a year or so, and then Frankie asked to marry her. I think Frankie has just wanted a way out of the house. So they got married, and they actually had a beautiful wedding. Frankie was really happy with his new wife, and he just went off.

We never really saw much of Frankie. He even stopped working with my dad. He just wanted his own life, and he seemed happy with his wife. Frankie just basically forgot us; he didn't really come around anymore. I think he was just happy to be out of the house and away from my mum and dad, but I couldn't blame him because life was just getting unbearable, especially for me.

All the other kids were growing up. They all had their own personalities. Maria was spoiled rotten; she got whatever she wanted. Harry – he did whatever he wanted to do, and whatever Harry wanted, Harry got. He was the youngest, of course. So the rest of them really just plotted along.

I found school really difficult. By then, my grades were slipping, and I really couldn't be bothered in school because I couldn't concentrate. During lectures, I kept wondering, *"What life was going to be like when I got home?"* I loved escaping to my aunt Jane's because I was treated like one of theirs. It seemed like an amazing life, a life that I always wished I had, and a life that I eventually got – but didn't turn out the way I wanted it to.

There were always struggles. Especially being one out of ten, I had to fight for my own place in the house, which I failed miserably. That is the reason I loved escaping to aunt Jane's.

At our place, no one really showed affection to each other. We never had *I love yous*, and even to this day, we don't. I am sure most of us have a household like this. This will make you have difficulty expressing your feelings later in life. Because you have learned to suppress it, you become a wallflower. You create barriers around yourself in order to not get hurt. We need to learn that being vulnerable is healthy if you care for someone.

Being vulnerable can help us to work through our emotions. It can foster good emotional and mental health. Vulnerability is a sign of courage. It helps build empathy and understanding for everyone involved.

Expressing your love and affection motivates the other person to continue doing the same for you. It will allow you to open yourself up to another person and can help you discover your inner capacity for pure and unconditional love.

Childhood traumas will always retain you, and you will always go back and revisit them. However, the key is to learn to cope and have strategies to take your life in control. You need to know how you're going to feel the next time the same situation comes up. It is an amazing feeling, knowing you have taken back your life – the part that was taken away by other people. You will be so proud of yourself when you'll realize how far you have come.

So, yes, childhood trauma does come back to you, and you will revisit it; but you will have better skills, a better mindset, and a more positive attitude. And you have the guts to stand up and say, "I AM A SURVIVOR."

People who have been abused tend to hide away because of shame. There is no shame in being abused. It wasn't your fault. You did not ask to be put into that situation. People put you there. And you, as the survivor, will shine because you didn't let all that anger upset you.

You need to tell other people about it. They can learn from you. The more you tell people, the better the response you get. So, as a survivor, you need to learn and have the ability to take back what was taken away from you.

Chapter 4: Wayne

There are times when you just connect with a person in an instant! Like you have known them for years. The same happened with Wayne and me. I met Wayne on my first day of senior school, and we've been inseparable ever since.

I must say, I have been very lucky when it comes to my friendships since childhood. I have always got the best people as my friends. Maybe, that was God's way of choosing my own family.

Friendship is one of the blessings of God. It is when you feel attachment, care, security, unparalleled love, and most importantly, sincerity. I believe that friendships can never be implanted or imported but developed internally.

In Wayne's case, it was like one body – as our souls are united. If one of us faces a hard time, the other automatically undergo the same situation. We were always there to provide a shoulder to cry on.

Wayne came from a similar background. His stepfather was an alcoholic, and he often beat up his mum and Wayne.

Wayne and I would go horse riding together down at Liberty Farm. We would go to the stables and look after the horses, after school, on weekends, and in summer times when his father would often beat Wayne. I think that's why we were so close in school because we had so much in common.

Wayne has been a big part of my life and a big part of my family as well. We used to go to my mum's with Wayne after school, knowing that if I went with him, she wouldn't be as mean and horrible to me as she usually was. Wayne once said to me, "I didn't realize it was that bad; the way she speaks to you." And I replied, "It is what it is."

Wayne was always invited to any event at our house. He bonded with all of my sisters well. Whenever he visited us, they all used to get so excited. His opinions really mattered before making any big decisions like before buying cars and etc. Sometimes I feel like life would have been a lot different to what it is today if Wayne wasn't there in it. I mean, I don't know how my family would behave? He always has and will always be a big part of my family.

I was in the paddock on a horse that needed to be exercised. Wayne had put the reins on the horse, but I didn't know that they were not attached to the bit. Wayne hit the horse from behind, the horse went forward, and I went backwards. Wayne and everyone else was laughing hysterically. I was lying there and laughing so hard.

We had a Show and Tell activity at school one day. So, Wayne said to me, "I've got to go to the farm, and

I'm bringing a horse." And that's exactly what he did; he brought a horse to Show and Tell. Everyone was laughing so hard, and Wayne and I were just looking at each other. It was a funny day.

When Wayne started working for an airline, I got to travel a lot with him. We travelled every week, going to Hong Kong for a few days and other places too. I had always been on the plane with him. So, wherever we went, there were long stopovers, and I was free. I loved that time, and I still miss it. We have a lot of memories together. I started travelling from a very young age because I had a partner to travel with. The best part is that I get to travel for free.

We have had many adventures together. We had our fair share of great times as well as shifty times too. We get it really going, it's like, if you have got an issue with one of your brother or sister, eventually you get through it. There were times when we agreed with each other, however, other times, we weren't.

Wayne and I also fought a lot, all the time, but like brother and sister, we were totally inseparable. Wayne and I mostly had fights over the relationship and stuff. But at the end of the day, I had always known that no matter how much we fought, we loved each other so much that no power on earth could separate us. It was more or less the same bonding I had with Julie, a friend I had made in infant school. We are still close to this day. Julie is one of my oldest friends, but I have great memories with Wayne as well of what we did when we were younger.

I settled into life with my Auntie Jane and her husband, Uncle Tommy, at their home because my mum didn't want me around. I thought I was so privileged to have a room of my own. I didn't have to share it with all the siblings. At our place, we all had to use water carefully because of its shortage. So to me, that was a luxury. They treated me like their own child. Their son Andrew was six years old when I first started babysitting for the other one. We had a lot of fun. I felt like I was part of their family. Uncle Tommy treated me like his daughter. I was 12 at the time.

One night, my door opened, and Uncle Tommy was standing there. He closed the door behind him, and he told me that it was time to pay back what they had given me. He climbed into my bed, and he sexually assaulted me right there. All I could smell were old cigarettes and alcohol. I lay there, silently crying. Tears were just rolling down the side of my face. I was legit frozen with fear. When he was over, he got up, walked to the door and closed it behind him. I spent the whole night crying about what had just happened. All sorts of emotions were coming through me.

I could never see that coming. All I could do was cry. I got up the next morning to get ready for school. I noticed the blood on the sheets. As if struck by fear and panic, I got them off and washed them before I went to school. I felt so alone. I felt there was nobody I could tell. I didn't even tell Wayne about it.

One night, Uncle Tommy came over from the pub, and I was lying on the floor. He came in and kicked so hard in my head that all I could see were stars, and that was when I thought, "*Enough.*" So I picked up the phone, and I dialled the police. The police officer came to the house. I told him about the abuse, and I told him that he had just hit me in the head. The police officers looked at me and asked me how old I was. I told him that I was 16 years old, and with that, he "advised" me to get out of the house and leave. He said, "If that's the case, you don't have to live here." I just looked at this police officer, and I thought, *"You're here to protect people, to help people, and you're standing there and telling me to leave? Where can a 16-year-old go with no love and support from anyone?"* The police officer just turned around and left. I stood there stunned. What a horrible man. Awful. Uncle Tommy just sat there and laughed. He thought it was funny. I felt so let down and so disheartened at that time.

As the days went by, the abuse continued; quite often. The light would shine into my bedroom, and I could see his footsteps outside the door and then I knew what was about to happen. I started to get really withdrawn and stopped talking to anyone. Auntie Jane kept asking me what the matter was. I just kept pushing her off.

One day I went home after school. Our dad was there, and he was in a foul mood. I didn't know where my mum was. I said something, and he beat me so hard that I was just numb. I just walked out the door and said nothing. I cried all the way to the bus stop. I even missed the bus. It was raining, and it was very cold. I sat on a bench, and I just cried and cried and cried. I felt like I was nobody's child. Nobody wanted me. They wanted me just to abuse me. I just sat on the bench, crying and waiting for the next bus. I went home to my Auntie Jane, and I didn't say anything. I sat there. I ate my dinner and then started doing my homework for school.

The abuse went on for two years until, one night, Uncle Tommy came home drunk. He started calling me a slut, a whore and all the names that no young women should be called.

I picked up a glass ashtray, and I threw it at him. It hit him straight in the face. He ended up having seven stitches on his face. I told him. "Next time, if you try to touch me, I will kill you." And since that day, that has never happened to me again.

I went to school one morning, and I met Wayne. Wayne told me that his stepdad was fighting with his mother, and he hit her so hard that she hit her head on the wall. Wayne flew into a rage, and he beat his dad so bad that he had to put him in the hospital. It was when Wayne and I both had said, "Enough. We're not taking any more of this shit. We're not standing any more people thinking that we are just there as punch bags." Wayne's stepdad didn't touch him again after that night because he knew if he did, he'd be back in the hospital, and Wayne said to me, "It was the best feeling I've ever had."

It was when I told Wayne about the ashtray incident with Uncle Tommy, but I didn't tell him anything else until I felt that it was time for me to talk about it. After some time, I told Wayne about the whole story, and then he said to me, "Wow, you're still full of surprises. No matter what you do."

Everyone has their own ways of recovering from the sexual assault they face. With me, I became very withdrawn. I didn't speak to a lot of people about it. I didn't even tell any of my brothers and sisters as well. And it only came into the light a couple of years ago when Dori my brother George and my cousin Robert met for drinks I became the topic of conversation it was George who told them about the the whole situation at my auntie jeans house at first they couldn't believe it they were shocked a few days later Dori called me and asked if it was true. Now, we were really close to each other. She asked me if it was true, and I told her yes. She asked me why didn't I tell anyone before.

I always felt like it is not the kind of thing you keep telling other people. It is very difficult for a woman to open up when you're sexually abused. It is like a fight within. I faced a lot of issues because of what I went through, effectively in my relationships and partners.

Whenever you decide to let people know about it, you go back and forth with yourself. I told my sister that the only reason it happened to me was because nobody saw me. Everyone was so busy in their lives that we didn't have time for each other. Keeping everything to myself was a difficult task.

However, the second it got out of me, I felt so relieved. It felt like something was off my shoulders. The heaviness I felt for all this time went away in a second. So yeah, it affected me in a lot of ways because I didn't speak about it, and I thought people would never understand my situation, but I was surprised that they did.

For me, recovering from it took time. The healing process was painful. I had to regain my self-worth, sense of control and learn to heal.

Mostly, it is extraordinarily difficult to accept the fact that you've been sexually assaulted. There's a stigma attached that comes with making you feel weak and dirty. People are afraid of how others will react. What if someone judges you? Stop respecting you? It looks easier to downplay. However, if you stay silent, it clearly means that you're in denial. You ignore the fact that you need help and reinforce your victimhood.

To all my readers and fellow survivors of sexual abuse, I want you all to know that you're one of the rarest, you're extraordinary.

If you ever feel difficult to come out, whether it be related to physical, mental, or financial abuse, just know that it is not your fault. You're not the one that should be ashamed. It is the abuser who should feel ashamed. Find someone who can trust with your life and let them know. Take that burden off you. It has been so long since you're fighting this battle within yourself. It is time that you clear your mind and start fresh.

You need to challenge yourself with the sense of isolation and helplessness. One can be left feeling vulnerable and powerless because of their trauma. You need to remind yourself that you are strong, and because of your coping skills, you can get through the toughest of times that come your way.

One of the best ways from which you can reclaim your sense of strength is by helping others, volunteering, reaching out to a friend who needs help, donating, giving blood, etc.

Apart from this, you should go to therapies as well. I remember my time when I started taking therapies. It was one of the best things. You have the sense that somebody is listening to you, looking out for you, and caring for you. They teach you a lot of hope, and you manage to get through what you need to get through.

In the end, everything makes you learn a lesson. You can take good out of every situation. Everything you will ever go through will empower you. You will learn to have empathy for people. You will listen to other abusers and compare them to your experience. It will help you understand what they are feeling.

Chapter 5: We All Wanted an Escape

One night after school, Wayne and I went to my mum's house and it was a very eerie feeling in the house. Something felt wrong. My sister, Dori, sat down, and we were told that my mum had throat cancer. I couldn't take that news in at the time. When my mum first found out about her illness, she had a difficulty swallowing it.

Thank God Wayne was there with me to support me. I couldn't imagine how hard it was for my mum to go through all that. He was constantly there listening to my fears. He was encouraging us and telling us that everything's gonna be okay. He never left my side, to be honest. He was the big part of my support. I didn't know how everything was going to be. I would constantly discuss my concerns and my fears with him, and he would just listened to me and gave me all the emotional support I needed. And now I think of it, I feel like it was one of the most beautiful friendship I had in my life.

My dad was away at the time because of the work. He used to visit over the weekends to take care of her. Throughout her illness, he supported her so much. He traveled home and was there for her full-time. If my dad was at work, one of the neighbours who didn't work would take her to her appointments.

The treatment lasted for months, and during this time, she lost a lot of weight; she didn't look well at all. My mum's health was really at stake at the time. Some days, she was really well and other days, her health both mental and physical, would be so poor. That was the reason we had to adjust out life according to the mum's treatment and stuff. We were all so worried because none of us knew what the outcome was going to be. Few days went by with her treatments and dialysis. But after therapy, she actually made a full recovery, which was surprising, according to the doctors. So she just carried on with her life the way she did.

We were all relived after she got recovered. However, obviously we were walking on eggshells because she still needed care and attention towards her health.

My mum had a major change in her behaviour after her illness. She was kind of unaffected by a lot of stuff; and I feel like it is natural. She didn't have that mental energy left in her to deal with the stuff. She turned into much of a really unbothered soul. Most of the time, she used to come back from her radiotherapy and just lie down in her room quietly. Even though she was one of the strongest women I know, in that particular phase, I felt like she lost hope from her life.

As far as we were concerned, all of us carried on with our normal routines. I kinda had mixed emotions from this situation. Even though I was really worried about my mum, however, it never really affected my personal life.

During that time, Dori wanted some money for her A-levels exams. She came home and asked my mum and dad if they would help pay for her A-levels. We had to pay for the exams at the time when we were growing up. My dad just laughed at her and said he hadn't paid for anybody's education, especially a girl, because they need to get married and get pregnant. They don't need an education.

As a woman living in an abusive household, I believe that all women must have an economic independence and security in order to eliminate and escape from the abusive relationship, whether it be with your parents or a partner. Doing so, will enable women who have experienced physical, mental, or financial abuse to become financially sound so that the the generational chain of abuse can be broken and their children won't suffer the consequences of being in an abusive relationship.

Dori was absolutely passionate about her education. So she went out and got herself a part-time job in the local bakery.

One morning, one of my sisters wanted to go on a school trip the next day. My mum had no money so she went into Dori's room and took away her money from where she kept it, without her permission. Dori was so upset by what my mum had done.

She just wanted to leave home. At the time, she was dating a guy called William. Their relationship continued, and Dori decided to go to London to be a chambermaid at some hotel. My mum would always nag her to send money home. My mum told her that as long as she had a bed under their roof, she had to send some money to pay the price. So, Dori would send money every week even though there wasn't a bed for her. But that was just how my mum was.

Frankie was married to Elizabeth, but their marriage turned out really rocky. They had a lovely daughter, Ann, and she was gorgeous. But the marriage was in trouble. I suppose Frankie only got married for the sake of leaving home. So eventually their marriage ended up in divorce, and they split. Frankie was broken, but he knew there was no salvage in the marriage.

Georgie, my second brother, was living with my mum, but they didn't end up being on good terms, so he left home too. I think we all just left our house at a very early age. Dori was 16, Frankie left at 17, and Georgie when he had just turned 17. It was all due to the kind of family life we had and because they just wanted to escape the abusive environment they were in.

Georgie seemed to have settled down in his married life. He got a job, and he was working hard for his family. His wife was expecting at the time too. Unfortunately, due to the bad economy, there was hardly any money. So he moved in back with my mum. There were already twelve people living there, which caused a lot of problems, especially with all the other kids. The baby came and my mother was beyond pleased to have a grandson. And the baby was beautiful.

Dori came back home after working in London for a long time. She decided to move in with William and it wasn't long before the two got married. It was a nice little wedding. We were all invited, and it was fun. But unfortunately, that marriage didn't last long either. So, my three elder brothers and sister had failed marriages. I think that's because they all wanted to leave home as quickly as they could.

It wasn't long after Frankie married again to a girl called Patt. By this time, Frankie had decided that he wanted to be a social worker. While I went to college, he finished college and went to university, where he got his PhD in psychology. It was pretty amazing, especially since he had a lot of support from Patt. They ended up having two beautiful little girls and he could never be any happier. Frankie loved them to death, and he had an amazing job where he was working with advocates about mental health issues and disabilities at the time. He worked in an institution, and he was so proud of himself. And rightly so, because he got his PhD.

As for Georgie, he loved his wife, but unfortunately, the marriage failed utterly. He went on to become a mountain rescue in Snowdonia, and with that, I was really amazed at what he had achieved.

Dori went to university and got her degree in accountancy. She became a director of finance for a group of hotels. She met an amazing guy there named, John. He was so funny and I always had a soft spot for him. Dori loved him so much, however, they never got married or had any kids but still they had an amazing time together.

There was an unsaid connection between me and my brothers and sisters where we all just accepted the situation we had at out home.

My mum was the youngest, out of 13 brothers and sisters. I never knew my grandparents. My dad was the eldest of 4 brothers. I can only imagine that my dad was beaten up by his parents and that's where he got his anger from and why he ruled with an iron fist.

My mum was 16 and my dad was 17 when they got married. She was pregnant with Frankie, at the time. Mum went on to have 9 more children. She loved being pregnant and having babies, but she hated it when we were grown up because she couldn't control us.

As we all started to move out, there was only Mum, Dad, Rose, and Harry. It was long after we all moved out, my mum found out that rose was expecting a baby. She was just 15, at the time. My mum was fuming, but what she forgot that she was the same age when she was pregnant with Frankie.

So, Rose grew absolutely beautiful, with a little baby growing inside. She looked so glowing and so happy. Then came the time when the baby was born, and Rebecca was the most beautiful baby you could ever imagine. She was amazingly beautiful and had blue eyes and blonde hair. She still has that blonde hair today. She even has daughters of her own now.

We all escaped our messed up house dynamics as soon as we got a chance to. The feeling of homeliness was never there. We all felt an extreme need to break the cycle of violence that perpetuatued our lives from the time each of us born.

I learned to become independent at a very early age. I was thrust into it because I had to survive to protect myself, and still, to this day, I have made myself strong enough and protected myself that no harm can affect me. I have started taking things positively in a way that saved my sanity for a bigger and better things to do in life.

Chapter 6: Life after Leaving Behind "Home"

When you hear the word family, it can bring an array of complex emotions to your mind. Depending on how your situation at home is, it can bring either negative, positive, or an equal of both of the feelings.

However, for me, whenever I think of my life back at home, it was mostly toxic and messed up, which turned my feelings into anger and frustration. There are times when just having a mere flashback of good memories can turn into having emotional distress.

Toxic and dysfunctional household results in nothing but a bunch of people fighting for their survival and trying to escape the situation as soon as they get a chance to. To get out of it, you must identify what you want out of it can help you develop a clear idea of the boundaries you want to set.

When I told Frankie that I would write a book about our life and how we grew up, he panicked. He said that he couldn't deal with it, and it would be difficult for him to remember flashbacks of everything he had gone through. I asked all my brothers and sisters about the book, but most of them never wanted to talk about life back at home.

Child abuse is common in many countries all over the world. Many children like me are beaten and starved to death each day due to the lack of parental love and poverty. I have been abused worse than an animal. Thousands of children fall prey to parental negligence, torture, mistreatment, and physical and sexual abuse by their relatives or caretakers. The last one is one of the most severe issues faced by us.

I always wanted to write for the people who have undergone child abuse and the children who face injustice on a daily basis. I think it's a book that conveys a very important message to young people, no matter where they come from, what have they gone through, and how they survived, especially in an abusive relationship. When you've got two violent parents who take their kids as scapegoats and take it out on them, it's nothing but a recipe for disaster. I mean, the only person that you can rely on or love is yourself. You can't love anyone else without putting yourself first. I would love to learn that – there are so many things I need to unlearn in order to learn something else.

I moved on with my life. Old things were ending; new beginnings were around the corner. Wayne and I left school at 16. I wanted to go to college. Wayne didn't know what he wanted to do, so he went ahead and started selling vacuum cleaners.

I applied to different colleges too. I went to college to get a two-year degree program in sociology. I wanted to work in healthcare. Through this education, I was enabled to have the ability to do something for the community and could share my knowledge and wisdom with other people.

Even after school finished, Wayne and I would hang out all the time. We even went on a holiday together. One day, Wayne told me that he was going to apply for a job to become a flight attendant with Dan Air, he was there for a short while and went on to work at British Airways. I was really excited for him. He went for his interview, and a couple of days later, he found out that he had gotten the job. He was ecstatic, and I was so pleased for him.

Throughout my degree program, I managed to pay for my fees and worked at several places.

My college was really great, and I had so much fun throughout my time there. The reason I chose the profession that I went into is that it gives people insight into how to deal with different people and their social needs. I was dealing with the physical aspects of their lives as well. That is how it gave me the chance to integrate myself into the community where I have to deal with different doctors, sociologists, social workers, etc.

In the beginning, I applied at so many places for the job, but everything needed consistency in order for it to show any results. There were a lot of rejections through the process of finding the right job for me, which was quite disheartening. It was mainly because I had knowledge and expertise of various things but no experience.

After some time, I decided to go and work for an agency called the Relief Nursing Agency as a Healthcare Associate. After I left college, a job came up that I looked at and thought, "Wow! That would be an amazing job for me to have." I never thought I would ever be able to do it. It came with many benefits, like a two-bedroom apartment and other stuff. The salary was pretty impressive too.

I decided to apply for the post, and believe it or not, I actually got it. I was so shocked. It was like my ticket out of round two. As I was living at Auntie Jane and Uncle Tommy's home, I thought that I didn't have to worry about violence anymore. I didn't have to worry about alcoholism or abuse in any way. It was a godsend opportunity to escape all that.

The workplace was a home where I looked after 50 old people. They all had their own rooms, and I would basically be their eyes and ears. So, in the morning, I would call on them all to make sure that they were okay and at nights before they all settled. During this time, I did find one or two people who had passed away in their rooms, that was the hardest and the toughest part of this job – to deal with their relatives and give them support.

So, now Wayne was working for Dan Air, and I was also working at a perfect place. We actually travelled quite a lot, Wayne and I. We've been to quite a few places and some places that people could only dream of at that time. We had a fantastic time.

Moving forward, one day, my sister, Maria, called me up on the block. And she asked me if I would be interested in buying their home, and I said, "Why would I want to buy your house when I have a two-bedroom apartment here?" To which she replied, "No, no! You can rent it out." The reason was that she wanted to buy a particular house for which she needed to sell the current one very quickly. I went inside and took a look at the home, and in no time, I had made the decision. I came back and told her, "Yep, I'll buy the house." And I did.

After I bought the house, I actually did rent the property out for quite a while. Then I met a guy called

Mark Grady who was a really nice man and was so funny. I met Mark because he was actually my hairdresser at the time. He was in the properties business as well. He had a couple of agents and salons, which he owned. So I told him that I had bought a house from my sister that I rented out. He told me a couple of ways how to buy and sell properties without using any or less money. He even showed me how to do it. That's how I bought my second house and rented it out, and a few others after that. I rented four homes in total, and that was enough for me to handle.

I had to have a guy managing the properties for me after the tenants had gone, and it was great. I mean, I was living the high life. Then, my sister Pauline, who was a hairdresser at the time, asked me if I would get a barbershop for her. She wanted it for her business, but she couldn't get it on a lease because her credit was so bad. So I thought about it, and I said, "You need this property, and I'm gonna get it for you, but you will only be an employee." She wasn't happy about that, but she had no option. She could either take it or leave it because she didn't have a job and needed one. So she agreed, and I opened Casey's Barbers. Casey was my maiden name.

I ended up having a portfolio of properties, including the barbershop and so on. It was going great. I had fast cars. I was going on vacations two or three times a year. Life was pretty amazing. After some time, Carol, one of the girls who worked with Pauline, wanted to manage her own shop. So I asked her, "What kind of management are you talking about?" She said, "Just a manager, not the owner." I thought it was okay, so I purchased the lease for the shop, and I put Carol in there.

Now, bear in mind that I still had a full-time job, a portfolio of houses, and two hairdressing salons. The residential post where I lived enabled me to do all this, and I mean, I just couldn't believe how my life had turned around.

Mark Grady was just so much fun to be with. I got all of this because of him. He had a number of properties and a couple of hairdressing salons, and he would be bouncing from one to the next. He had a lot of experience, and he taught me many things.

A few years later, Mark headed for Australia. He sold most of his properties before he left for Australia. I still see Mark now. I mean, I've visited him quite a few times. And he did the same thing in Australia. But he had such an amazing head on his shoulders. After going through a lot in his life, he became a successful entrepreneur and taught me how to be on myself. Mark has always been my inspiration. He achieved so much in life in a very short period of time. That is one of the reasons why I love and adore him with all my heart.

My life continued after that. Wayne and I would travel a lot. Meanwhile, Wayne started dating a guy named Kevin. He was a fantastic guy. I loved Kevin, and most importantly, Wayne was really happy with him. They were together for 13 years when Wayne had a suspicion that Kevin was cheating on him.

Kevin came to visit me when I lived in Philadelphia. He was kind of weird, and I didn't like what he was doing or where he was going, but I wouldn't tell Wayne because I didn't want to upset him. I knew there was something up. So one night, while Wayne was home, Kevin said he was going to the gym, and Wayne decided to follow him. As expected, Kevin didn't go to the gym. He was actually cheating Wayne. When we found out, he just went ballistic, and Kevin became a psychotic lunatic. He was threatening to kill. Kevin really put Wayne through the mill.

They ended up in court because they had lived together for so long. They had to split the assets. But what really pissed me off was that Kevin had no assets. It was Wayne who bought the home. It was Wayne who did it all the hard way. Kevin was only a chef working for an agency. He never had a full-time job. Wayne had to split the assets and give them half everything, including the shares because it started working with BA. I had been really sad because Wayne had never had another partner since then. He didn't trust a soul after that, and I guess it's because he was hurt so much. It happens when you are in a relationship that you thought was amazing, but then you never know it will end. It was heartbreaking to watch Wayne go through that.

The message I wanna give my readers is that everybody struggles through life, it can be financially, academically or professionally. I obviously have struggled both emotionally and physically in terms of my career. Nothing was served on a plate to me. That is the thing, you must be consistent for fruitful results. One must take control of their life.

The only way to overcome your struggles is to sit down with somebody and tell them your life story, what happened to you, how you got there, and where you are today.

At first, I was in turmoil about whether I should go to therapy or whether I should tell someone about what happened to me. Then, one day, I was sitting there, and I thought to myself that if I don't share it, this will be going to haunt me for the rest of my life. After that day, I signed up for therapies. I told everything to my therapist. One should know that just like how doctors cure your physical health, our psychologists are a doctor for our mind and soul – they cure our mental health. Both of them are equally important.

It is completely understandable that there are tons of questions going through your mind, what should I say? How are they going to react? What will be the outcome of it? But once you'll the initial step, and you take that leap of faith, everything will turn out to be so smooth and flows really well.

Talking to someone will help you put your life back together into pieces. The healing process will begin. If you don't talk to anybody and keep suppressing your emotions, it's nothing but a recipe for disaster. You need to be totally honest with them and with yourself as well. You can't sugar coat it and just lay it out, and once you have done that, the road to recovery is a lot easier.

Chapter 7: Mum's Death

"Too many people push us to 'get on with life' too soon after a significant loss. We need to be able to grieve, but...we also need to adjust our expectations of ourselves."

— LIZ SCHMITZ-BINNALL

It is no doubt that a mother is an integral part of our lives. Whether we grieve for the death of our mother (someone who birthed us) or a mother figure who played a big part in raising us, it is the bond that we grieve for, the attachment that we carve after they leave our lives. Sometimes, you are not even so close to your mothers, but only the sense of her presence of her is enough for you to live your life and stay motivated.

A British psychologist, John Bowlby, stated that children are born to seek attachment and love from their caregivers. This attachment is totally based on the responsiveness and the nurturing of a mother or a caregiver.

Therefore, it is understandable that grieving that attachment and the relationship of love and affection is extremely difficult. It is proven through research that children who had lost their mothers at an early age often scored lower with regard to resilience than those who have not.

There are times when people do not have good relationships with their mothers. However, they are surprised at the intensity of their grief reaction because of their mother's death.

The death of a mother is one of the extremely difficult things people go through in their lives. Whether they possess a great relationship, a terrible one, or somewhere in between, this is something that has a major impact on their lives – and the same thing happened to me.

Things were moving on with my career and my businesses. Then, I got a phone call one day to say that my mum had been taken to hospital. She had to undergo a six-hour operation. It was quite a shock to everybody. But it was sad; they would give us six months. My sister Irene was my mum's full time caregiver. Mum spent those last months fighting for her life. She was diagnosed in April, and then, unfortunately, she died in September.

My mum's death came as a shock for all of us. My family took my mum's death very hard. Even though she died peacefully surrounded by all her loved ones. It solidified what an incredible woman she was and how many people she touched while being here on earth. She was dear and loved by a lot of people. Unfortunately, I was not there when she passed away.

Death is extremely painful for those left behind to grieve, especially in my mum's case. Losing her was one of the hardest battles I had to go through. I was truly not prepared. The fact that she was no longer on earth with us, this realisation hit me square in the face.

When I lost my mother, I realised how it feels to lose someone you love. Perhaps, there is no proper way to describe the grief and intolerable pain that tears you apart, which is like a stone in a heart and makes tears run down your face when you remember each moment spent with your loved one.

Memories of my mum will always follow me wherever I go, and however far while I live my dreams with the gentle scent of her perfume and the shimmering of her laugh.

I didn't particularly do anything special to survive my mum's death, I just continued to stay alive. Sometimes, I think that I still haven't processed the pain of losing my mother. It wasn't that terrible – there were little shreds of mercies I had which I can never forget.

If I ever was at my worst, I had my fair share of friends and loved ones that were able to soothe the unbearable.

Eventually, all of my siblings and I moved on with our lives while keeping our mum's memories alive in our hearts. We often have family get-togethers. Me and siblings began having a very close bond after my mum's death. Even though I was subtly jealous of the bone, they all shared it with my mum. My mum was an incredible woman, she was beautiful inside out. However, the sad part is that everybody got to see it except me.

Harry, my youngest brother, was the one who was taking it really bad. He turned to alcohol and drugs. His behaviour was irrational. He just couldn't cope with my mum's passing away. After all, he was a blue eye, and everything he wanted, he got it. He wasn't even 21 when she passed away. But he managed to get himself involved with some unruly people due to all his drug and alcohol habits. I think it was my dad or Maria's husband who actually paid these guys off. Harry worked with Maria's husband. He was dating a nice girl who he idolised. They went on to have to beautiful boys but due to his drinking and taking drugs she refused to let him see them he was devastated.

My mom was only 51 when she died, and Harry was 21. And she'd already bought him his 21st birthday present, a gold bracelet. We were all there at his birthday party. I was there too. But as I said before, I never said much at family gatherings because I didn't have anything in common with them. They all talked about the kids and what they were doing. I didn't have children.

For anyone who has lost their mother, please know that people will expect you to move on. We all must have our deserved time to grieve. When it's fresh and new, you might think that you will feel like this forever or you will never be able to get over it – but you will.

If you're not acknowledging your feelings or if you are in denial, that doesn't mean that they don't exist and impact our lives. Throughout the struggles of my life, one thing that I have learned about grief is that it isn't supposed to be logical and linear. You must be very careful with the people you keep around you. Make sure that they love you and they are extra tender to you. Sometimes the most bi-hearted people around you say or do something which may cross the boundaries you have set for yourself. It's human nature, they make mistakes, even I still do it myself. Mostly, those missteps may be forgivable. However, you will have the right to which ones aren't, and that's important.

If all of this is awfully similar to you, or if you could relate to any of these situations, it is because we have all grieved in some way. We may collectively experience the events and wave after wave of loss somewhere in the past. I want all of you to know that we know how you feel. We know how it feels to lose someone you love.

Have you ever seen a subway stop between stations? Try to sense the second it begins to lurch back into motion until you can't tell the difference between standing still and moving – this is what grief is like but with fear and fury and sadness and a terrible blankness that nothing can soothe. You are unaware of the fact that when the subway will start to move again and you can't magic it into moving. You can just wait and see and make sure that you're still holding on when it starts to motion again. You will be surprised by the things you are able to survive. You won't believe how much strength you bear – I still don't.

Chapters 8: Thriving through Life

One might think that a person born into such unfortunate and uncanny circumstances is likely to stay in the same circumstances for the rest of their life. Perhaps this statistic is true, along with the statistic that less than 1% of such unfortunate beings rise to be extremely wealthy and possibly one of the richest people known to mankind.

I was one of those uncanny, rare people, yet looking back, it was odd how I never felt special or superior in any regard. Or maybe I did in my own way, but I never let it manifest in a way one might think I was arrogant, unreasonable, and haughty.

Let me start at a time when my life was golden and glamourous and how slowly and gradually it took a turn into a quieter, toned-down, domesticated path of life by my own choice.

During my college years, which were spectacular, by the way, I happened to have made the first important and huge purchase of my life. I bought my apartment while I was still a student, and by that time, I had worked multiple jobs to lead such a lifestyle. Not only had my grades in school gotten me far, but I believe my sharp and street-smart wit and common sense had proven fruitful in my professional life too. I was finding it easier than most naïve and pampered children my age when it came to thrive on my own as a grown adult.

There were things I had been seeing from a young age that many of the children my age and older than me had neither seen nor experienced. And in a way, I was now grateful for them, although I still believe a child should not have to go through what I had. God forbid if someone has to go through an abusive environment. I wish everyone to pass through these difficult times and shine brighter than ever.

However, things went differently. I was a grown-up with my own apartment and a college degree. Not long after, I was an established grown-up with not just an apartment and a college degree but also many prospective businesses.

My array of businesses grew and flourished, and before long, I was independent, wealthy, happy, and thriving. Thank goodness for what I have achieved in a very short period of time.

Unlike my career, I wasn't quite sure about my love life. My belief is that most people think that love is a profound experience where you find "the right person," and when you find your soulmate, you will just "click." Many of our stories perpetuate this. They ascribe the mystical element to love. I agree that when you are in love, it is something really special, but I feel like it is also ordinary. Many of us experience love a few times in our lives. The element of mysticism sometimes leave us feeling powerless, and I think it doesn't really serve us.

Have you ever wondered if you have met that "right person" or soulmate? We all do. As far as I believe, everyone finds their soulmate once in their lives. However, in order to find a soulmate, we must understand that we humans are never meant to be alone, and the purpose of a soulmate is that they complete each other, they challenge us to grow together and to help each other reach our potential.

Everything in life comes at its destined time. It is purely a matter of self-knowledge when you realize that a relationship is not just a simple need for fulfilment and attention but an essential part of your spiritual and psychological development, that is when you're most likely to meet your soulmate.

I did find love a couple of times. I had a few serious relationships that I genuinely thought would make it till the end, only to be sabotaged by me. And I say sabotaged because that is how my family and friends at the time thought. From my own perspective, however, I saw myself as too young, hopeful, and fresh to get cuffed so early by not just a legal bonding but a legal commitment that would tie me down to one location, a few restricted career paths, and very little mobility in terms of living arrangements. Not that I was planning on moving anywhere outside the UK anytime soon. I just did not see myself as someone willing to settle down so fast when I was only beginning to live my life to its fullest.

One of my boyfriends, in whom I genuinely saw a future, proposed to me, and I said yes. We were engaged for a while before I ended the relationship. It was not an impulsive decision at all but rather a very well-thought-out and insightful move. While it may have been somewhat of an emotional dip for me, it helped me throw myself into my businesses and flourish even more.

I have been engaged once. The guy was Steven, and we went for about three to four years. But then, there was a time when I thought I didn't want to continue with it anymore. I didn't want to be with him. I realized it late, but Steven wasn't the type of person who would take risks and chances and knowing me, my life was always dependent on the risks and chances I took. He was the type of person that would plug along with everyday life, and I expected more from my life partner. I knew I wanted more. I wanted something better, but I didn't know what it was and what I wanted, but one thing I was sure of was that it wasn't Steven. So, in the end, I called off the engagement. I won't lie, it was devastating in the beginning. Obviously, I had an attachment with him. You can't go through life for four years and not have feelings for them. It was tough on me, even though I broke it off. It was tough because you had to live on your own again. Once there were two, and now, just one. So you have to learn to be on your own again instead of thinking about 'we' it's just 'I,' and that is what you have to do.

There was always something that was stopping me from committing to somebody. I had no idea what it was, but I just couldn't cater to the idea of living with just one person for the rest of my life. I had a difficult time coping with this fear of commitment. I always thought that why do I feel that way? Why do I not want to commit? I always thought maybe it was because I wanted something bigger and better in my life, and I hadn't found it yet. I was in search of it until I actually found the one I wanted. His name was Keith.

I was in love with Keith. He was everything that I ever wanted; he was smart and intelligent as well. When I first met Keith, I was at the hospital. It was like all my fairy tale dreams came true at that moment. I instantly knew he was the one I was looking for. He was my prince charming until, obviously, things went a little bit different and when they started to fall apart, but this story is for later.

I had many opportunities to date doctors and many other highly professional people, but it always turned out that I wasn't interested in them. He was the one that I wanted. He had my heart – and to give somebody your heart is like giving them your soul.

He supported me with everything that I wanted to do. If I wanted to change careers or I wanted to take a different path with regard to some career choices, I would always talk to Keith about it, and we'd weigh up the pros and cons. However, at the end of the day, it was always my decision.

In the midst of all the ups and downs regarding my relationships, life went on. I met people, socialized, and continued to do wonders in my career.

My cousin, who was my mother's sister's son, Mark Roscoe, owned a casting agency in Liverpool that was doing very well. Mark and I were quite close, so I would visit him at work sometimes. Whenever I could check up on Mark to ask him how he was doing and what was new, he would be working on films or TV commercials. He was really busy with several top film projects that were going on in Liverpool. It was like being related to a powerful drug lord of some sort; he had all the contacts, strings, and PR one could imagine within and outside of the UK. And mostly, much like myself, he traveled a lot. Mark taught me how to buy properties with little or no money at all. I suppose out of our poor and pitiful childhood living standards, all of us children had established ourselves quite well as adults. However, it was I who really took our successes and assets to the next level with the help of Mark; and that is why we were so close.

There was a period when Mark had to visit Miami for a very long period, about six months or more. He asked me to come with him. I agreed, and within a short span of time, without much of a notice period, I set for my half-a-year-long trip to the United States of America to enjoy one of its most popular states in the world.

Something about this trip hit me differently, and I could not tell what was right then. It was perhaps the lifestyle that I had adopted there, or maybe it happened at a very comfortable, mature, and well-established point in my life. Even though I had been to the States many times before, this time, everything about it felt a little different and unique. It felt like a prospective home to me in more ways than one.

I packed my bags, took a month off from work, and got managers to take care of my business. Mark had a beautiful apartment in Miami. It was one of those ultra-modern contemporary penthouse apartments that cost a fortune. It overlooked the ocean and had a view of much more than just the water. It felt like a resort that I never actually thought would be a home to me for so long. It was simply beautiful.

My life during those six months was quite interesting and intriguing.

Mark had numerous friends. We had some good times; we would be hard and fast and party throughout the evening. Be that as it may, Mark would need to work morning, noon, and night. I didn't accomplish any work at all. I relaxed more often than not, either on the oceanfront or at the pool. And afterward, we'd go out to supper and get to know one another as time passed by. I really began to feel comfortable in the United States.

In any case, I had never felt like that in the capacity of feeling comfortable, and I even started contemplating whether to remain or live there. Toward the month's end, I returned home right when Mark returned to Liverpool.

Just like this, I have had many traveling experiences in my life. Wayne and I would travel everywhere. We would hop on to the plane whenever we could. We have been to so many places, and it was a lot of fun. The privilege I had was that Wayne used to work in airlines, so it didn't really cost me much to travel. We are traveling companions. We went to the Caribbean, Africa, Shanghai, Hong Kong, and many exotic places as well.

One of the best travel experiences that I remember is my honeymoon with Keith. It was dreamy and magical, just everything a girl wanted. It was amazing.

What's more, I began taking a gander at my life. I thought I'd achieved such a great amount at such a young age. I realized that it was a huge milestone that anyone could achieve at a very young age.

One thing I want to advise my readers when making career choices is that look at everything. I repeat, LOOK. UP. EVERYTHING. Calculate the pros and cons, write it down, look at it, walk away from it, come back, look at it again, and then make a decision. Decisions that are made in haste are never fruitful and will cause a lot of issues for you in the longer run. However, if you look at the things practically and you take the time to evaluate them, only then you're going to make the right choice.

Always remember that whatever decisions you're going to make, we make it at that timc. It may not turn out to be fruitful at a later date but needed at that time. However, always evaluate the circumstances – what you have, where you're going, and what you want to achieve. Never do it in haste.

In my career, I have always wanted to work in a public job. I have been an outgoing person, and because of my past history, I never wanted to be in a mundane job. I wanted to be where I was literally helping someone. I wanted to have a feeling that I was achieving something, and I wanted the people I was taking of to know that they were in the best possible hands. I always knew from an early age what I wanted from my life. My sole purpose was to go and help people, no matter what. I never wanted an office job.

I have had my fair share of hurdles that come my way. I had literally no one who would support me. I had to completely rely on myself. Nobody told me whether it was a good or a bad idea with whatever decision I made. I thought they would tell me or listen to me about what I wanted or where I was going because nobody really cared; I don't know if it's a good thing or not, but that made me strong. That was the driving force for me. I think that nobody helped do it. I did it all on my own.

And yet, I had times when I was totally alone. I had times when I wanted to scream and get someone to listen to me, but nobody was interested. Everybody thought that I was living in the limelight. But I had some lonely dark times. You don't talk about those lonely dark times to people because people don't want to know, people have got their own things going on, so they don't really want to listen. Dark times come in everybody's life. You to bring yourself out because if you don't, you're going to stay there for the rest of your days.

Through all of my life experiences, I had tremendous growth within me, and I learned how strong I could be in difficult life circumstances and situations. I was contemplating the pros and cons of my potential choices. I wanted to make a very calculated decision for my life. One bad step, and boom! Your life can change drastically, either in a good or a bad way. I never knew what my life had stored for me.

Chapter 9: A New Start in the USA

Life becomes hell when your fight is within you. Often in life, we all have to choose between two things or make difficult life decisions, either big or small. However, this decision-making can create conflicts sometimes. For me, it was the decision of whether I should stay in the USA and do what my mind felt peace at or go back to where I was already settled. No matter whatever era or age you are, you've definitely encountered someone saying, "Follow your heart." If you will ever come to me for advice, I would advise you the same because that is what I have blind faith in.

However, following your heart is always about intuition. It can sometimes conflict with the messages we get regarding how important it is to be rational. I believe that if you follow your heart, you tend to achieve higher satisfaction in your career as well as in life. Being a firm believer in the follow your heart thing, I actually always did what made my heart happy. Even so, I wouldn't say it was an easy choice to make, but I came up with a conclusion.

After two or three weeks, I'd settled on the choice that I really needed to proceed to live in the United States. I discussed it with a few people, and they thought I was insane and needed to quit any pretence of all that I had in the UK. It was anything but a simple choice to make. I had been mulling over everything for quite a while. I was wondering if it was worth it to pack up what I had spent years and years building upwards from scratch just because one particular year, it felt "right" to move. I wondered why it had never occurred to me before to want to move here and become an American national. It was all quite confusing, and I did not know whether it was worth it or not.

I consulted my friends and family. Some stood in an agreeable position with the move, others not so much.

Finally, I made up my mind that this was the place I needed to be. So I put all my organisations as well as every one of the properties available to be purchased.

My family and everybody were very stunned. I thought to myself, be that as it may, I have settled on this choice. I needed another life - a fresh start. The time had come, and I was truly frightened. But I was also invigorated, simultaneously thinking about what my new life would be like.

Wayne had a friend, Paul, who lived in California. He called him and told him that I needed to come to the US. So I wound up in San Diego, California. I had nothing but a suitcase and some money in my pocket. I settled in with Paul for some time. We had a great time together, but then it was time for me to settle out.

San Diego is a delightful spot encircled by seas. It is where you can simply relax without any pressure by any stretch of the imagination. So I celebrated for a brief period. And afterwards, it was the chosen time for me to get my Green Card.

Paul had another friend named Rudy, who was in the military. He would come all through the port. Rudy was an astonishing person, so brimming with fun and life. We partied together and had a lot of fun. At the point when he returned to port, it would remain for two or three months, and afterwards, they would need to leave once more.

One night we had all been sitting out, drinking in the nice weather in the evening air and soaking in the goodness of a well-paying life in the company of great friends. Everything was perfect.

Rudy turned to me and said, “Hey, you’ve been wanting a nationality here, haven’t you.”

“Yeah,” I gave him a lopsided smile, unsure of what he was getting to.

"Well," he chuckled, "Why not just marry me?"

"Yeah, right!" I guffawed, truly thinking he was joking.

Rudy sat up and looked straight at my face and said solemnly, "I'm not kidding. I quite genuinely mean it, Suz. You should marry me for the purpose of attaining a Green Card as soon as possible. It also works for your living arrangements."

It began to dawn on me that he was right. He had a very valid point, mostly because many people did this, and it worked out perfectly fine for them. So I agreed. And soon enough, Rudy and I got married.

It took little time for the vacation and partying phase to be over, with the new priority being making a stable home in America. I started working with adults with learning disabilities, mental health issues, incapacities and psychological well-being concerns. It was pretty much like a highly specific old home; an extraordinary line of work, a great job. However, it was exceptionally stressful since it involved a great deal of travel and movement, and I needed to move between different clients and customers. I really wanted to. I loved moving and checking up on and monitoring the progress of all these clients, and it made me care for humanity in a different way.

Most importantly, it had me grateful for my life thus far. I saw psychological issues like PTSD and such, where the elderly people I was looking after suffered a great deal. I reflected on the abuse and horror I endured as a young, innocent and impressionable child. It was a wonder how I had not only made it out in one piece mentally and intellectually and as a well-rounded adult but also as successful, happy and satisfied as I had been. I found a new form of appreciation for the wonderful life I had been living and truly felt like the one up there had been keeping out a special eye for my loved ones and me. I mean, it truly was a wonder how my mental awareness had not fragmented into many different personalities to endure the abuse or how I was not an extremely paranoid or damaged person emotionally.

It had all ended up working out so well for me. And so, I truly loved my work. And I loved helping people.

I actually got a job at a hospital in San Diego, and I settled into that. And one evening, I met Keith. Keith showed me how to use all the medical systems and stuff at the hospital. The first time I met him, he was teaching me computer systems on the medical base. There was an instant attraction between us.

Keith was an astonishing person. He was so enchanting and had the ideal grin. And he was very handsome. One day he asked me out on a date. It was one of the most magical experiences of my life. We had so much fun. We walked home and talked continuously.

Keith and I began to date. And we dated for some time. It was the best part of my life. We had so many things in common. We both played tennis together; the society we lived in in San Diego had private tennis courts, so we used to hand out a lot over there. Other than that, we spent our time shopping and did a lot of the craziest things that we had never done before.

The more time we spent together, the more it revolved into something that this is the guy I want to get married to. He was just so much fun to be around. He was intelligent, and he taught me a lot of things, either work-related or life-related. It was like a team of two. We were just eighteen, and it was just magical. Everything about him was a complete package for me as far as I was concerned.

People believe that when they meet their other half, it feels like a life-changing experience. They say that it feels like you have known the other person for ages.

However, I never knew what happens when two people who are destined to be soulmates cross paths. Obviously, never in my life, I have seen healthy relationships growing up, and it made me believe that I would never be able to realise whenever I meet my potential partner until I met Keith. And then everything started to connect.

Whenever you cross paths with your other half, it will seem like you could be with the person forever. You both have mutual respect for each other, and you begin to have a deep and powerful feeling right from the first encounter. You feel an effortless connection. Most importantly, when he or she comes into your life, no power can keep you two apart, and the universe would do anything to pull you two together.

He was an executive at an organisation and worked as a network administrator. He worked in the neighbourhood emergency clinic managing their organisation and was their organisation support. Keith and I met one night for supper, and he let me know that he was going to Atlanta. His brother-in-law possessed a clinical software organisation, and he had extended an employment opportunity to Keith. So Keith requested that I go with him. I took a gander at Keith and thought, "It really works how far we have come as a couple? How do I know that this relationship will not end up like all the previous ones I have had? What distinguishes it from those? How will we settle, far from where I had rooted myself in this foreign land, and how will we work moving forward, especially with the status difference?"

I had been quite wealthy in the United Kingdom, naturally. Owning several many businesses and houses had gotten me up the social and financial strata. However, moving to America is a lot costlier than what one initially calculates it to be. The expenditure goes many times multiplied by that initial amount that a person willing to move has to consider to spare. The truth is, what seemed to me to be like peanuts became quite the fortune. For me, back then, the move had been quite worth it. Still, I went from being the owner of many businesses to an employee in a meagre job that I luckily happened to like.

Keith, on the other hand, was like what I had been in the UK, except wealthier, because he belonged to a rich, reputable family. It was quite the "Crazy Asians" drama for a bit, where I sensed that, despite flourishing financially well-doing, his wealthy and scandalous family did not seem to fully approve of our relationship, even though nothing had been initially expressed to our faces. It took me a while to sense the disapproving thoughts.

All these thoughts led me to conclude that if I were to be anywhere in America, I would be with Keith because what was between us was divine and rare. I was still married to Rudy, and we lived in the same apartment. Of course, Rudy and I were married for legal benefits and nothing other than that. Our relationship never manifested into anything more than friendship. However, for legal work's sake and because he was my friend, along with Paul and Wayne, I informed the three of them of my decision. They not only approved but hyped me up to move to Atlanta with Keith.

And so, not long after I hauled my way over to the States after having winded up everything in the United Kingdom, I once more packed a lot of my belongings and work-life and moved to Atlanta with him.

Little did I know, that move would be the beginning of a series of moves over a span every few years with Keith. I still convinced myself that wherever I was with Keith, I was home.

Chapter 10: Moving to Atlanta

Moving to a new city with your potential partner is a big step in a person's relationship. Whether it is living in the same apartment or separately in your own spaces, moving to a brand new place is exhilarating as well as risky. Sometimes, you do not even have control over your overwhelming emotions. You get to experience exciting things together. There are times when things are not going smooth; you need to deal with it calmly.

I will not say that moving to Atlanta was a bad choice for me, but it somewhat brought me back to the initial stages – from where I started. You will get to understand this later in the book.

As soon as we got to Atlanta, we settled into a corporate apartment for a month after moving to Atlanta. I was deciding which direction I wanted to take my career. Keith was trying to cope with settling at his new place too. We were starting a new life together, from scratch. I had so many thoughts going in my head regarding the decision that I made. It was a wholesome feeling, though – moving in with the love of your life and planning to start a new life together.

It is obvious that the longer you date a person, the more likely the situation of living together comes up. After all, when the two people have actually planned to live together forever, why not start that "forever" soon? It can be good before getting married to the person as well. Whatever it is, this decision comes with several reasons why you are moving in together with your significant other. However, one thing you all must note: you MUST know the reason why you're doing this. Why are you leaving your already-settled lifestyle for that one specific person? I honestly thought that being a live-in boyfriend and girlfriend would be a breeze. We all see those happy cohabitating couples on TV shows.

However, what we never see is the time and commitment it takes for the both of you to invest while compromising each other's habits. Nothing like that exists in TV land.

Personally, I think Atlanta is a great place – so charismatic, full of amazing people, and full of life. The city grows on you. If you want good food, you can undoubtedly find it in Atlanta. If you are an athlete, Atlanta is for you. If you are into art, theatre, or opera, it's Atlanta. Friendly people? Atlanta. History? Job opportunities? Better health care? You can definitely find it in Atlanta.

Atlanta was very vibrant as a city because there were so many cultures there. The city has the tendency that it gets evolve in you. I found it to be intriguing and an eye-opener. However, in every situation, bad follows a good. As the city had a wide range of diversity in it, on the other hand, there was slavery, and violence kind of stuff present too. For, I am the kind of a person who doesn't like discrimination in any sense. It is still common there to this day. You can literally see the segregation between whites and African Americans in the city. The fact that people are tortured just because of their colour doesn't sit right with me ever.

As far as my career was concerned, I didn't want to go back to work with adults having learning difficulties, but I got a job. I wanted some change, so I thought about doing something in the medical field. They had programs for medical assistants who would work alongside doctors. I would do all the technical stuff while the doctor did everything else. I knew I had the ability to learn more.

I decided to enrol myself in a school for the cause of becoming an MA. Soon, my classes began. Whilst I was in class, I met Vanessa. She was a great girl, full of fun, and we used to sit next to each other. We really hit it off. We spent most of our time in class together doing coursework and working on different projects. It is one of the best feelings to find people like you in a new city.

Soon after, both of us eventually graduated and went our separate ways. But we managed to stay in contact through all this time, and I am grateful that we are still really close friends to this day. I ended up getting a job in a hospital called St. Joseph of Atlanta. It was a big cardiac hospital. At the same time, Vanessa went on to work in different fields.

At first, I was quite shocked at the fact that I actually got a job in the emergency department there. It was a huge achievement for me. However, there were so many things that I was experiencing for the first time. I've never seen or heard about gunshot wounds or victims coming in who had been shot, and it was quite a cultural shock for me because it was something I've never seen.

Yet, it was quite common with everybody else there. It was like they were prone to it.

People came in every day with different gunshot wounds, stab wounds, and cardiac problems. The good thing was I am a fast learner. I tend to put all my efforts and work hard to achieve my goals – it is one of the qualities that helped me gain what I had in my life. I finally settled in, and I began to really enjoy what I was doing. It wasn't long after a news came of husband who shot her wife who was in ICU at St. Joseph of Atlanta Georgia Hospital because they had no health care insurance. They later locked the hospital down and the husband was arrested. Imagine how desperate he was that it made him do what should never have happen.

I faced struggles in this regard. Everybody has struggles, you know. Anybody that goes through college, university, or so forth in life faces struggles. I am not saying that life is all fancy schmancy with the glitters and stuff. We always lose something in order to gain success in our career and life in general. I had anxieties too. Everything was so new for me. I was vulnerable in the sense that it was a new state, new people, and a new career. I had to move forward with a big change in my life. However, having the ability to overcome the situation can outgrow all your anxieties and vulnerability. I tried. I tried to overcome the situation.

Keith had settled into his job and even met some amazing work colleagues. He hired some great employees, and we had a really good time together. We would all meet up, go out for dinner or drink together, and have a political and social life. We both were having one of the best times of life.

Keith and I talked about marriages and engagements, but nothing was ever set in concrete. Suddenly, one day, Keith came in and asked me to marry him. It was a huge milestone for us. I was a bit taken back, but I said, "Yeah, of course." So, it was time now for me to divorce Rudy. I had my Green Card by then. I'm glad that it happened the way it did because I didn't want to drag Keith into the whole Green Card situation. Keith wanted to come to England to meet my family. So we started looking at flights and stuff.

Once I was out, Keith's mum called him and asked if I was around, and he said, "No, Suz's out." Then she started explaining to him, "Do you realize she was married?" And he said, "Yes, I do." Unbeknownst to me, times that I'd gone around to have dinner with Keith's parents, they would ask me all sorts of questions. I didn't think anything of it because they were Keith's parents, and I guess they just wanted to get to know me. Or did I know that Keith's dad, who was a retired FBI agent, had done a background check on me? There was nothing to be found other than the fact that I was married. He was quite taken aback by the fact that Keith knew all about it and that I was totally honest with him. The greatest difficulty that I had to face all this time was that I don't think Keith's mother was happy with our decision to get married.

So we headed off to the UK to meet my family. Everybody loved Keith, and they fell in love with him. They thought he was an amazing guy, and they all clicked with him. Keith and I then got engaged. We hadn't planned our marriage yet, but we talked about it. So eventually, we set a date and started preparing for our wedding.

Keith's brother-in-law and his sister lived in Delray Beach, Florida. Their property was right on the ocean, and it was a perfect setting for the wedding. So, we asked them if Keith and I could get married at their property, and they were happy about that. They said, "Yep, perfect." The day finally came. We had an amazing wedding. It was an oceanfront beach wedding. It was magical. I had seven bridesmaids and the whole nine yards. It was the perfect day, and Keith and I were so happy. He was the perfect husband, very attentive, and everything I needed was there. I loved him dearly.

Imagine you've been dating someone for a decent amount of time, and you know that it is the person for you - the person you want to spend your life with, and suddenly, that happens. The dating relationship takes a turn into a life-long commitment. Now it might initially give some jitters. However, the exhilaration of this is uncontrollable. The excitement to finally call them yours, you start to share a life with them is just simply an amazing feeling and the thoughts you have in mind are a mixture of so many things.

After a few years, things started taking a turn for the worst in the office where Keith worked. There were accusations that the company was in trouble and some accusations of insider trading. I am not too sure because I didn't get to know the full story. One of the reasons I didn't want to know is because it didn't affect me. At first, it didn't affect any of us that much. We were cautious, but we continued with our lives.

Keith's sister and his brother-in-law had their own private jets and yacht. We would spend a lot of vacation time on their boats and then fly wherever we were going to visit. I was living the American dream. Things started to decline for Keith at work because they knew that his brother-in-law owed to the company, and they weren't sure whether Keith knew what was going on. But he didn't, and neither did I, and we didn't want to know, but it got difficult for him. So he decided that he was going to leave.

He came home one day and told me that he had given the notice and that we would return back to San Diego. We set our property out there. We had rented it out. We didn't sell it, which was a good thing. We kept it because if we ever needed a home to go back to, we knew that we'd have a beautiful place waiting for us. We had orange, peach, and lime trees. We had the pool, hot tub, and the whole nine yards. We had an amazing house. It was beautiful. So we got back, and Keith got back into the IT field. However, after a while, he came home, and he said that he was getting bored with it and he wanted to do something different.

Grey, the guy who cleaned and maintained our pool, had his own business. He would build pools, fix leaks, and do all the engineering stuff. Keith was talking to him, and grey said to him if it's something you want to do, I can help and give you some of my clients, so Keith said yeah, great, that would be amazing. I'll take some of your clients, and you can show me what I need to do, where to get all the equipment and how to do it.

Eventually, Keith started his own business. He was doing really, really well, but I noticed things were slipping with Keith; the monthly bills that he would have to send out in monthly invoices to clients, and he started to get lax on it, and I wasn't sure what was going on. Keith would come home and have a drink, and it didn't bother me at first. I didn't drink alcohol ever. I preferred not to have anyone around me who would drink, but it was fine. I compromised on it.

However, his mum and dad lived around the corner from where we lived, and if we had an argument or something, Keith would be on the phone with his mum, telling them that we had an argument and telling them what was over and stuff like that. I thought that it was really low of Keith to do something like that because that was between us and not his parents.

Keith was the youngest of five and the only boy, so his mum spoiled him rotten. Keith could do no wrong, but a string started to get worse and worse. His business started to slip and eventually stopped working. I continued to work. I got a job at Scripps Green Hospital in La Jolla, which is one of the prestigious hospitals in San Diego. Sometimes, I would come home late. If I were on a late shift, it'd be 11 o'clock at night, and he would be in bed. Or, if it was early, I'll be home by 3 in the afternoon. All Keith would do is sit there and drink. Honestly, that started to become a problem because I didn't like alcohol. I didn't like people drinking around me.

We started to argue about this. And again, he'd be on the phone with his parents to tell him that we'd been fighting and arguing, but he never told his parents what it was all over, and neither did I. Because, at the end of the day, it wasn't their business and it was only between him and me. But he always made me look like the bad cop where his parents were concerned, and it started to show.

It got to the point where we were arguing all the time. I told him he had to go to work because he would sit there and drink all day, and I told him that one day he would leave me a widow at an early age if he didn't stop whatever he was doing. And he said, "No, I won't. I've got it under control." But he hadn't got it under control. And bit by bit, our relationship started to fall apart.

Chapter 11: Back to San Diego and Many Battles

Nowadays, this world is lurching from one crisis to another in an instance time. We all have experienced a worldwide pandemic, which literally changed how we conduct our day-to-day lifestyle, social turmoil, political and economic uncertainty, as well as an array of natural disasters. Then there come our personal traumas which we are dealing with in the midst of all the crisis, like losing a loved one, unemployment, declining health, divorce, tragic accidents, or violent crime. For many of us, this is a major time of unprecedented struggles and upheavals.

Either the source of disruption in our lives may be a personal tragedy or global emergency—or both. Living in chaotic and difficult times can surely take a heavy toll on our mood, outlook, and health. It can also leave us feeling incapable and overwhelmed by anxiety and stress. Some of us may be grieving all that we have lost, flooded by a slew of conflicting, difficult emotions, or uncertainty about how to carry on with our lives. We may even feel that our lives are totally out of control, and we may feel powerless to affect whatever may happen next.

Even though there's no way to avoid adversity, sorrow, or distress in life, there surely are ways which can help us smooth the rough waters and regain a sense of control in our lives – that is, resilience. It is the way to cope with the change, loss, and trauma that have been inevitable in our parts of life even before these extraordinary times. Building a sense of resilience in yourself can help you adapt to life-changing events by bouncing back from hardships and tragedies while coping with these turbulent times.

As I said, things in my life went on like this too. Keith kept looking for new jobs. He continued drinking more than before.

Eventually, his brother-in-law asked him if he wanted to go and work in Philadelphia. Keith told me that he had been offered the job. And I said, “Yes, let’s go.” I said that because I didn’t want Keith to be drinking anymore. At least he had a job, and he wouldn’t be sitting at home drinking all day. So we packed up our bags, rented the house out, and went to Philadelphia.

The office was actually in Pennsylvania, an hour away from Philadelphia. So we found a place to rent, and we settled in, and Keith started to go to work. The first thing he would do after coming home was to have a drink. He wouldn’t even eat dinner. There were many nights that I had to throw dinner out because he didn’t want it. All he did was drink. I started working with a family as a private nurse – a great family, and I'm still very close with the family to this day. I wasn't sure whether I wanted to work in a hospital or not. So I decided to do my EMT (Emergency Medical Technician) job. I ended up getting a job at East White Land Fire Department. It was another good mark on my portfolio. The company was amazing. We had so much fun at work. But I dreaded going home because I didn't know what I was going home to because Keith continued to drink.

You may be wondering why I never tried to send him to rehab for his drinking problem. Well, I did. I did, and he refused. I believe that caused a lot of problems in our relationship because he thought he didn't have any problem. As far as his mother was concerned, her precious stone didn't need any help. She thought it was all my fault. Everything went down to me.

Anyway, Simon, one of my nephews, was doing firefight training over here in the UK. I asked him if he wanted to come and spend some time with us in the US and see how our firefighters work. Simon did that. So my fire company made all the arrangements and got him insured for the company. Simon ended up coming out. He became a member of the East white land fire rescue service, where I worked. Simon was with us for six months, but he noticed how our marriage was dying and how bad it was getting. He was quite shocked because he said to me, "Auntie Suz, I thought you guys were so happy." I said, "Yeah. So did I, until, he started to drink."

When Simon came to live with us, Keith and he got along so well. They had an amazing bond together.

Simon still misses him to this day because they were really, really close together. They used to go out together. They went on different vacations together too.

As his drinking was getting out of control and I was getting angry and frustrated with him, I threatened to divorce him many times, but of course, I didn't. I stayed with him. Keith and I couldn't have children. We got married in October, and in November, they found I had a tumour. So I had to have a total hysterectomy. If we had kids, things would have turned out differently, but I will never know.

So Keith's parents sold their home in San Diego and moved to Florida. When we moved back to San Diego, I thought maybe things would be different now that his parents were not there anymore. Well, it turned out I was wrong. Our fighting was getting worse. Keith would often call the police because Keith was great at playing the victim, and I was always the one who was held accountable.

There were so many events when I thought of leaving Keith, but I could never do it. I loved him so much that I thought I could fix him. Even though deep in my heart, I knew I would never be able to do it, I never wanted to give up on him. He was the love of my life. Every time he did something wrong, I always tried to justify his actions. That's a sad situation when you love someone so much, and yet they choose to provide you with nothing.

Keith always tried to use violence or manipulation to maintain his power over me and control me. His actions resulted in me feeling anxious and scared, and I had a lot of trouble sleeping and concentrating. I started to lose my confidence. It had a devastating effect on me. It kind of affected losing a sense of security and safety in me.

It happens to everyone. This kind of abuse can have a long-term effect on us, both physically and mentally. It can affect our good relationships, and we are more likely to use controlling and manipulating behaviour ourselves. There are so many signs that someone is being abused in their relationships. Some of them are:

- They seem detached and withdrawn.
- They are bullied by other people.
- They may experience physical problems, like headaches or cramps.
- They have difficulty coping with their work and academic lives.
- Mood swings, and
- Use of alcohol and drugs.

Back to the story: one particular night, Keith and I actually had a huge fight, and he called the police for the simple factor that I threw something at him, but it missed and hit the TV instead.

The police came and asked who the house belonged to. I was not prepared for what he said. He told the officers the house belonged to his parents. Unbeknown to me, he had the property turned over to his parents, so if we divorced, I wouldn't get a penny. The police told me I had to leave.

In California, the laws are very stupid, I must say. I mean, I was arrested for destroying my property. I was quite shocked at the fact that I was arrested and booked for this. Keith came out and asked the police officers to let me go but they turned around and told no because I was arrested for criminal damage. So I was put in the back of the police car, and off I went. They booked me in, and I was taken to a women's jail.

I ended up in jail in downtown San Diego. It was quite a frightening experience. You were forced to like strip, and you had to put on the jail's uniform. You have to wear underwear that probably a million inmates had prior to you. It was double-checked to see whether you had that underwear on. It was so humiliating.

The guards shouted at us to turn and face the wall. I was stirring for around 15 minutes when the guards shouted at us to turn around and move. So I phoned Keith. I called him from the jail and told him to get me out of here and bail me out. He straight up said no. I couldn't fight with him over the phone because people would obviously be listening to my phone calls. I started to look around for someone to bail me out. Somebody to get me a bail bondsman and get me out of jail I phoned my family and Francis. My sister put up the money.

I never spoke to any of the inmates; I just lay on my bunk. We were called to go and have breakfast. The food was disgusting. I refused to eat it. One of the inmates said you should have taken it and would have eaten it; I didn't say a word.

It was pretty scary because I was in a dorm with about 20 other inmates. Some of them were in there for drugs, burglary, and a number of other crimes that they committed. All I did was smash my own TV.

My sister Francis finally be able to bail me out after being in jail for two days. It was such a relief to get someone to get me out. So I put up the bond myself, and I was released. I asked to appear in court the following Tuesday. I didn't even go home to Keith. I just walked into a hotel, which was near the home where we lived. And the following Tuesday, I went to court. The case was thrown out; there was no case to answer to. So I was released to let go.

I went home to Keith. I didn't even bother picking a fight with him because I was just totally disgusted. My family were absolutely gob-smacked by the fact that I was arrested and put in jail for breaking a TV. Our marriage hit rock bottom. There was no coming back, and again, we had another fight. Keith being Keith picked up the phone and called the police again. The police asked who the house belonged to and Keith told the police his parents so I left that house for the last time

I said, "Where the hell should I go? There's nowhere for me to go." And the police had the audacity to tell me to go downtown to Saint Vincent DePaul – they deal with people who have nowhere to live or nowhere to go.

So, I went down to St. Vincent DePaul and asked if they had a bed or anything where I could stay. They turned around and told me that they had no beds available. So I was literally sitting in a doorway. Wherever I was, I was in downtown San Diego somewhere. I just cried, cried, and cried. I thought, *"How did my life ever get this crazy?"* And I knew what had caused all of this; I knew it was the alcohol. I knew it was an addiction. How could I have ended up with someone who was an alcoholic after everything that I'd been through when I was a child? After everything that

I had achieved on my own, I ended up with a husband who was an alcoholic?

I couldn't go back home. After all, Keith got a restraining order. I was literally on the streets. I was just watching the sunrise. As the sun was rising, I couldn't believe what I was seeing. I saw rows and rows and rows of tents. I thought, *"Where the hell is this?"* This was a part of San Diego that I had never seen before and a part of San Diego that I didn't even know existed. People just started to wake up, and I just saw people coming out of these tents. There was this huge marquee in the middle of all these surrounding tents. I wanted to know what that was.

I stopped and asked somebody where I was, and they told me that I was in Tent City. I said, "What the hell is Tent City?" And they told me, "This is where all the homeless live. This is where the homeless go at night." I was shocked! I was shocked to the core because what

I saw were babies, kids, and adults crawling out of these tents. I asked somebody what that huge marquee was that I was looking at. They told me, “If you are lucky, you get to spend the winter there.” They told me that it was done by raffle. If you wanted a bed for the winter, you were given a raffle ticket. If your number came up, you got a bed for the winter in the marquee, and you got food as well.

I just couldn’t believe what I was hearing and what I was seeing. So I just sat there for a while and watched. I was really upset by what I got to experience because it was something that I had never ever seen before and never really realized existed. I asked one woman, “Where do you go to get a shower, and where do you go to eat? She told me that they would go to St. Vincent DePaul, where they would shower, or there was a missionary across the road.

All of this made my heart sink. I couldn't believe the fact that how blessed I was. It was the time when I realized how ungrateful we could get in life. We happen to curse God at the minor inconvenience that happens in our life, while there are people who don't even know if they'll get food to eat or a bed to sleep in at the end of the day.

Chapter 12: What It Feels Like To Be Homeless

Homelessness is a national crisis for everyone: there are so many people who are lacking to afford like, like college students, lower and middle-class individuals, as well as the working poor. They experience unexpected catastrophes. They all are swelling the ranks of the homeless. Experts say that an average person who would be out on the street for two or three months after losing a job or source of income can be considered homeless.

Homelessness is not just a problem of physically handicapped, substance abusers, or people with mental illness. It can happen to anyone.

There is discrimination against the poor in our society, especially the homeless, which makes it difficult for them to take care of their basic needs, or more complicated tasks like securing employment with living wages. Even a glass of water is a challenge for them. Nobody wants them around.

You may be able to walk anywhere, yet you're still bound. Transportation is not free. In so many ways, homeless people are constantly reminded that they are nothing without money.

Even if someone wants to find a job, it's difficult when you're homeless. Employers look at you cynically when they discover you live at a "no fixed address."

The longer they remain homeless, the more difficult it is for them to return and meet the mainstream standards of society. Being homeless is destabilizing, depressing demoralizing. Homeless people lose their base, a foundation from which they can begin to function. It becomes hard to focus. Constant obstacles in life chip away at their self-esteem, and their healthy personality wither, disintegrates and scatters.

They become scared, angry, frustrated, bitter, and distrustful. They're always tired and overwhelmed. Small tasks feel like chores as depression saps their energy. Stress clouds their judgment and biasness. They grab at anything that seems like an opportunity, yet they feel like they're getting nowhere.

It is pathetic to ever be homeless. In developed countries, affordable housing for people like them should be a right and not a privilege.

For me, one night, being homeless made me feel like the night was never going to end. I really don't know how to describe what it felt like. One can never imagine how it feels to be homeless. Seeing all of it, I felt very emotional. I was uncomfortable because the floor was hard, and it made my back really hurt. I felt vulnerable. I wanted to rescue all of the homeless people there and give them shelter. If only I could do a bare minimum for them.

While I was thinking through all of it, one of the homeless people told me that she was going for breakfast. She took me to a missionary called God's Extended Hand Missionary, which served the homeless people in downtown San Diego. So, I actually went in with this lady. She told me to sit down and that they would bring breakfast. And they did this by adding volunteers who would hand out breakfasts to the homeless.

She also told me that if I wanted a shower, I could go to St. Vincent DePaul, so I went. Little did I know that I had a shower with 30 other women over there. I started speaking to some of the homeless people. Some of them had told me that they'd been on the streets for a very long time due to alcohol and drug addiction. Then I spoke to all those who had been on the streets because they lost their home because they couldn't pay the rent, and my heart went out to these people. It upset me so much. And there was one particular girl I spoke to, she was so young, and this was at the time of the crash of 2008 and the credit crunch. This made me realize that most Americans are only one paycheck away from being homeless.

I had nowhere to sleep that night. The lady that told me to have breakfast with me that morning said that the same missionary normally has beds. So I went on. They didn't have a bed. So again, I spent the night on the streets, huddled in a doorway. There was nothing but the clothes I had on me. I didn't feel sad for me. I felt sad for those other people, for those young kids who had no way to live. The addicts had no help. It was the saddest phase of my life, and I never wish to go through that again.

The next day, I saw people helping each other – the homeless were helping each other because who else could help them? Nobody. And it was in the middle of the afternoon when a fight broke out. I saw this guy pull out a knife, and he slashed this kid right across the face. His face just opened up, and I stood there shocked.

I wanted to go and help him. But I couldn't speak for the fear if I intervened, something would happen to me as well. That was the hardest thing for me to do. Because all I ever did was help people keep my safety apart. I knew the missionary that had fed me breakfast would open up again at 3:30. So after watching what I'd seen, I walked over to the missionary, and I just stood up by the wall, bent, and was crying silently. I wasn't crying for myself. I was crying for him. Because I couldn't help him and because I couldn't help myself.

At the end of the day, I had dinner at the missionary. I actually got a bed there. I spent the night in the church, and I lay under the cross. Just looking up at the cross and thinking, "God, how can I end up like this?"

In the morning, everybody got up, and we left. I saw a crowd gathering. I walked over to where the crowd was gathering and saw two guys, there were police officers around. I saw two guys putting a homeless person into a body bag. I asked one of the bystanders what had happened? And they told me that he had been sleeping on the sidewalk that night and got hit by a car. I asked this person whether they knew where these homeless people go when they pass away. They told me that they get buried in the Potter's Field. I asked him what Potter's Field was, and they said, "It's a grave. These are unmarked graves where the people who know nobody are buried."

That's when I decided to leave this place. I thought to leave this place as soon as possible. This was my fourth day on the streets now, and I thought, *"I can't. I've got to go and get myself away from here because my mental health was really suffering badly."* So I called my sister Dorie, with who I am really close. She was shocked at the fact that I had been on the streets that long and why I didn't call anyone. I said that it took me a while to find the public phone. Dori was grieving she was broken hearted but amongst all her grieve she still reached out to make sure I was safe.

So she got me into a beautiful hotel that night, and I ended up soaking in a hot tub, but I couldn't sleep. I went shopping to get some clean clothes. She put money into a bank account for me, and I went shopping to get some clean clothes. I couldn't get out of my mind the images of all those people on the streets.

While Dori put me into a hotel, my sister Francis was looknf for a flight home to get me home . But I didn't have my passport with me. It actually route was out of date. So they called the British Embassy in Los Angeles. I made my way down to Los Angeles. I brought it to the British Council, and they issued me an emergency passport, and soon, I was on the flight. I arrived home with nothing but the clothes on my back. I was broken, empty, a Mia shadow of myself, and I thought, how am I going to put myself together? Two of my sisters picked me up from the airport, and they knew my mental state was bad. So I had a hot shower, got changed, and went straight to the hospital.

I was in the hospital for six weeks on a mental health unit. I never thought I would feel human again after everything I went through. I had the most amazing mental health team that worked with me every single day and for that I'm truly thankful. I still think about all those poor people on the streets. People see the USA as this amazing place to live; but that's only in the movies if you lose your job and you can't pay your rent or mortgage, you have no health care you end up losing everything. You only get 13 weeks off unemployment benefits. When that runs out and still haven't found a job, you're on your own and they only place that's left is on the street. From then on, it's a down would spiral that some people never recover from. All the people I met on the streets had the same story to tell which boiled down to the MIGHTY DOLLAR.

Whilst I was there, my sister Dori told me that Keith wanted to talk to me. I said I don't think I wanted to talk to him. However, before she left, I told my sister to ask him to call me. He did call me. I didn't really know what to say to him. I just said that I'm safe. He didn't even know I had left the United States. None of my family informed me because they were all disgusted with what he had done. The hospital staff were a bit concerned about the call, and I said that it was fine and I could handle it.

After six weeks of being in the hospital, it was time for me to leave. They were trying to find me an apartment, and they couldn't find one that was suitable for me. So I went to stay with Wayne. I was there with Wayne for about two months and social services called. They told me to find the perfect apartment for me – they did. It was a beautiful, absolutely beautiful apartment.

The difference between the US and the UK is when people are in dire straits, the UK is there to help, while in the US, people are thrown on the streets. If you can't pay your taxes or find a job, you're on your own, which is the scariest thought of all. So they fit it up to my apartment. I had a brand new everything – appliances, washing machine, beds, knives, forks; you name it, I got it. There was nothing that I needed, and if I did need anything, they got it for me. So I settled into my new apartment. I decided on what I was going to do with the rest of my life.

The experience of being homeless and having a mental illness are mostly interrelated, which increases an individual's ability to attain employment, vulnerability, and sustain their tenancy.

Mostly, for people, changes in their mental health can affect their ability to live independently and affect their accessibility to afford decent housing.

Chapter 13: Keith's Death

I settled into my new apartment. Things finally started to work in a flow. That's when Keith called. He wanted to come over to visit me in the UK. I told him I wasn't ready for that. And I asked him if he stopped drinking, and, as expected, he didn't – once an alcoholic, always an alcoholic. Anyway, he continued asking, "Could I come over?"

So I asked my sisters what they thought about this idea. They asked me if I was ready to see him. I said there were a lot of things I needed to ask him, a lot of questions and answers that I needed. So Keith came over to UK. Simon and Keith were pretty close while Simon was staying with us in the US. Simon picked him up from the airport. I told Keith to stay for two weeks. So we did stay for two weeks. And was he drinking? Yes, he was! Was he drinking the amount that he was before? No!

After two weeks, it was time for him to go. And he sat there and cried for me. I don't want to leave you. I said, "Look, you've got a flight! Now go!" Simon took him to the airport, and Simon said he was beside himself. I said, "Simon, he made a choice. So he has to go home."

Keith and I stayed in contact, and he asked me again, "Could he come over to visit for a second time?" My family asked me was I sure that this was something I wanted. I said, "I don't know." So I left Keith waiting on my answer.

Harry and I, my youngest brother, kept in contact. I would go and visit, and some days, he would be totally wasted. I couldn't get a conversation out of him. And other days, it was quite lucid. And we would laugh, and we would joke, but he was still battling alcoholism. I would go and visit, or I would go on appointments with him.

And we became pretty close. I started working for St. Johns Ambulance Company as an EMT. Once, I had a pretty rough day, and I'll never forget what Joel said to me, "Can this day get any worse?" And I said, "I hope not." And we both said our goodbyes. So I got home from work, and there was a police car outside the apartment block where I lived. I really didn't think anything of it. There were two police officers sitting inside. He said, "I'm looking for apartment 2B." I turned around, and I looked at this police officer, I said, "I live in 2B." He said, "There is just something I wanted to ask you, don't worry about it."

I got into the apartment, and I sat down. And the police officer knelt down in front of me, and I thought, "What's going on?" And he said, "I have some bad news for you." I said, "Okay?" He said, "We found your brother Harry dead, this morning. People were trying to get hold of you." I said, "I don't really use my phone while working." I didn't even bother checking to message anything.

I hurried into the car, and I was totally stunned because I had spoken to him a few days before. They told me they didn't know whether he'd gone to the Royal Liverpool Hospital or Whiston Hospital. And the police officer said to me, "Is there any way I can take you? Or any way or anyone you want to contact?" I said, "No, it is okay." I just sat there and cried.

I had to inform my dad, so I called him. I couldn't tell the rest of my sisters, but I did that. I just got in the car and drove to my sister's. They were shocked, and they were screaming about which hospital he was in. I sort of didn't know. I didn't know whether he was in Whiston Hospital. I didn't know whether he was in the Royal. So we got to the hospital. And yes, he was there. So we all went up, and they brought him up to us. My sisters were shocked. I was really upset, but it didn't shock me because I had already seen him. I have spoken to him. I had been with him.

Anyway, he had the post mortem. And obviously, everybody thought it was alcohol that killed him. He had no alcohol in his system that day. The post mortem said he died of natural causes. He was 39. We all left, and we all went our separate ways that night. It wasn't a good night for me. I didn't sleep at all. I didn't know what to do so I called Keith, and I told him everything. I thought maybe, given his past history, he would understand. He asked if he could come over, so I said okay. He came for another two weeks.

Whilst he was there, he asked me, "Could you come to live in with me?" And I told him, "No! Because he was still drinking." He swore to me that he would stop. We went home. We started the paperwork for him to come over here to live with me. It took quite a while; all the paperwork was done. And he was granted his

Permanent Residency Card. He rented the house out in California and came over here to live. A lot of people were quite shocked that I took him back after everything he put me through. He met some of my friends, Jen and Ken. All four of us would hang out Jen is a real good friend of mine, so Ken and Keith would hang out and go to the pub. Keith would even go to work with Ken. They had so much fun just hanging out, but Keith never came home drunk. But then he started to slide. And his health started to fail.

He was taken into hospital on one occasion, where he was constantly throwing up blood. And they managed to stop the bleeding, and they told him that he must stop drinking. So he went to a clinic, which would enable him to stop drinking. He did for a little while, but then he started again. He ended up back in the hospital, through the same thing, bleeding in the stomach. With the knowledge to stop the bleeding, they told me that he'd be out the next day. But I got a phone call at one o'clock in the morning to tell me that Keith had been rushed into intensive care. I needed to go to the hospital. So I went up, and they told me that he had a massive seizure, and he stopped breathing.

While he was in intensive care, the doctor came to me and said, "Look, this happened again, he is not going home." I said, "Okay." I called his sisters, I told them that Keith was in intensive care, and he wasn't doing well. All his family knew that Keith had a drinking problem. They all knew he was an alcoholic.

So two of his sisters came over. They started throwing their weight around, telling the doctors not to feed him or not to give him any fluids and just to let him go. I was dumbfounded by what I was hearing. I couldn't believe that the two people who were sitting there were his sisters. This is something me and my family could never knew that why his sisters were acting so weird. Even though, despite the age gap between them and their brothers, they had a pretty good relationship with each other.

Anyway, the medical staff were getting very concerned about the behaviours of his two sisters. They even talked about putting Keith on to a safeguarding issue, which meant his sisters couldn't come near him. When they found this out, both of them left and flew home.

Keith pulled through, and he looked so healthy and so good. Keith started drinking again, and his health was failing. I got up in the morning, and he didn't look good. So, I took him to see the doctor. She told us Keith had pneumonia.

He was taken to the hospital. The next morning, I got a phone call telling me they had moved him to intensive care. I felt sick. I couldn't breathe. I remember what the doctors told me if he came in again, he won't be coming home.

I went to the hospital. He was sitting up and talking to me. I tried to get him to eat and drink, but he refused. He was sleeping a lot, and I sat at his bedside day and night. The last thing Keith said to me was just holding me. I held him so tight I didn't want to let go.

I phoned his sisters and told them they needed to come over. I never lifted his bedside, praying to god, please let him live. Everyone left, and I was alone with him. I laid next to him, just holding him.

Keith passed away on 24 December 2016. The nurse had to phone everyone because I couldn't do it for the next couple of weeks. I was just walking around num all my family did all the funeral. Arrangements I laid Keith to rest. None of his sisters came to his funeral.

After whatever he made me went through, I never thought I will ever be able to forgive him and I really couldn't. Whenever I could think of him, all I could remember was my difficult times with him. However, as the time went by, I started to heal from it all and I was in the right place mentally. I was also consulting a mental health team at the time, they played a major role in it too. They were there 24/7 whenever I needed them. So yes, I healed, but I was so cautious about everything after that. Even when he was alive, the more I saw him, the more I was able to forgive him.

I never want go through it again. I just want to stay where no one else can hear me, and no more loved one will go, fortunately that wasn't the case, you know? But yeah, I can't move on. I don't want to move on because of the fear factor. I spent all my life running away from alcoholics and in the end this happened. I don't want to repeat the same mistake twice.

I'll never forget Tent City. I'll never forget the homeless people that I met and the stories they told me.

If only people in San Diego, California would go and see how these people are, how they look after each other, and how they take care of each other. If you're cold, they'll give you the shirt off the back. If you're hungry, they'll give you the food that they are eating.

You don't get that anywhere else. The homeless have a special bond with each other because they're all living the same life. They don't have to compete with anybody, with the brand new fast cars or the bigger house. They are simple people who lead simple, sad lives, but they cope. They cope so well.

I've never been back to San Diego since that day. If I am ever there, I will go back to Tent City. I will sit and spend time listening to the stories they have to tell because every face have a different story.

I ended up homeless on the streets. I was there for four days or four nights. These people have been there a lifetime. Some of them don't even know who their families are. Apparently, they are alone, but they are not because they have each other.

I hope whenever I go back there, I would do anything to help them with whatever I can. They are amazing people. They live in danger every single day, and nobody cares! Because nobody knows, and to be honest, nobody wants to know. It's quite sad! I have spent endless hours listening to Catherine and Meghan. In my opinion, in comparison to both, HRH Princess Catherine can be more empathetic towards these issues and understands what true suffering really is. I know I lived it. If anyone needs security, it's homeless.

Chapter 14: Life in the UK vs the US

People say that your world changes at the death of your spouse. Well, I couldn't agree more! It is true. You mourn and are left with feeling grief and sorrow. You go through a lot of emotions – shocked, numb, and fearful. At times, you even feel guilty for being alive. You may even get angry at your spouse for leaving you. I want to tell anyone reading this that it is okay to feel all of these things. There is no "perfect" way to mourn. Everybody has their own ways.

It is both physically and mentally exhausting to grieve. There is an overflowing of emotions. Simultaneously, in the chaos and dealing with the feelings of loss, you have to deal with the pressure and stress of getting your life back together, which is literally torn apart. Moving on is the difficult part. It is different for everyone; some people feel better and get through it early, while others take time.

Just something else that I want to add in that is that you are not alone; it is how I feel too. To get through all of these feelings love deeply, forgive easily, find inner peace, and strength, only then can you truly be free.

When Keith passed away, I was allowed to grieve for Keith. One of the reasons is that I was in the UK at the time. He was admitted to an amazing NHS hospital. I didn't have to pay a penny for Keith's treatment. However, if I were in the US, I would keep getting doctor's bills and phone calls. I remember some of the times when I was in the hospital, and I needed treatment, I wasn't even at the hospital for less than a couple of days, and the medical bills started coming through the door. Then, the doctors' offices were calling me constantly.

Things in the United States are not what they seem. I have seen three presidencies – Clinton, Bush, and Obama. Obama brought in affordable health care, which included treatment for substance abuse. It didn't take long before clinics were being set up offering addicts treatment. They had boots on the ground touting businesses targeting the most vulnerable, the homeless, and addicts on the streets. I suggest that my readers watch a movie called BODY BROKERS on Netflix to understand what I'm talking about. People got rich very quickly by exploring the neediest because they knew once they got clean, they had nowhere else to go except back on the streets. It became a vicious cycle. They really did nothing for the people of the United States. Then came Trump, who did more in his time as a president than any president in recent history. People had more money in their pockets. They were happier. Gas prices were low. The tax was low. Then Joe Biden got into power, and the pandemic hit. It is when George Floyd died and the riots took place. So many innocent people lost their lives at that time. It is when the United

States went down hard. Millions of people lost their jobs and homes. Yeah, they got unemployed; they got it for a year, and since then, they have been on their own.

Vanessa, my dear friend, was a project manager in a company with a six-figure salary. All of her savings went away to pay the mortgage. She has two old age parents who need round-the-clock care. Vanessa would have to pay for that care out of her pocket. Now, she has a job with a minimum wage and is struggling to find care for her parents.

Another example is Karen, one of my dear friends. She has three beautiful boys. She is a divorcee at a minimum wage who is trying to keep a roof over her children's heads.

Likewise, Pam, who I took care of, had to return home to her ailing parents who live in military accommodation. Once I was in the States for Thanksgiving, I went to stay with Pam and her parents for a few days. It was deplorable because half of the people that lived there were veterans. Most of them were drug addicts. They would offer me weed and other stuff as I walked through the apartment complex.

I even spoke to some of them. Most of them started with prescription painkillers. Most of the homeless people on the streets in the United States, their addictions were caused through painkillers, doctors, or pharmacies. Pharmaceutical companies deliberately push medications onto their patients, even though they know that they are addictive. Doctors earn thousands upon thousands of dollar a year through these painkillers addictions, while pharmaceutical companies earn trillions of dollars a year.

Government should be forced to build social housing and pay for the treatment of the addicts they've created.

Homelessness is one of the major issues in the US. There are more people homeless on the streets today in the United States than there ever was before. Having no place to sleep or having no food to eat can be unimaginable for many people, but it is a part of their daily lives for the homeless. The thing that saddens me the most is that people are not even aware of the concept of homelessness which has been happening in major parts of the world. In contrast, the people who know about it is keeping a blind eye towards this issue. The way they are treated in US is not good, at all. I would say US have its dark side, and I have seen that dark side on couple of occasions. It was hard for me to survive.

You know, I came back to England because I knew my country could take care of me, and they did. Not only me, but they also took care of Keith and gave him the best health care anybody could ask for. The situation is terrible in the US. People think the United States is a wonderful and brilliant country if you have money; it's not if you don't.

Once, I spoke to my friend Karen. She said that the average person living in the United States needs a combined income of at least 80,000 a year. And that's to pay for their health care insurance. Karen believes that the United Kingdom is an amazing country to live in, and yes, it is!

If only I could bring Karen and her boys here to the UK. They hold a very dear place in my heart. It saddens me to think that she is struggling and trying to put food on the table.

Another dearest friend of mine, Kristal, was on a call with me the other day. She has two beautiful boys, named Wyatt, who is five and Gabrielle, who is eight. Those boys are just so wonderful. She's going through a divorce and trying to survive on whatever money and child support she can get. She's been living in someone's basement for the last four months to make sure the boys had a roof over their heads.

After a lot of research, she finally got home. It is a three-bedroom house, which is going to cost $1,400 a month. She only earns $1,600 a month. She doesn't know how she is going to survive. She may have asked for a roommate. One needs to be very careful on who gets to move in with them, but I am sure she is sensible. I am sure one day, she will find someone who will protect her and the boys.

Kristal is a kindergarten teacher with a minimum wage. I'm not so sad about her divorce, because her two boys are going to be with her, because her ex-husband does nothing. What an asshole! He doesn't want to take care of and protect the boys. He hasn't even asked to see the boys. Anyways, she moved on so fast, and I am so proud of her for everything she has achieved.

Living in the UK means access to a good standard of health care. People have the right to give their children an education at no cost in public schools. As they have a diversity of people there, one can make connections and settle in with their lives very easily.

In the end, I want to let my readers know that I know how it feels to lose a spouse or a partner. Never think that you are alone. It is devastating, whether it is followed by illness or sudden death. Amidst the intense emotions, I would suggest all of you go easy on yourself and take care of your health. Grieving can be hard, but try to move on with fulfilling and positive life for yourself and cherish the memories of your relationship with your loved one.

Chapter 15: My Father's Death

My life after Keith went dull. The time was just going with its own pace after Keith's death. It was pretty hard for me to move on, even though I had my family around. There were days when I just didn't want to get out of bed. The days I didn't even want to brush my teeth and had no motivation to even go to work – I had to drag myself to stay active. It was awful. After his death, I had to rebuild my life.

Mark Grady called me and said I have booked a ticket for you and you've got to be on that flight. I had to leave my comfort zone, which I built around. It protected me while I healed. I had no other choice but to go to Australia because Mark had paid for the ticket. As soon as I got there, Mark met me at the airport, and we went to his house.

I went to see Mark twice that year. We had so much fun together. I returned home after my second trip I was healing not only physically but also spiritually with the help of my friends. But one day, I got a call that brought my life to a standstill. It was Mark; he asked me if was sitting down and I said yes. He proceeded to tell me he had cancer. I was speechless. I was in shock. I couldn't speak. I still remember those words in my head saying, "Oh lord! Please no, not Mark. Mark has no brothers or sisters and his mum had dementia, he was all alone. I dropped everything back, my bag, and headed out to Australia. Mark went through chemotherapy every day. The treatment had done a number on him. He would come home and sleep a lot. I would encourage him to eat and drink. He got a phone call from Andrew, his doctor, and told him he would have to come to the hospital. Mark was yellow, his liver was failing, and he was very sick. It was Christmas Eve, and I was alone in

Sydney. It brought back so many sad memories for me. I was broken-hearted, crying and praying to God, “Please don’t take mark from me.” Mark’s health improved, and he was doing so well. I headed back home, and it wasn’t long before I got a call from Mark telling me he was cancer free. I was so happy and was dancing around my living room. You would have thought I had just won the lottery.

It wasn’t long after that the pandemic hit. Wayne’s mum had been ill for a while. It wasn’t long before she became gravely sick, and Wayne had taken time off work to care for his mum. She passed away peacefully at home. Wayne was inconsolable, he idolised his mum, and there was nothing I could do for him except to be by his side. I knew how that pain felt, and I couldn’t take it away from him.

I finally started feeling alive again. Even though my heart was aching, Keith left me penniless, and his sisters sold the property. I walked away with nothing. The house was never put back in Keith's name, so on paper, his parents still owned his house. His mum was deceased and his dad was 92, they never told him that Keith has passed away. As far as they were concerned, they owned the property. They may have taken all his assets, but they couldn't take away my heart and all those amazing memories I had and too me they our priceless.

A house came up for rent in the old neighbourhood that I had grown up in rose had purchased the family home many years before it seemed like I had done a complete circle who would have thought I would end up back home. My dad also moved back to our old neighbourhood he lived about 600 yards from Rose and I. I started often visiting my dad and doing some shopping and groceries for him. Rose and Maria had a great bond with my dad that no one could ever break. I was kind of jealous of that bond, so I started spending more time with my dad. I took him shopping did anything he wanted me to do. At night, I would go around and have tea with him. Before we went to bed, we talked about a lot of things. My dad and I actually started to bond. I actually felt that it was meant something.

I travelled a lot after Keith passed away to the United States to stay with Vanessa, Kristal and Pam. When I got back from the States, Rose said that my dad really missed me and missed our chats at night. So, when I came back, I told my dad about all the adventures and where I am and what I did.

One night, I was sitting with him, and he said to me, "The reason I was so hard on you is that I had to toughen you up." I looked at my dad and smiled. I thought I was a child but I knew that was the nearest I was ever going to get an apology. I didn't say anything. Soon after, it was time for me to leave. When I was about to leave, I asked my dad to make sure that he locked the door after I'd left. We gave each other a long hug. That hug made me feel absolutely amazing, and as I was leaving, Dad said, "I love you and am so proud of you." I looked back at dad and replied, "I love you too, dad," and walked out the door. That night, as I was walking home, it hit me instantly that all that pain and sorrow that he coursed me when I was a small child didn't matter anymore because my dad and I had bonded. We actually started to get to know each other the only thing I regret about my dad he never gave me away on my wedding day.

As time went by, I spent more time with dad. We laughed and joked. I took care of him and gave him everything he needed. The pandemic was hard on every one of us, especially my dad. He was one of the first people to be vaccinated. It wasn't long after that that my dad got ill. Rose called for an ambulance. My dad had got pneumonia. He also had dementia. The first night he was in the hospital, a nurse called Rose asking if she could come and sit with my dad because he kept taking his oxygen mask off. Rose asked the nurse if Maria could be with her, and they said yes. Dad wasn't in a COVID ward, a blessing that enabled Rose and Maria to be there. I became ill and was taken to the same hospital. Whilst I was there, I got a text message saying that dad had taken a turn for the worse and was really poorly ill. I asked a nurse if she could find out what ward dad was in. She came back and told me. I asked if I could go and see him. The nurse took me in a wheelchair down to see him. Rose and Maria looked so tired. They had been there all night and had no sleep. The three of us held Dad's hand, and it was long before he slipped away peacefully. I bent over him and kissed him. A single tear fell on his cheek. I generally wiped it away. I miss my dad, and I miss our long talks and the jokes we shared.

I miss my dad. I missed all our chats together with tea. I miss calling him and talking to him for hours. I have learned a lot from my relationship with my dad, and that is, it's never too late to build bridges and mend hearts. As long as you live by that, only love and truth will be told.

I still struggle every day with losing my dad and losing Keith. But I have grown so much in so many ways. I work hard, I play hard. I travel. I go and meet my friends. But, I live a quiet life now – on my own. I'm quite happy with that right now. I don't have anyone to tell me where I can go, what I can, or what I can't do.

If I ever feel the need to go somewhere, I just pack my bags and leave. I have no restrictions. I am now living my life to its fullest.

I've never even been on a date since Keith passed away. It's been six years now. Yeah, I go out, but I like the comfort of my own home. I'm just enjoying my life. I must say that Mark had really played a huge part in getting me out of that rut and that dark hole I was in when Keith passed away.

We were blessed because, at the time, no one was allowed in the hospitals to visit. The only reason why Maria and Rose were was there only because my dad kept taking his oxygen mask off, and they needed somebody to sit with him. I happened to be a patient in the same hospital at the same time. We were privileged to be with my dad when he passed away. All those poor people I could not stay with their loved ones during the pandemic was heartbreaking. And I thank God every day that I got to spend that time with my dad. I pray that everyone else who have lost loved ones can find some source of peace. And always remember, tomorrow's another day.

The death of your loved one can feel unbelievable at times, especially when it strikes one of your parent. They are the ones whose presence in your life may can never be wavered. Even if you grow up and successfully reached your adulthood, you'll still need and expect to have your parents for many years to come. The loss of their guidance, love, and support can leave major emptiness and pain that seem impossible to heal, even if their death was expected. Or, maybe you and your parent were had a complicated relationship, which results in a roller coaster of conflicting emotions. Even then, it is difficult to cope up. I want all of you to know that whatever you are feeling is valid. Do not let anybody make you feel like you're "overreacting" while in the process of mourning. Give yourself some time and everything will fall into its place perfectly.

Chapter 16: Pandemic and its Toll on Us

Pandemic and COVID-19 have affected the lives of millions of people around the world, especially around me. As well as having grave health consequences, the pandemic has also crushed our aims and objectives, upended our family dynamics, and sabotaged our financial stability. Subsequently, the global crisis brought by the pandemic significantly affected our mental health.

I wasn't doing very well health-wise before the beginning of the pandemic. When I first heard about it, I was extremely terrified. I live on my own, and I was struggling through lockdown, due to which I suffered depression. I mean, who else didn't. Each one of us had a tremendous effect on our minds. At points, I really felt alone too. Things got pretty messed up financially, emotionally, and everything else. It was dealing with a lot of stuff which was mentally exhausting for me.

At the start of the pandemic, as I was racing a lot during the fall, I actually designed to be careful because obviously because my dad was still alive during the pandemic. And I have to take care of him because of his state of disease. There was no way was I going to compromise his health. So I juggled some of my work and stuff. And to make sure that was safe, I did that and quite a few times for him.

Even though certain things have impacted my life during the virus, I was lucky enough to not contract the virus even once during the whole situation. However, as the circumstances got intense, the fear grew more. Considering my past experiences, I kept thinking the worst. I was not at all in the mental capacity to deal with losing people I loved anymore. The fake news that people kept spreading all over social media made it worse.

The pandemic came with travel restrictions as well. For someone who loved to travel, it was another struggle to go through. I had no choice but to stay at home whilst dealing with my anxiety, depression, and reliving past memories.

Despite the negatives, the lockdown has also proved to be the care for my soul. I believe that there is no one-size-fits-all technique to practice healing. Every one of us needs to understand what works best for us that can lead us from grief to the process of healing and moving on. My formula to deal with the midlife crisis is: *"little heart and soul, mixed with a few shreds of courage."* You need to put in a little effort in everything you need to achieve in life, followed by having confidence and courage in yourself that you are made to achieve bigger things in life – and that is how I dealt with my pandemic mental health crisis.

As the whole situation affected my life, it also had a toll on my friends' lives. Every one of them has a different story.

After my father passed away and the travel restrictions were lifted, I had to take a flight to Philadelphia to see Kristal. The pandemic and the lockdown really did a number on her husband to the point that she had to take her two sons and leave because she no longer felt safe. Her husband had suffered huge mental health issues, and so she felt like her life was in danger. Soon after she left her house, Kristal

filed for a divorce from her husband. I hope she finds peace wherever she goes in her life. She is one of the strongest women I know.

Whilst I was there in the USA, I popped in to see Pam and her partner. Like everybody else, she, too, was suffering from the consequences of the pandemic. She and her wife had to move in with their ailing parents because both of them had lost their jobs. Overall, the financial situation was pretty tight for them too.

Another friend of mine, Vanessa, lived in Atlanta. She was on a six-figure salary working as a Project Manager. However, as soon as COVID-19 hit the world, she lost her job too. She is now working for Delta Airlines on a minimum wage.

The overall situation in the USA went really bad because of the lockdowns and pandemics. Everyone I know who lived there was affected terribly.

When I was returning back to the UK, Kristal asked if I would ever return to live in the USA. I told her that it was a huge possibility, and maybe not too distant future. But I haven't wholly thought about it. For now, I would just say that it was quite an experience visiting my friends in the USA.

I still have much to think about in my future plans. Even though nobody knows what is actually destined for us, however, one must always be prepared for new adventures life throws your way.

We were all challenged with considerable disruptions in our daily lives during the COVID-19 pandemic. It is not hard to feel stressed or overwhelmed as we experience all the changes rapidly. However, this is the time when our extreme self-care and good mental health must come in handy.

For a lot of us, being mean to ourselves is natural – it has become a default way of talking to ourselves. If you noticed that you were especially hard on yourself during the pandemic, you aren't alone. Even if you've tried to work on this in the past, pandemic came with a lot of stress that made it harder to stay positive.

I hope things will work out best for all of my friends, family, and my readers. Now that the pandemic is over, I want all of us to make the most of our lives and get back to some sort of normality.

Pictures of Family and Friends

SUPERC

LEADBETTER & MURPHY

Printed in Great Britain
by Amazon

87309380R00133

Educating Maggie

Debbie Chase

This is a work of fiction. Names, characters, places, and incidents are products of the author's imagination or are used fictitiously and are not to be construed as real. Any resemblance to actual events, locations, organizations, or persons, living or dead, is entirely coincidental.

World Castle Publishing, LLC

Pensacola, Florida

Paperback ISBN: 9781629899701

eBook ISBN: 9781629899718

First Edition World Castle Publishing, LLC, August 20, 2018

http://www.worldcastlepublishing.com

Licensing Notes

Cover: Karen Fuller

Editor: Maxine Bringenberg

Table of Contents

Chapter One

I was never a Margaret, always a Maggie. What my parents were thinking when they named me on the day of my birth, fifty-four years ago, I had no idea. "Your granddad wanted the name Margaret," my mum told me, just as my mum wanted my middle name to be Eleanor after my grandma, who died when I was one. "At least she had a chance to look at your pretty little face," she always told me, "You were the first grandchild." But it will always stand that I, Margaret Eleanor Benson, (changed to Margaret Eleanor Sears when I married Ray, of course) was always a Maggie, never a Margaret.

Just as Stephen was always a Stephen, never a Steve. Stephen Gates. I was in love with him at school, and used to gaze at the back of his handsome head in math classes from my seat behind him. I liked the way his dark hair laid in whorls at the back of his head, curling around and around like tiny mazes. I imagined my fingers becoming lost in those mazes, the pads of my thumbs touching his silky soft hair. He always seemed so self-contained, remote, and I was desperate for him to notice me.

He was a clever student, good at math and English, so much so that he went on years later to become a headmaster in a posh school down south somewhere. I heard all this by rumor; through the grapevine so to speak—my mum grapevine. Once we left school, I never set eyes on Stephen Gates again.

I married Ray on a beautiful autumn day bright with scarlet leaves bathed in sunshine, but with a chilly wind that caught you unawares. I remember I had goose bumps on my arms beneath the flimsy white sleeves of my wedding dress. Ray was a good man—steadfast, loyal, and never looked at another woman; unless you count that drunken New Year's Eve with Audrey Rivers from across the road. Peeking from my sitting room window, I could see her right now, tripping along the pavement in high heels and fake fur; and my God, she must have been pushing sixty now.

"Mutton dressed as lamb," as my mum always used to say. She wouldn't say it now, though. My mum, slumped in a nursing home for the past couple of weeks, struggled to recognize me, her own daughter, let alone fake fur Audrey Rivers.

I didn't marry until I was thirty and Ray fifteen years older than me. "You're marrying your father," my mum always used to say. "You lost him when you were so young, only sixteen, to that awful express train, and he knew that I didn't like him working on the railway. I remember him telling me that the money was good. Didn't do *him* much good though, did it?"

Ray and I had had a good marriage for a long time, but around our fifteenth year he had to go and spoil it all by wanting to move to nearby Hampthwaite. He expected me to up sticks and leave Cobby Village. Unthinkable! There was no way in this whole wide world that I would leave Cobby, my village, my home. Everything I wanted and needed was right there in Cobby. The emerald green countryside that seemed to reach up as high as the sky, and the cows and the sheep slumbering in the fields. The canal thick with paddling ducks and swans, and the river that wound its sparkling way along its green banks. If I peered really hard from my bedroom window, I could see the school where I'd fallen in love with Stephen Gates. And just around the corner was Cobby College, where I'd spent a very happy year learning to type on an old Underwood typewriter—as well as being lured behind the bike sheds and given lessons by the local boys on how to smoke and how to kiss.

Bloomers the Bakers nestled cozily on Cobby High Street between the dry cleaners and the post office, while nearby was the little ancient church and the tiny graveyard where Ray now lay in perfect peace, a great stone angel sprouting from his headstone and gazing with vacant eyes at the sky. There was nowhere else like Cobby. Even the sun seemed to shine warmer, and the stars, splattered across a midnight sky, were clearer and more beautiful than anywhere else. I couldn't tear myself away from any of that, now could I?

I remember Ray pleading with me, telling me that a beautiful house was coming up for sale and pointing out how unusual this was in the tiny village of Hampthwaite. "Andrea and Les Dowling are selling up," I remember him saying.

"They've got the best house in the village, and it could be ours, Maggie." I refused so many times that eventually he stopped asking and succumbed to a deep dark silence and hurtful looks, which I never managed to penetrate—no, never, not even to the day he died.

Hmm, I thought to myself, a vague memory tugging at me. *Andrea and Les Dowling? I'm sure that Andrea is the sister of that poor Johnny Emmerson, who was killed so tragically in a car accident a year or so ago*. He'd been a councilor, and was instrumental, actually, in setting up Cobby Town Council with two of his buddies—a good kind man, attractive too, with his head of thick graying hair and startlingly blue eyes.

Now that was a thing. His widow, Kath Emmerson, had lost her supposedly wonderful Johnny, and I've got to say she certainly looked like a shapeless sack in her grief. Yet within that first year she had moved to a lovely place along the tow path, gotten herself a very good job as town clerk to the Cobby Town Council, and nabbed herself a very attractive boy toy, too—town planner, Paul Timpson. She'd seemed to flourish and bloom like some sort of exotic plant, and for all I knew could be Kath Timpson by now.

I'd seen the two of them in Cobby Village only the other day, walking along arm in arm, gazing into each other's eyes, totally besotted by the look of it. How did people move on so quickly? Ray had been gone for more than four years, and I was still finding it difficult to put one foot in front of the other, let alone achieve all that Kath had. Was there something wrong with me? Or was there something wrong with her?

I didn't think she, Kath, realized how much gossip she caused around the village at the time. The whole place was rife with rumors. I remember a customer in Bloomers almost having a stroke because of Kath taking up with another man so soon after her husband's death. She was so put out that she dithered between sausage rolls and corned beef pasties for ages before making her final choice. If you ask me, it was mainly jealousy that caused all the tittle tattle.

Anyway, what was I doing standing stock still in my sitting room reminiscing about the past? I couldn't do anything about it now, could I? Although guilt at not moving to Hampthwaite still crept up on me at times, and I could see in my mind's eye Ray's hurt puppy dog eyes.

Checking my watch, I noticed the time and, panicking, dashed upstairs to get ready for work. I was due in Bloomers the Bakers for a twelve o'clock shift.

Gazing into the mirror, I decided that there was no point in doing anything with my hair which, limp and unwashed, hung around my pale face so that I bore a very sad resemblance to that old rocker Iggy Pop. *Never mind,* I thought. *The hair net and baseball cap that I have to wear for work will cover it up anyway.* I dabbed minimal make up on my skin, which I noticed was becoming festooned with lines like one of those maps that Ray and I used to take with us in the car on long journeys. It was all GPS now, though, and maps were becoming as outdated as egg timers.

Maybe I should do what Kath Emmerson did and go to a beauty parlor for a makeover, change my job, and grab myself a boy toy. Looking hard at myself now though, I really didn't think I had the energy for it. My old cat Arthur, laid out long like a tatty rug on the end of my lonely bed, narrowed his yellow eyes suspiciously as, sighing heavily, I grabbed my bag and my coat and left the house, hunching my shoulders to my ears as I walked out into the nippy spring sunshine.

~*~

Customers were queuing out the door when I arrived at Bloomers, and I could see young Jeff and Lillian, rushing around behind the counter serving sandwiches, pasties, and sausage rolls. The smell of freshly brewed coffee and hot chocolate hung in the air like a mist, and I could still detect the lingering odor of bacon and sausages from this morning's breakfast rolls. A few people sat in the small café area eating their lunch and, as I walked past to go into the back room to get changed, four familiar faces swam into view.

Hmm, what a coincidence, I thought. *I'm sure that's Kath Emmerson's daughter, son-in-law, and grandchildren. Lizzie, I think she's called, and I'm sure his name is Martin—a nice man, attractive in a kind way—and the two kids, Layla and Joe.* Good looking too—the little girl had eyes like patches of bluebells just the same as her grandad's, Johnny Emmerson, and a good-looking daughter come to that, lots of dark curly hair and ruby red lips. The little boy was just—well, cute. I often wondered what it would have been like to have a little grandson just like Joe. For that matter, I often wondered what it would have been like to have a child of my own. Kath Emmerson was a very lucky woman!

Changing into my uniform of black trousers and a T-shirt overlaid by a blue apron—Bloomers…the Best Bakers by Far, depicted in white swirly letters on the front—I gazed at myself in the mirror, securing my hair with a scrunchie and piling it into the hair net and cap, turning this way and that to make sure I looked okay.

"Whatever happened to my plans to work in a school?" I asked myself. I remembered that while in college, learning to type, working in a school had been my aim, my dream really, and now I couldn't even remember where the dream had gone.

I recalled Ray asking me the same question. "I know you're happy at the bakery, Maggie, but it's a far cry from your hankering to work in a school, isn't it?"

I don't know what I used to say to him, probably that yes, I was happy at Bloomers, but the time had flown by, and….

"It's never too late, you know," he always said. And perhaps he was right.

I noticed, on going out into the shop ready for work, that Lizzie, Martin, and the two children had gone and a man sat alone at one of the tables, sipping from a cup of coffee, a caramel custard doughnut laid on an outspread paper bag in front of him. He looked rather nice too, having black hair with the odd grey snaking through its thick depths like highlights. His nose was very straight, and he had what my mum would have called "sexy full lips." I also noticed that he had a square chin, with a dimple so deep it looked to have been scooped out with a teaspoon.

I didn't like him sitting there at that dirty table, ringed with coffee marks and sugar scattered like snowflakes across the surface. I noticed a couple of empty cups standing by forlornly, their rims smeared with pink lipstick marks. Why didn't people clean up after themselves?

"What can I get you, love?" I heard Lillian say to a potential customer, a little old lady with a shock of messy grey hair who was squeezing the life out of a six pack of bread rolls with long knobby fingers.

"These fresh?" she asked with an accusing glare. I left her to Lillian who, after all, was shop manager, and grabbed a cloth and cleaning fluid and went to wipe the tables.

Two young girls walked past the shop, tight black leggings clinging bravely to jaunty buttocks and glaringly white midriffs on display. "A sight for sore eyes," I commented to young Jeff as he peered at them through the plate glass window, eyeing them from behind a poster—advertising Bloomer's latest chicken curry pasty as being the best ever, and so low in calories—as I diligently scrubbed until the tables were clean.

The man moved his doughnut on its paper bag plate so I could wipe around it. He picked up his coffee cup and took a long swallow. I could see the Adam's apple bobbing up and down in his throat.

"Do I know you from somewhere?" he asked suddenly. He put his head to one side and frowned, his eyes, the color of a good sherry, narrowed, his gaze appraising. "You look so familiar...."

I was just about to say no, I don't think so, when a sudden memory overwhelmed me, and I wished that I could sit behind him on an uncomfortable wooden chair and see if his hair still grew in whorls like tiny mazes on the back of his head. Oh my God, why hadn't I seen it straight away?

"Well, I never," I heard him say, as if from a long, long way away. "I can't believe it. Is it really you, Maggie Benson?"

"No, actually," I remember saying. "I'm Maggie Sears...."

And then everything went black and tiny bright dots flew around me, and the ground heaved and rolled and then hit me hard in the face as I fainted.

~*~

The care assistant on duty did a double take when she saw me coming through the nursing home door that evening. She was the younger one, Tracey—as opposed to the older lady, Winifred, who mainly worked the weekends, I think—a rather large girl shaped like a Weeble, with a face like a full moon and a heart full of golden treasures. As usual, the buttons on her pink checked uniform seemed to scream in agony across her chest. The familiar odor of urine overlaid with lemon furniture polish assailed my nostrils.

"What have you done to your face, Mrs. Sears?" she asked as I walked into the home's communal sitting room, where my mum could sometimes be found hunched in a chair and staring vacantly at the flickering television screen. The room was clean and tidy as usual, with chairs of all different colors and sizes ranged around the walls. The focal point of the room was the TV, which was switched on, but no sound came from the mouths of the actors on the screen, who looked as though they'd spent at least two weeks under a very hot sun lamp. Why didn't somebody turn the color setting down?

"Oh, nothing to worry about," I assured her briskly, knowing full well that a vast bruise covered my left eye and cheek so that I looked as though I was wearing thick black make-up, like a glam rocker from the seventies. "Where's my mum?" I asked.

"In her room," she replied, still staring hard at my battered face. "A bit peevish today—didn't want to socialize."

Glancing around the communal room, I noticed a couple of old men snoozing in their chairs, eyes covered in veiny lids, bobbing balding heads hanging low, and wondered who exactly my mum was supposed to socialize with and if she could come to that. I laughed at Tracey's use of the word peevish, odd in one so young. She laughed too, and said, "Well, I mean, cranky then, like a fed up little kid…you know what I mean?"

I nodded yes and smiled, then made my way along to Mum's room to find her lying in bed, her head sunk deep into a thick white pillow. She was so thin now that she barely made a mound beneath the starched white sheets and garish pink bedspread that the nurse had tucked around her like a straitjacket. I looked at the doctor's notes hanging at the end of the bed, but couldn't make heads or tails of them. The markings on the pages looked like hieroglyphics to me, and I was supposedly quite an intelligent woman.

I stood looking at this tiny person in the bed for a moment or two, mentally comparing her to the mum from years ago, from another life it seemed, when I was a young girl. Had this tiny frail person really worn tight sexy miniskirts that showed most of her long, tanned legs, and back combed her hair so high it had towered rich and dark on top of her head? Had her soft breath really tickled unbearably deep into my ear, making me squirm with pleasure as she cradled me closely and sang about a tiny house by a tiny stream?

Oh, Mum, I suddenly thought. *Where have you gone*? And for the first time in I didn't know how long, I missed her. I missed my mum. I felt like stomping my feet and crying like a petulant child, and demanding that my mum come back to me. *What's brought this on*? I thought to myself. *Was it the blast from the past that I delved into this afternoon*?

I sat down on the chair at the side of the bed and reached out and put my hand on hers. Hers was so little now, and wrinkled as a claw. "Mum," I said. "Guess who I saw today? Guess who came into Bloomers? Go on, have a guess."

We used to play this guessing game when I was young and living at home, and she would join in by shouting out random names, trying to guess who I'd seen that day. She did none of that now but just lay there, her eyes closed, barely breathing, it seemed, beneath the thin sheets.

Disappointed that she wasn't having one of her lucid moments, I turned away and went over to the window, where I gazed at the home's beautiful gardens bathed in what was probably the year's first golden spring sunshine. A gardener dug the borders with a glittering spade, his shirt sleeves rolled up to reveal hairy muscular arms. Sweat stood out like little beads on his forehead, and a robin fluttered around the dug-over earth, hunting for the worms that would now be wriggling to the surface. I opened the window a tiny bit so that air, fresh and sweet, poured into the lifeless room.

"Yes, Mum, who did I see today? Who made my heart beat so fast that I could barely breathe when he looked at me from his sherry brown eyes?"

I heard a voice, a tiny scratchy voice, like a bird cheeping from its nest. "Stephen Gates?" I spun around so fast that I almost toppled over. Her eyelids fluttered as she valiantly tried to lift them, and a small smile hovered around her lips. "You always liked him," she whispered. "He must be getting on a bit now though.... Not that good looking young man anymore."

I sat down beside her and put my hand on hers once

again. "Only the same age as me," I told her. "Oh Mum, let me tell you all about it."

Chapter Two

I hugged the day to myself like a special present as I lay in bed that night, still wide awake, and sleep so elusive it seemed as if it was something that happened to other people but not to me. I felt as though I would never sleep again. I slid out of bed, the polished floor boards cool beneath my feet, and went to the window and peered out from between the flowered curtains. Just darkness outside, and the shape of trees etched like paper cut outs against a dark blue sky strewn with messy tendrils of clouds.

Images of Stephen Gates ran through my restless mind. Stephen as a young man, and now Stephen as an older man who was Stephen, but wasn't. Still attractive enough to make me feel weak at the knees, so much so that I had fainted. Oh my God! He'd been such a gentleman though, helping me up from the floor, his hand firmly grasping mine, a gentle arm around my waist as Lilian and young Jeff hovered uncertainly in the background. I remembered him asking young Jeff for water and gently putting a plastic cup to my lips, the concern in his eyes disconcerting yet touching all at the same time.

"Well, well, Maggie Benson," I remembered him saying, shaking his head in disbelief. "Maggie Benson…who would have thought it?"

I tried to tell him again that I was Maggie Sears now, but my face was throbbing, especially around my left eye and my cheek, and opening and closing my mouth seemed to require far too much effort.

"Ooh, I'll tell you what," said young Jeff, standing casually, arms crossed over his scrawny chest, Bloomers baseball cap teetering on the back of his head. "You're gonna have a right old shiner there, Maggie…."

Getting back into bed, I snuggled down beneath the duvet, feeling tired now, and my eyelids heavy, drowsy, beginning to close, technicolor images of Stephen Gates running like a film just behind them. I remembered the shape of his lips, and the way they moved as he asked for my mobile number, and then recalled his long fingers moving across his phone as he saved the number and promised to text to arrange a meeting. Leaving the shop, he lifted his hand in a little wave, and I watched his retreating back as he disappeared amongst the dense crowds of shoppers.

~*~

"Stephen Gates, eh?" said the ratty voice of my sister, Lynette, as it travelled quickly through my mobile into my waiting ear. "What's going on then, Maggie?"

"God, I don't believe it. How do you know about him?" I asked, and then said, feeling a sudden burst of irritation, "You can say hello you know, Lynette."

In a very high pitched, silly voice, she said, "Oh yeah, hello Maggie," then carried on. "Mum told me all about it."

"Mum?" I asked. "What…she remembered?" The wailing of a small child suddenly rang out, so I pulled my mobile away from my ear before it deafened me.

"Shh, Jenny," I heard Lynette say. "Sorry about that, Maggie, I'm looking after our Steve's Jenny today."

I felt a sudden pang at the thought of Lynette being able to spend whole days with one of her many grandchildren.

"Getting back to Mum—yeah, she's very lucid at the moment. If you ask me, she's not as daft as she makes out." There was a short silence which, momentarily surprised by her comment, I tried to fill. But as usual she beat me to it and, changing the subject, said, "You ought to watch out for him, that Stephen Gates. I've heard stuff over the years. Twice divorced—"

I butted in then. "No Lynette, you're wrong there. Not twice divorced, once divorced, and he was very young then. They didn't even have any kids, and now he's a widower, actually."

"Whatever," she replied, sounding just like the moody teenager that she used to be.

I shook my head wearily and closed my eyes, conjuring up an image of my sister. I pictured her pacing restlessly around her large shiny kitchen, her vigorously straightened blonde hair falling forward like a curtain, shadowing her dinky upturned nose, full fleshy lips—not surgically enhanced, I must point out—and that deep V between her eyebrows that she hated so much.

Lynette was eight years younger than me—a drunken red

wine night with your dad, Mum always said—but bossy, so bossy. Yet she hadn't always been, not when we were children. Life had shown her that even though I was the older sister, I was the one that had finally got married when everybody thought there was no hope, whereas she had snared Dave, the boy from next door, and married him when barely out of her teens. Poor old Maggie had never had children, but Lynette had popped out four in very quick succession, and now had a great brood of grandchildren. This proved beyond any doubt that she knew best, had more experience with life and the world in general, and could boss her older sister until the cows came home.

I took a deep breath before saying, "He just turned up in Bloomers. I couldn't believe it. Even thought I was seeing things—you know, hallucinating."

"Yeah. Even though I was only a kid, I remember you fancying him at school. I suppose it must be a bit of a shock to see the love of your life as an old man. Is that why you fainted, do you think?"

"Don't be daft, Lynette; and he's not old," I replied patiently. "Only the same age as me. And just because he's suddenly turned up, it doesn't mean that we're destined to end up together."

"Best to let sleeping dogs lie," said Lynette darkly.

Pulling my mobile away from my ear, I stared at it disdainfully, listening to Lynette's voice as it echoed tiny and tinny like Minnie Mouse, and thinking irritably, *She's so full of those stupid sayings;* A fool and his money are soon parted; Absence makes the heart grow fonder; and her favorite seeming to be, Ask a silly question and you'll get a silly answer. Where she got them from I had no idea. I didn't remember Mum or Dad using sayings like that.

"Anyway," I said, trying desperately to bring the conversation to an end. "I'm due at Bloomers soon, so I'd best go—"

"Hang on a minute Maggie. What are you going to do then?"

"If Stephen Gates texts to arrange a meeting, then I'll go. It will be good to catch up with an old friend."

"Hmm. Well watch out, and don't forget," and here she quoted, "Sometimes it's better to be alone—nobody can hurt you."

I had no answer to that one.

"And anyway...." She paused here and took a deep breath. "What about Ray?"

"Ray," I said, totally mystified. "What about Ray?"

"Well...he was your husband...."

"He's gone, Lynette; he died, remember? He's been dead for four years. I loved him—well, I still do—and I miss him, but I've been on my own now for four years!"

"Okay, keep your hair on," she replied impatiently. "I just meant—oh, I don't know. How do you think he'd feel if you went out with another man? Or, how would you feel if he went out with another woman?"

"Lynette," I repeated as patiently as I could. "How can Ray go out with another woman? I don't know what sort of dating rules they have up there, but...." I trailed away, for once lost for words. "But anyway, Ray is dead. What—do you think he's looking down and watching me or something?"

"Well yeah, maybe. Anyway, Mum said you looked just

like a glam rocker when you visited her at the home last night. You know, all that black around your eye." Manic laughter followed this statement. Half-heartedly I laughed along with her, and then made what was for me a very curt goodbye and hung up after promising that I would let her know if Stephen did get in touch to arrange a meeting.

I padded into the kitchen and put on the kettle for a much needed shot of caffeine, my mind whirling with the conversation between myself and my sister. All that stuff about Ray—and what on earth was that comment about Mum? I could hear Lynette's voice again; "If you ask me, she's not as daft as she makes out!" What did she mean?

Mum had been admitted to Green Gates Nursing Home in Cobby only a couple of weeks ago. It had been a heart-breaking decision for me and Lynette, but Mum was confused and vulnerable and couldn't even cope in her retirement housing flat any more. It was felt that she needed specialist care, and the doctors and nursing staff at the home were brilliant with her, so kind and attentive. Tests were being carried out so that a correct diagnosis of her illness could be made. She wasn't daft, she was ill. Seething, I poured boiling water into my favorite aunty mug, steam rising in a great plume, bathing my bruised face as if I was in steam room. Taking a deep breath, I inhaled the intoxicating odor of coffee beans.

I sat down at my lovely scrubbed pine table and gazed around the kitchen—at the lemon painted walls and pristine white ceiling—and smiled to myself as I noticed the countless uneven brush strokes. Decorating had never been one of Ray's good points, which was a minor thing when I recalled all the things that I'd loved about him.

Sighing heavily, I took a sip of coffee, thinking again about Lynette and her comments about Stephen Gates. She knew nothing about him—she'd only listened to rumors. And all that stuff about him being old had made me want to scream.

I'd lied to her so I could get off the phone—I'd said I was due at Bloomers but I wasn't. It was one of my days off, and I was looking forward to having some time to myself. And really, it was just as well I wasn't at work looking as though I'd done ten rounds in a boxing ring. I thought my face would have put the customers off their sausage rolls, and that was saying something. It didn't seem as if anything in the world could put Bloomer's customers off their favorite pastry fix.

Lynette's comments about Ray puzzled me too. Did she really think that he was sitting up there on a fluffy white cloud watching my every move? I shook my head. My sister, my only sibling—always a Lynette, never a Lynn—always a strange one. She hated being called Lynn, and even Lynette, come to think of it. Even when she was a child she had moaned at poor old Dad, asking why he'd chosen such an awful name. "Thank your lucky stars," I always told her, "that you weren't named Margaret!"

Groping in the cupboard under the sink, I found a couple of acetaminophen and swallowed them down with a glass of tepid water. Hopefully they would ease the throbbing pain that was turning any chance of a smile from me into a grimace.

I heard a ping from my mobile, and looking at the garishly lit up screen saw that it was a text from an unnamed number. Peering closely, narrowing my eyes—I was so useless without my reading glasses—I could just about make out the message.

Hi Maggie, it's Stephen. I said I would send a text and here it is! It was really good to see you yesterday after such a long time. Do you still fancy meeting up? Text me back if you do. It would be good to hear from you. PS hope your face isn't too bruised! x

Well, well, I thought, my good humor miraculously restored. *He hasn't wasted any time in contacting me, even after seeing me in my Bloomers uniform, which isn't exactly attractive*! I read the message again, trying not to smile too much because of my sore face. *Hmm,* I thought with a sudden pang. *Don't make too much of this, Maggie Sears – don't get your hopes up. He's probably just being friendly and has absolutely no thoughts of romance. Come to that though, do I even want romance? What do they say about first love? That first love is almost always unrequited.* I giggled to myself and thought what a fantastic quote that was. Lynette would certainly love it!

I picked up my phone, thinking hard about what I was going to say, and was on the verge of texting back, my fingers on the screen, when I suddenly thought, *No, not yet*. I placed the phone firmly on the table. *Yes, okay, I know, I'm older now and I really should know better, but I still remember those heady teenage years and the power of playing just a little bit hard to get*!

~*~

The 11:34 a.m. train from Cobby to Skelmanthorpe chugged out of the station exactly on time. Beautiful pots of gaily colored plants stood proudly on the retreating platform, and leafy hanging baskets swung serenely in the spring breeze. Clouds of steam spewed from the train, obscuring my vision for a moment, and I almost expected Jenny Agutter to appear amidst the vapor, arms outstretched, saying plaintively, "Daddy, Daddy, oh my Daddy." That part of the film *The Railway Children* struck a chord with me, and always brought tears to my eyes.

I snuggled into my seat and gazed out the window as the stunning Cobby countryside sped by in a green and brown blur. Taking a deep breath, I tried to calm the erratic beating of my heart, but all I could think of was the forthcoming meeting with Stephen Gates, and my heart skipped yet another beat. How glad I was that circumstances had brought him back to Cobby, his home town.

I glanced down at my dress, a simple black and red shift dress that I hadn't worn for ages. I'd even put on heels and applied discreet eye shadow and a soft pink lipstick, blow dried my hair, and sprayed perfume on my neck and my wrists. Looking in the mirror, all ready to go, I had to say I'd been pleased with the result.

I felt strange though, vulnerable, as if I'd forgotten how to dress up, how to make up my face, style my hair. Since Ray died I'd barely done a thing to myself. I didn't need to dress up for work anyway, and with Ray gone—well, what was the point? I suppose I thought I didn't need to dress to impress any more. Well, perhaps now there *would* be a point. I shrugged and thought carelessly, but with a hint of excitement, *Who knows?*

Gazing from the window, I thought how glad I was that I'd decided to take the train today. When Stephen had mentioned meeting in Skelmanthorpe because he had a meeting there today, I'd definitely been of two minds about it, and had thought that I would drive as I had on the rare occasions I'd gone to Skelmanthorpe.

For years travelling on trains had filled me with dread, bringing morbid thoughts of Dad into my mind. His death had affected me deeply, but time had eased the memories a little, and the sound of engines clanking along railway tracks didn't upset me as much as it used to. In the early days, trains had been demons—hissing, spitting demons.

To make it even worse I'd been so young when the accident had happened—only sixteen, and Lynette a little girl of eight years old, who didn't quite understand where her daddy had gone. Mum had been devastated. In fact, to be perfectly honest, I didn't think she'd ever recovered. On the surface, perhaps, but not really, not properly.

As the train slowly glided into Skelmanthorpe Station, I saw Stephen before he saw me. He was standing on the platform wearing a smart grey suit underneath a long black overcoat, and mirror shiny shoes. The train stopped with a deflated hiss and his gaze became searching, his neck straining from his shirt collar. He seemed oblivious to the crowds scurrying around him like busy ants. A shaft of sunlight streamed from a sky as blue as Johnny Emmerson's eyes. Stepping from the carriage, I raised my hand in a wave, and catching sight of me, he raised his as, smiling broadly, we walked towards each other.

~*~

The older lady, Winifred, was on duty when I arrived at the nursing home the following day. Unlike Tracey, the younger care assistant, Winifred was very thin, her long buttoned-up-to-the-neck overall making her look as tall and rangy as a giraffe, totally at odds with her large flat feet encased in thick pumps that resembled those of stereotypical flatfoot police officers. I was tempted to say "Evening all," instead of "Evening Winifred" as I walked through the door.

"Hello, Mrs. Sears," she replied. "How are you today, dear?"

"I'm fine," I told her. "Mum okay?"

"She's getting on a treat, even had her hair done. Oh, by the way, our Christine had her little one last night—another boy, Archie, nine pounds two."

"Nine pounds two!" I exclaimed. "Wow Winifred, that's wonderful. I'm so pleased for you. How many grandchildren now?"

"He's the eighth," she replied, as puffed up with pride as a chicken ruffling its feathers. Then she quipped, "Just think, number eight—two fat ladies click click click." Winifred had a great brood of children and grandchildren that she updated me on regularly. She carried on speaking, but the shrill ringing of the phone cut her short and she answered it, saying, "Good evening, Green Gates Nursing Home, Winifred speaking, how may I help you?" in a voice so la di da that I barely recognized it as being Winifred.

Dad's voice flashed through my mind. "Hmm," I remembered him saying. "Putting on the Florence, eh?" He often made that comment about people putting on a posh voice, like Mrs. Bouquet from that old situation comedy, *Keeping Up Appearances*, on the telly. Smiling, I shook my head at the memory as I climbed the stairs to Mum's room.

Mum had indeed had her hair done and it looked great, softly waved and highlighted with a rich chocolate that looked good enough to eat. To my surprise she wasn't in bed as she usually was, but sitting in a comfy wing chair that stood by the window overlooking the gardens. She looked tiny and frail, lost in the deep soft cushions. A fuzzy pink bed jacket hugged her shoulders.

At the sound of the door opening she turned her head, and for the first time in what seemed like forever I saw recognition in her eyes. Opening her arms wide, she said, "Hello, my Maggie. Come here and have a cuddle."

I rushed to her and, kneeling by the chair, took her in my arms, hugging her hard, her bones feeling so small and fragile I was afraid she would snap in two like a tiny wooden tooth pick. "Oh Mum," I said, holding her by the shoulders, pulling away and studying her face. "You know who I am." Tears like tiny drops of rain teetered on the very edge of my lashes, poised, ready to fall. I tried to blink them away.

"Yes," she replied. "I do. I've been somewhere though, haven't I, Maggie? Have I been gone a long time?"

Crying hard now and finding it difficult to speak, I nodded my head.

Chapter Three

Bloomers was busy, and it was only just after eight in the morning. I'd been there since before six and was longing for a break. The taste and smell of hot strong coffee and spicy cinnamon buns spun around and around in my mind, competing for first place with intriguing thoughts of Stephen Gates. Stephen was still winning, but for how long? My stomach rumbled alarmingly, a great loud gurgle, much to the amusement of a group of scruffy work men clad in paint spattered denim dungarees, who had appeared like a mini army at the front of the queue demanding their breakfast.

I kept going into a Stephen induced haze, recalling his sherry brown eyes, the deep dimple in his chin, and his hair, which still grew in whorls like tiny mazes on the back of his head. I'd had a sneaky peek when returning from the ladies' room in Ziggi's Pizza Parlor, where we'd gone after meeting at Skelmanthorpe Station. I'd made up my mind that after all this time I *still* wanted to run my fingers around and around in those tiny mazes. But what about Stephen? What did he want? I wasn't sure. He still seemed as remote and self-controlled as ever, as well as being friendly, funny, and generally good company. A somewhat strange combination, I thought.

I glanced up at the queue that snaked out of the shop and across the courtyard, almost reaching the door of the pound shop opposite. Several customers sat outside at our plastic tables and chairs, even though it was spitting rain and tiny drops soaked little rings into their sandwiches and coffees. Wind, snow, ice, rain, whatever—the weather never seemed to bother Bloomers' customers when they were intent on munching away at their breakfast bacon and sausage.

A small man with a pot belly and a limp ponytail trailing down his back like a tail shouted hysterically at Lillian because there was no omelet left to go with his bacon. He was on the verge of tears, his voice sounding scratchy and sore. Marta, fairly new to the job, a sturdy polish girl with thick legs and a heavy accent, demanded that he apologize for his behavior, and he said he would if she would give him a baguette with extra sausage and bacon for free. Such terrible bribery—what was the world coming to?

"Break time, Maggie," said Lillian, giving me a nudge in the ribs. "You look as though you could do with something to eat, love."

I sank wearily onto one of the hard wooden chairs in the break room, allowing the events of the week before to run through my mind as I took a first tentative sip of hot restorative coffee, almost burning my mouth in the process. Stephen had been so kind and gentlemanly as we stood on the platform staring at each other, quite shyly I thought, now that the meeting was actually there and was real. He complimented me on my clothes and my hair, then steered me around the busy streets of Skelmanthorpe, a firm hand cupping my elbow, while talking earnestly and pointing out various landmarks of the town.

"Look," he said. "There's the gym that I go to, Hale & Hearty."

No wonder he looks so fit, I thought to myself before saying, "Oh yes, it looks very grand, and the orange logo of the stick man and woman running together is brilliant."

"Yes, it's a fabulous place, with a lovely big swimming pool and new state of the art gym. The swimming pool looks out onto a lake, which is very scenic. It was a former school, I think." He pointed with his index finger. "See that extension?" I nodded. "That's where the pool is, and the steam room and sauna."

I stood on my tiptoes and stretched my neck so that I could see over the drystone wall into the pretty gardens surrounding the building. The lake shimmering in the sunshine and dotted with a few ducks and a couple of elegant swans looked as though it had been taken over by a gaggle of honking geese that seemed to leave a layer of green slime wherever they went.

Stephen then said mildly, "There was a fire there recently, and the whole of the extension had to be rebuilt."

"A fire?" I said, glancing at him. "Oh my God, I hope nobody was hurt?"

"No, luckily no one was in the building at the time." As he looked at me, his sherry brown eyes seemed to sparkle in the sunshine. "You'd never guess it was rebuilt. They've done a brilliant job."

"How did the fire start?"

"I've heard it was arson," he replied darkly.

Before I could ask any more questions, he raised his hand as a young couple appeared from the building through a massive oak door. "Melanie and Rob," he explained. "They both work there. Melanie in reception and Rob is a personal trainer and lifeguard. Nice couple." I remembered nodding my head and stealing a glance at them as, smiling in acknowledgement, they walked past hand in hand. They were an attractive couple, very toned and fit looking, and I'd bet you a fiver—if I was a betting woman—that they had a lot less fat on them than a rasher of Bloomers' bacon.

"Do you like pizza?" Stephen had asked me suddenly, out of the blue.

"Yes I do," I replied, thinking for one wild moment that we were going to go to Gerry's takeaway on High Street that sold everything from burgers to curry, and eat greasy pizza sitting on a bench in the park. But no, Stephen grabbed my hand, which gave me a lovely tingling sensation right in the pit of my stomach, and led me to the older part of the town, where I tottered on my heels down secret back streets, the roads windy and cobbled, to Ziggi's Pizza Parlor. Traditional Italian music played softly from the open doorway, and the smell of baking bread and melting cheese hung in the air. Impressed, I remembered looking up at him, exclaiming, "Wow, what a find. It's like being in Italy…for real." How childish I must have sounded. I noticed that his lips, as red and inviting as cherries, curved into a smile.

I remembered how we'd talked and talked, firstly about

Diana, Stephen's wife, and about Ray, and then how he'd told me that he'd always liked me at school but thought I was way out of his league, and had been far too scared and nervous to talk to me, let alone ask me out. "Then we moved away as a family," he said sadly, "down south, and I suspected that I would never see you again. But here we are now, together...." My heart soared at his words and, for the first time since Ray died, I felt hopeful again, young and foolish and capable of anything.

"What a pity you didn't ask me out," I told him. "Because I always liked you too. I liked to look at the back of your head when I sat behind you in math class...your hair grows in tiny whorls like this." I made circles in the air with a wayward drunken finger. "No wonder I've never been any good at math." I liked the sexy wrinkles that fanned out around his eyes as he roared with laughter.

At the end of the evening he kissed me once hard on the mouth. Then, cupping the back of my head in the palm of his hand, he kissed me again, softer this time, until, like the flickering candle that had stood on the table between us in Ziggi's Pizza Parlor, I thought I would melt.

Coming abruptly out of my reverie, I glanced at the clock and saw that I'd gone five minutes over my break time. Hurriedly I glanced in the mirror, tweaked my cap into place, and pinched my cheeks poppy red before going back behind the counter and into the mayhem that was Bloomers the Bakers.

~~

"Delirium?" I repeated, not sure if I had heard correctly. I leaned in nearer to the doctor, thinking that perhaps I should get my hearing checked after Lynette and I had finished in here. I glanced around the room which was surprisingly plain, almost as bare as a cell with white unadorned walls. A green blind hung slightly crooked at the window—I longed to straighten it, but what would the doctor say? "Mrs. Sears, really, that blind is no concern of yours!"—through which dust motes danced in a stream of hazy sunshine. The air felt moist and close, even though through the window I could see that clouds were forming, fluffy and rich, blocking out the sun.

The results of Mum's tests had come back, and I was not at all sure that the word delirium was what we had expected to hear, Dementia maybe, even Alzheimers, but definitely not delirium. Although, after the long lucid conversation I'd had with Mum the other night, I wasn't sure what to think.

The doctor said it again as he leaned forward against his light wood desk and put his fingers into a steeple. "Yes, delirium—brought on by repeated urinary tract infections, water infections...."

"Really?" questioned Lynette. "Can that really happen?"

"Oh yes," he confirmed, peering at us over the top of his tiny half glasses, the frames of which were silver and thin and looked as fine and flimsy as cobwebs. "Especially at your mother's age. We often find that older people are far more susceptible to this condition." The doctor, who must have been pushing seventy at least, smiled warmly at us. Doctor Russell, as it said on his name badge—a pleasant looking man, his eyes, an unusual light grey, twinkling behind the little glasses.

"Please don't worry," he assured us. "Your mother can

be treated, just as your local doctor tried to do. But obviously the antibiotics he gave her weren't strong enough for such an infection. We've already started administering some stronger tablets, so they should clear it up and hopefully restore her to something like normality."

"Delirium sounds almost medieval," pointed out Lynette. "I thought you were going to recommend that she have electric shock treatment or be tied to a ducking stool and submerged in icy water for an hour. Or maybe even put a frog on her chest." She giggled as I shook my head slowly and wondered, *Why oh why does my sister have such a strange sense of humor?*

Doctor Russell smiled at her and shook his head. "No, we will certainly not be carrying out any of those practices. The medical profession has come on in giant leaps and bounds since then."

Lynette smirked at him, then glanced at me from the corner of her eye. Ignoring her, I asked the question, "Will she be able to go home yet, Doctor?"

"No," he replied gently. "I'd rather your mother stayed in Green Gates for a few more weeks so that she can be monitored. Any infection must be cleared before she leaves, and we also need to make sure that she is lucid."

"She recognized me when I came in to see her yesterday," I told them. "I had a good long conversation with her, the first one for ages." I then added, "It was so good to have Mum back."

Doctor Russell smiled sympathetically and said, "Excellent. That means the antibiotics are kicking in already."

Lynette and I were strangely silent as I pulled my little yellow Fiat out of Skelmanthorpe Surgery's parking lot and headed back to Cobby. Typical for spring, the sun had disappeared behind banks of misty clouds, and the day, which had promised to be fine, had turned cold and wintry. Cool white flakes danced like tiny fairies from a low pewter sky. Golden daffodils, shivering in the breeze, lined the windy roads, a vibrant splash of color amongst the white rimmed hedges and bushes.

Wishing I'd worn a coat, I turned the heat up a notch, glancing at Lynette as I did so. Her profile with its tip tilted nose was unchanged since she was a tiny baby sleeping in her cot, and I had a sudden memory of holding her close and kissing her downy cheek. I smiled to myself as I thought of her reaction if I did that now. I thought it would be quite aggressive. "What on earth do you think you're doing, Maggie? Get…off…me!"

"You okay?" I asked her. "Warm enough?" I turned the radio down slightly, drowning out Ken Bruce, who was rambling on about Pop Master and the Tracks of my Years. It seemed that Adele was in the hot seat for her choices this week.

"Getting there," she replied as she hunched her shoulders almost up to her ears. I noticed that she wore her smart work uniform of a navy-blue skirt and jacket, teamed with a multi colored blouse, with Bedrock & Rose, the Estate Agents Who Care to Get You There, embroidered on the top pocket.

Lynette worked part time for Bedrock & Rose, and apparently was very good at her job, having just the right sort of persuasive personality for buying and selling. It seemed that she'd been instrumental in setting Kath Emmerson up in her little house along the tow path. "She fell in love with the place straight away," Lynette was always fond of saying.

We discussed Mum's situation as I drove carefully and slightly nervously along the narrow roads, hoping against hope that a car wouldn't suddenly appear going the other way, when Lynette abruptly changed the subject. "Well, how did the meeting with Stephen Gates go then? You've been very quiet about it. Actually, did he even get in touch?"

My stomach gave a great lurch and my palms felt slippery on the wheel as I replied, "Oh yes, sorry. I meant to let you know. He did get in touch, and we met in Skelmanthorpe and had lunch."

Lynette giggled. "Oh, is that it? Is that all that happened?" And then in a silly baby voice she added, "We met in Skelmanthorpe and had lunch."

Ignoring her sarcasm, I said, "We had a lovely time. Stephen is very charming. We went to a really nice pizza place called Ziggi's Pizza Parlor. Do you know it? Nice place—quite up market."

"Pizza?" she exclaimed, wrinkling her nose. "No, I don't know it. Are you meeting again?"

"Oh yes, I hope so," I replied. "We said we'd text."

"What's he doing back here in Cobby anyway?" asked Lynette. "Why did he leave the glamorous south?"

Concentrating hard on the roads, I said, "Yes, I wondered that myself. As you already know, his wife died and he didn't want to stay in the house—too many memories—so he decided to sell it. Then the job of headmaster came up in Cobby High School, which clinched it really."

"Oh, I see—he was lucky enough to get the job, and the rest is history," she butted in.

I nodded. "Yes, that's about it, although maybe not just lucky to get the job, but qualified enough, clever enough. And don't forget he was a deputy headmaster at a school down south."

"Hmm," Lynette slowly shook her head. "Smitten, are we?"

I grinned and we exchanged sideways glances. "Certainly not," I replied.

"Where does he live?" she asked.

I had to smile as I told her, "He lives in a rather nice detached house on White Church Lane."

"Never." She turned her head and stared at me, wide eyed. "Not the notorious new housing development on White Church Lane? Well, not so new now, but the one that Johnny Emmerson was involved with just before he died?"

"That's right," I said. We exchanged a grin. "All that hoo-ha about the green belt, and what happened?"

"The development went ahead," Lynette finished for me. "Well fancy that; what a coincidence."

"Not really a coincidence," I replied. "He just happened to buy a house in that development."

Lynette replied, "If there was no such thing as coincidence, there would be no such word."

I kept quiet. Now really—what could I say to that?

On arriving in Cobby I noticed that the weekly market had been set up in the center of the town, and the whole place was bustling. A large white banner, emblazoned with the words Cobby Continental Market, courtesy of Cobby Town Council, had been hung amongst the budding blossom trees. The streets were choked with traffic and the pavements with shoppers. There was no doubt that the market was a hit. I caught a glimpse of Kath Emmerson flitting around the stalls, conspicuous in a bright red suit.

"I need to go home, I forgot my Bloomers uniform," I told Lynette. "Can I drop you here?" I glanced across the road, where I could see Bedrock & Rose huddled between Sweet Things, a tiny, old-fashioned confectioners, and Wilson's, the pharmacy with its dimpled glass shop front. She nodded and started to get out of the car when she turned back and said, "You might be better on your own, Maggie—at least no one can hurt you."

"Unrequited love and all that?" I said, a small smile hovering around my lips.

"I'm serious," she replied. "You're better on your own...."

"Lynette...," I called, but she'd already slammed the car door and was on her way, stomping across the road to the estate agents. I shook my head, wondering what on earth was eating away at her now. Something was bothering her, but what? She seemed a bit put out that my meeting with Stephen had gone well, but why would that be? Maybe it was just worry over Mum. But then again, it had all been good news on that front this morning.

I carefully maneuvered away from the side of the road and out into the milling traffic, the brightness of my Fiat standing out against the mundane black, silver, and white vehicles. As I drove I thought of the one thing that I hadn't told her. I didn't know why I hadn't, as she would probably have been pleased. She was always telling me to get away from Bloomers and find myself a better job. I frowned as, thinking about it, that wasn't really much of a compliment.

Cobby High School was advertising for a new member of staff for their secretarial team, and Stephen thought that I would be an ideal candidate. "You have all the relevant qualifications," he had said. "Typing and word processing, knowledge of email and several Word packages." How glad I was now that I'd kept up with the trends over the years. He told me that he had his own personal assistant, but that they were looking for a secretary to work closely with the examinations officer.

"She's the one that's leaving," he told me. "Relocating to Norbury, I think. Laura Miller. It's a part time post, three days a week, lots of contact with the kids when they're doing their exams. You'd love it, Maggie. There's nothing like working in a school. I'll email you all the details and an application form."

"What about Bloomers?" I'd asked him stupidly as I took another sip of wine, staring at him, taking in his whole face—the scooped-out dimple, the slightly stubbly cheeks and chin, and the deep sherry brown eyes. My heart was beating so hard, I thought he would hear it and say, "Good God, Maggie, what's up with you? Your heart sounds like a herd of galloping horses." All he said though was, "Maggie," as he softly stroked the palm of my hand with his thumb, which was most disconcerting to say the least. "You need a change from Bloomers. Didn't you always say you'd like to work in a school?"

I nodded dumbly.

"Well then, you can do anything you like—leave Bloomers, anything!"

He opened his arms wide as if to encompass the whole

world, and with the quiet ambience of Ziggi's Pizza Parlor around me and red wine coursing rapidly through my veins, I certainly felt as if I could do anything and that the world was there, ready and waiting for me. All I had to do was grab it—and maybe this was my chance.

Chapter Four

"Well, well, you do look smart," said Mum as I walked into the communal area of Green Gates that sunny July morning, "What a fabulous outfit. Where are you off to then?"

She was sitting in a comfy chair at one of the large bay windows that was swathed in what looked like hundreds of yards of pink velour material masquerading as curtains. The sun blazed yellow as egg yolk in a cloudless blue sky, throwing myriads of light onto the room's plain cream walls. The garden looked as beautiful as ever, the well dug borders full of brightly colored flowers and bushes and the manicured lawn shimmering emerald in the heat.

I bent forward and kissed Mum on the cheek, which felt soft and papery beneath my lips, and then lowered myself into the chair opposite. She looked good, her hair still beautifully colored and styled. Dark blue trousers and a light blue and white striped top adorned her small frame—although she did seem to have put on a pound or two since she'd been feeling better—and her face was made up—a tiny bit of eye-shadow, a dab of lipstick.

"I'm going for an interview," I told her.

"An interview? What's all this? You never said anything."

I glanced around. I didn't really want anybody to know where I was going today—I'd look a fool if I didn't get the job. But apart from an old man dozing in his chair the room was empty. The television was still on—I didn't think it was ever switched off—droning in the background like a hive of busy bees. The color setting was obviously still set far too high, as a woman with a very red face and bright yellow hair was reading the news.

"Well," I explained. "It's for a job at Cobby High School, part time, on the secretarial team, mainly working with the examinations officer. It sounds really good."

"Cobby High School? Well, I never. What about Bloomers?"

"Well, if I get the job, I'd have to leave Bloomers, wouldn't I?"

The care assistant, Tracey, bustled into the room, cutting our conversation short. She carried a tea tray laden with matching flowered mugs, sugar bowl, and milk jug. "I saw you come in, Mrs. Sears," she said brightly, "And thought you might fancy a cup of coffee with your mum. Ooh I say, you do look smart."

I glanced down at my black trouser suit teamed with a red blouse, and felt that, because of the compliments that I was receiving, I'd made the right choice when getting dressed that morning. "Thank you, Tracey," I said. "You're very kind—for the compliments and the coffee."

I was hoping desperately that Mum wouldn't tell Tracey where I was going when she blurted out, "She's going for an interview at Cobby High School."

Tracey's pale blue eyes almost popped out of her head. "Mrs. Sears, that's wonderful," she said. "I— "

Whatever words Tracey was going to say were left hanging in the air never to be heard as her mobile phone gave a sudden loud beep. With a quick, "Oh, I must answer this," she hurriedly left the room, her rather large bottom swaying beneath the too tight overall.

"I didn't really want anybody to know, Mum," I whispered. I poured us both a steaming hot coffee, adding plenty of milk and sugar to Mum's cup. I knew just how she liked it.

"Why ever not?" she retorted, pursing her lips together, then picked up her cup and saucer and took a long swallow before putting it carefully back on the table. "You should be proud you've got an interview. It's not everyone that gets picked these days, you know. In my day you could get a job just like that," She clicked her finger and thumb together. "But today it's not that easy. You've done well to get this far, Maggie."

"I might not get the job," I said.

"Of course you'll get it," she said breezily. "You're a clever girl, you are."

Good old Mum, she always did make me feel confident in myself. But enough was enough. I didn't want my head so big I couldn't get through Cobby High School's door. I changed the subject by saying, "Anyway, how are you, Mum?"

"Oh, so much better, Maggie. I really hope the doctor says

I can go home when he's on his rounds today." She paused, and then said in a tiny yearning voice, "I can't wait to go home."

I patted her hand that lay like a tiny bird's claw on the arm of the chair. "I know you can't, Mum. But we have to make sure that you're all right, don't we?"

She nodded, then said—quite slyly, I thought—her eyes downcast, looking through her lashes, "How are you getting on with Stephen then? Still seeing him?"

Thoughts of Stephen coursed through my body. I felt his hand in mine, his lips against my cheeks and my hair, his sherry brown eyes looking at me, appraising me, and complimenting me, the clean soapy smell of his skin. I didn't remember ever feeling this way before—well, I suppose I had with Ray in the early days, but....

"Oh yes, Mum," I stammered. "I'm still seeing him."

"You're blushing, Maggie," she said, and screeched with laughter, a sound so loud that even the old man sleeping in his chair opened one lazy eye to see what was going on.

"Stop it, Mum," I chided her, then took a healthy slug of coffee. She was right though—my cheeks were burning, and I almost expected to hear the wild clamor of a fire engine as it arrived to put out the fire. "He wants me to meet his son and daughter," I told her. "Very soon, I think."

Mum nodded her head and said coyly, "It must be serious then. But you always did like him, and I think he liked you. I remember you writing his name inside a big red heart on your school exercise books." She giggled. "If it wasn't Donny Osmond or David Cassidy you were mooning over, you could be sure it was Stephen Gates."

"Mum," I said. "That was a long time ago…." But yes, I could remember doing it, writing his name on my school books, coloring in the red heart with a felt tip pen. How silly I'd been.

"Have you been to his house yet?" she asked.

"No, I haven't," I told her. "We've been meeting up in the pub or restaurants or going for walks—or drives."

I conjured up a picture of us sitting in Stephen's car on the worn leather seats, the soft salty taste of his lips on mine and the warmth of his arms around my neck. Stephen was far from remote now. In fact, we were acting like lovesick teenagers—and in our fifties!

She nodded, and then went off on a tangent and said, "Keep an eye on Lynette, will you, Maggie? I have a feeling something's not quite right there."

"What do you mean?" I asked. "Not right where?"

"With her and Dave, of course," she replied. "What did you think I meant?"

"What—you think Dave might be having an affair?"

"I'm not sure," replied Mum. "Maybe that's the case"

I put Mum's comments about Lynette and Dave to the back of my mind as I drove away from the nursing home and to Cobby High School. My stomach was fluttering so much at the anticipation of the interview that I knew I'd never be able to concentrate on anybody else's problems at the moment.

Anyway, it was totally out of the question that Dave could be having an affair. He was crazy about Lynette, and didn't even seem to notice other women, let alone be interested in anybody else. *Think about it later, Maggie,* I thought to myself as I parked my little yellow car in the spacious parking lot and made my way to the school's imposing glass entrance doors. Stephen's words ran through my mind. "There's no need to be nervous about the interview, Maggie. In fact, the worst part will be trying to get past the bulldog in reception."

I had spent some time mulling over this, puzzled by his words, but all became clear as I approached the reception desk, because if a human being ever bore any resemblance whatsoever to a bulldog, it just had to be the receptionist. Trying to keep a straight face I said, "Hello, I've come for an interview. My name's Maggie Sears."

"Take a seat," she barked, pointing to a long line of plastic chairs that stood against one wall. "I'll tell the interview panel that you've arrived."

Afraid that she might growl at me if I didn't obey, I sat down timidly on one of the hard chairs, my heart beating so hard now that I could barely breathe. Discreetly I wiped my sweating palms along the sides of my trousers. *Hurry up and call me in*, I thought to myself. *Let's get this over with.*

Glancing around I noticed, from several large signs on the walls, that I was in the reception area – surprise surprise – and that the cafeteria was to the left and the upper grade level area to the right. Groups of students wandered along the corridors chatting and laughing. I noticed a boy walking along quite aimlessly, I thought, peering intently at each classroom door as if he was lost. He wore scuffed shoes, and a grey rucksack hung limply from his rounded shoulders.

A couple of girls giggled together as they sauntered past, wearing very short skirts, their long legs clad in thick black tights. Cleverly they hid their black kohl rimmed eyes behind long veils of hair. I shook my head and laughed to myself as I recalled turning my school skirt up at the waistband to show as much leg as I possibly could—probably for the benefit of Stephen Gates. Some things never changed.

Just as I was wondering again if I would be sitting on this hard chair for the rest of the day, all night, and maybe forever, a small blonde woman appeared, wearing a bright cerise skirt suit that clung rather closely to her curves, and called my name. "Maggie Sears. please. Maggie Sears." She carried a clipboard and a pen, a pair of glasses on a gold chain hanging around her neck. Nervously smoothing down my trousers and my jacket then taking a deep breath, I stood up and followed her.

~*~

The sun was beginning to sink slowly into the horizon in a bright red hue as the taxi pulled up outside Stephen's elegant house in the "notorious White Church Lane Development," as Lynette called it. A gentle breeze pushed gold rimmed clouds in a darkening sky and stars began to twinkle. The nights seemed to be drawing in already, even though it was only the end of July. The tiny garden with its square of lawn and rich earthy borders dotted with flowers was neat and tidy, and a dark green creeper covered the walls of the house, softening its harsh angles and hiding the new sandy stone. Stephen stood in the doorway, illuminated by the glow of the porch light as I walked uncertainly and very nervously along the path that shone in the near darkness. He wore a crisp white shirt open at the neck tucked into black trousers. He looked slightly tousled, and a touch of designer stubble coated his cheeks and his chin. He looked good, sexy, and my heart beat quickened until it was fluttering like little wings. Tonight I was meeting Jake and Vanessa, Stephen's son and daughter, for the very first time. Stephen had already told me all about them, so hopefully, there would be no surprises.

"Maggie, darling," he said. "I think congratulations are in order." He held out his arms and pulled me into their safe curve. I smiled and put my face to his, inhaling his scent, citrusy and sweet. I traced the little lines at the corners of his eyes with the tip of my finger. In the darkness of the hallway his lips brushed mine and his hands cinched my waist, pulling me even closer. I pressed my curves against him.

All at once a door was flung open, making me jump, and a face appeared, moonlike in the gloom. Tearing myself away from Stephen and narrowing my eyes against the sudden glare of light, I could see a girl. She was tall—a lot taller than me, and I wasn't small—and well built. Her short dark hair curled around her smooth pale cheeks and neck. She wore blue jeans and a white T-shirt with a rainbow motif on it that stretched taut across her breasts. I didn't know it yet, but she bore a striking resemblance to her mother when she was young.

"Hmm, what's going on here then?" she said and stepped back, opening the door wider so that I could see into the sitting room.

A couple sat on one of the two large leather settees that, together with one single arm chair, were grouped around the inglenook fireplace that housed a Much Wenlock wood burner and a large basket filled to the brim with shiny black coal and logs. A large orange rug dominated the center of the room, and a dark wood sideboard covered in a snowy white cloth stood against one wall, upon which stood many framed black and white photographs. Lamps shone cozily from each corner.

"What a lovely room," I commented.

Stephen, grinning like a boy, said, "I do my best, Maggie."

The young man, although he didn't get up, raised a hand and the woman smiled with striking red lips. A slight young woman a few months pregnant, she had shoulder length blonde hair that was curled at the ends, and light blue eyes that appeared almost sightless. The young man looked so much like the Stephen that I had known at school that I had to pinch myself to make sure that I hadn't somehow gotten into a time machine and been transported back to the seventies. The only difference, apart from being a little bit older than Stephen was at the time, was that Jake had a small pointy beard and was dressed down in such a way that he appeared almost scruffy.

"Whoops," said Stephen. "Sorry about that, Vanessa. I was just giving Maggie a welcome kiss."

"A kiss?" she almost growled. "Is that what you call it?" She stood with her hands on her hips, her face a black scowl, marring her prettiness.

Stephen laughed heartily, throwing his head back as I blushed to the very roots of my hair—was it embarrassment or a hot flush?—and Vanessa, taking advantage of this, said, "I'm Vanessa." She held out a warm limp hand, which I tried rather unsuccessfully to shake. "My girlfriend, Lucy, was hoping to be here tonight, but unfortunately had other plans."

Well aware that Vanessa was waiting for my reaction, I said, "Oh, what a pity. I guessed from the rainbow motif on your T-shirt that you would have a girlfriend. I'd love to meet

Lucy next time. Have you been together long?"

Surprised but not wanting to show it, Vanessa muttered, "Um…oh yes, around eighteen months." She sat down heavily on the single leather chair, then reached to the coffee table for a pint glass foaming with amber liquid.

"Eighteen months? It must be a good relationship."

Vanessa nodded as Stephen took my arm and led me to the sofa. "Sit down, Maggie, sit down." He pressed a large balloon glass of red wine into my hand. With a nod of his head Stephen indicated the couple on the sofa. "Maggie, my son Jake and his wife, Lauren."

"How do you do," I said, nodding to them both and taking a tiny sip of wine. "When's the baby due?"

Lauren, taking a drink of what I assumed was mineral water, leaned in towards me and said, "We have a date for the end of November."

"A lovely Christmas present then. Do you know whether it's a boy or a girl?" Valiantly I tried to make eye contact with Jake, but his gaze, as slippery as an eel, kept moving away.

"Yes, it's a girl," said Lauren happily. "We can't wait to see her, can we, Jake?"

Unable to help himself, he smiled at Lauren, right into her eyes, and said, "No we can't."

Lauren leaned in towards me again and said, "We're going to call her Rebecca." She looked to her husband again. "Aren't we Jake?"

He nodded again and smiled, his eyes still skittering away from mine.

Hmm, I thought to myself. *He's going to be hard work.*

Stephen caught my eye and gave a pained, "Well, what

can you do?" sort of grin.

Vanessa butted in. "I don't want to appear to be prying, Dad, but I heard you say something out there about congratulations being in order?" She took a long swallow of the amber liquid.

"Oh yes." Stephen smiled and looked at me. "Maggie is the new member of our secretarial team at the school. She came for a very successful interview and got the job."

"I couldn't believe it," I told them. "I didn't for one minute think I'd get the job."

For the first time Jake fixed me with a hard stare. "Why did you go for the job if you didn't think you'd get it then?" Everybody looked at him, and I noticed that Lauren frowned, her pretty face troubled, probably wondering why he was asking such a question and in such a tone of voice. I noticed that he was drinking a very dark, almost orange liquid, from a squat glass tumbler. It looked like whiskey, smelt like it as well, oily and smoky.

"Well," I replied. "I'm a bit out of practice with office work. I've worked in Bloomers for many years—"

"Bloomers?" he butted in, wrinkling his nose. "What, Bloomers the Bakers? The one in Cobby?"

I nodded, heat rising in my face for the second time that night. He put the squat tumbler down on the small occasional table at his side and sat forward, his forearms on his knees. A grin swarmed over his face and he slowly shook his head. "How on earth are you going to do such important school work—particularly with the exams—when," and he said this scathingly, "You've been working in Bloomers?"

"It's not such a bad place," I began. "I've worked there for a long time, and enjoyed it mostly."

Jake shook his head again and said, "Well, what can I say? I'm just surprised you got the school job, that's all."

"Jake, that's enough," Stephen said harshly. "Maggie got through the interview with flying colors. She's got all the necessary qualifications, and I've no doubt that she'll be very successful in the job. She's got just the right personality and drive for it as well."

Before I could make any comment, Lauren suddenly said, "Ooh," and everybody turned to look at her, taking the attention away from me.

What a clever girl, I thought.

She had both hands flat on the huge mound of her stomach. "She's moving—Rebecca's moving." She grabbed Jake's hand and put it over hers. "Feel Jake. Vanessa, come and feel. Stephen...."

Then she looked at me, her eyes so pale, like the blank eyes of a statue, searching my face. "Maggie...?"

Slowly I leaned across and laid my hand next to Jake's and Vanessa's. Stephen put his close to mine, and we all felt the baby as she rolled and heaved within the confines of Lauren's womb.

I hoped that the situation with Jake and Vanessa would improve after that, but the evening dragged on and on, and even though the meal that Stephen had prepared was excellent, I really couldn't taste a thing. I felt harassed and bullied, particularly by Jake, and desperately wanted the evening to end. Eventually I began to feel hopeless and tired, and pleading a headache, asked a worried looking Stephen if he would ring for a taxi.

It arrived almost straight away so our parting was hurried and, because of the presence of other people, also abrupt and curt. Stephen kissed me chastely on the cheek and we promised to be in touch. As the taxi drove away, I turned and waved from the back seat until he became a little black dot, until the car rounded a corner onto the main road and he was gone.

I arrived home to my quiet empty house with sad thoughts of the evening running through my mind. My old cat Arthur greeted me at the door with a plaintive meow, as if to say, "Mum, I'm so glad you're home. I want some treats—I want Droolies."

I slumped onto the settee, kicking off my shoes, feeling considerably downhearted. I really hadn't expected Stephen's son and daughter to take to me straight away. After all, Stephen had told me that this was the first relationship that he'd been involved in since their mother had died. I suppose I'd been prepared for some animosity, but not for the scathing remarks from Jake about the job in the school and the pitying looks from Vanessa. I'd felt intimidated by two people young enough to be my own son and daughter. How could this be?

Lauren had been lovely. Such a kind, caring girl, and it was so obvious that Jake was very much in love with her and looking forward to the birth of their daughter. I sensed that Vanessa would come around eventually, particularly as I'd shown an interest in meeting her partner, Lucy. Had she thought that she could shock me when she announced that she was gay? I'd gotten the impression that this was the case.

Whatever Vanessa had intended, Jake had succeeded in denting my confidence, and I questioned myself now as to whether or not I really was capable of doing my new job. The elation that I'd felt on being successful was totally gone. Maybe I should forget about it and stay at Bloomers. After all, I hadn't given my notice yet.

Wearily I stood up and made my way into the kitchen, where I put water in the kettle and flicked it on to make a cup of hot chocolate. Hopefully it would help me sleep. Otherwise I suspected I would lay wide awake all night.

My mobile gave a loud beep, startling me, and I almost knocked my mug over. It was a text from Stephen, saying how much he'd enjoyed seeing me this evening, but also profusely apologizing for the behavior of Jake and Vanessa. *Maybe next time we should all go out for a drink together, or maybe go to a restaurant or even Ziggi's. Let me know what you think, Maggie. I hope you feel better soon x.* I had to smile at the little tearful face that he'd put after the kiss.

I recalled how Stephen had tried so hard to make things right with everybody this evening. He'd tried to jolly us along by telling the story of our meeting in Bloomers after so many years, how he'd immediately recognized me even though I was wearing a hair net and a baseball cap. "She took one look at me," he joked, "And promptly fainted. I don't think I made that good an impression on her."

Lauren had screamed with laughter and clapped her hands like a child, saying, "Oh, I wish I'd been there." But Jake and Vanessa had exchanged glances and told me a long, detailed story of their mum and dad's romantic courtship. I listened dutifully and exclaimed at the black and white photographs that they thrust in front of my nose. I commented on the resemblance between Vanessa and her mum, and said that Diana had been a very attractive woman and that I could understand the depth of their mourning. *After all,* I thought. *I'd been through the very same thing with losing Ray.*

I awoke the next morning feeling jaded and hung over, which was surprising as I hadn't drunk that much wine the night before. It was probably because I hadn't slept very well. Awful thoughts of the evening came hurtling back at me, and in my mind's eye I saw Stephen's tight worried face when I asked him to order me a taxi. I made myself get out of bed even though I felt as if a cold hard stone was lodged right in the very pit of my stomach. I padded to the window and peered from between the bedroom curtains at the day outside.

The sun, dodging between fluffy clouds, shone weakly, lighting up my somewhat bedraggled garden in a somber yellow glow. I sighed heavily as I thought of Ray busily working out there for hours and hours, sometimes all day. It had been his pride and joy, and I certainly wasn't keeping it up to his high standards. I glanced at the sky and fervently hoped that he wasn't sitting on a cloud, shaking his head and lamenting my poor gardening skills.

Suddenly my mobile rang, and picking it up I heard Lynette's voice. "Well, how did it go last night then, Maggie?" There was no preamble with Lynette, no "Hello Maggie, how are you?" I smiled to myself, but at least she was ringing and taking an interest.

I related the whole sorry tale, telling her all about Jake's nasty comments about my new job and the condescending tone to his voice when I told him that I worked in Bloomers the Bakers. I told her about Vanessa, and the lovely Lauren and the forthcoming baby.

"What did Stephen say when you left early, Maggie?"

"He didn't look very happy, but I think he understood how I felt. Anyway, it wasn't that early, around half past ten, I think, and he sent me a text message later apologizing for his children's behavior. I think Jake, and maybe Vanessa as well, think I'm incapable of doing a good job in the school."

"Well, Maggie, if I were you," said Lynette, "I'd show them all a thing or two and give your notice at Bloomers, take the job in the school, and make a really good go of it."

Surprised at Lynette being so supportive, I stammered, "Well, yes, you're right, that's exactly what I'm going to do, and I'm going to do it today."

I suddenly felt as light as a feather, so light that I could float away up, up into the ether, into the stars—and maybe join Ray on his fluffy white cloud.

"Good for you," she replied wholeheartedly. There was a tiny split second of silence, then Lynette said, "Maggie, I think Dave's having an affair...."

Ah, I thought. *So that's what Mum meant when she said she was worried about them, and maybe that's what was wrong with Lynette the other day too when she got all touchy in the car.* I didn't say anything about either of those things, but replied, "No, Lynette, Dave wouldn't do that."

I pictured Dave, a gangly man, six-feet-four inches tall, with a shock of black hair and a face as ruddy as I imagined a farmer's to be, which was weird because he had a desk job in computers. They'd been together since they were fourteen years old and, as far as I was aware, he'd never been interested in another woman. Lynette was little, less than five feet tall, so I thought he'd always been protective of her, and she bossed him to death, which he loved. No, Dave would never have an affair.

"What proof have you got?" I asked her.

"You want proof? Well, just listen to this," she replied nastily. She began to read out a text message which she said had been sent from Dave's phone, but had, obviously by mistake, popped up on hers. "'Hi Lena, hope you're available at 7. I want to have a look at the hotel room. I need to try out the bed for size and comfort. Are there facilities for aromatherapy and massage?' What do you think of that then, Maggie? A sext, that's what it is!"

"Oh my God, how strange," I replied. After a few heartbeats where I really didn't know what to say, I managed to blurt out, "It's obviously a mistake. Actually, it sounds as if he's just having a look at the room, don't you think?"

"No, I don't," she snapped. "It's a sext, that's what it is, and the only mistake is the fact that it's come through to my phone and not that other woman's."

"Calm down, Lynette," I said. "I'm sure there's a reasonable explanation for it. Dave's just not like that."

"I don't want a crowded marriage," she blurted out.

"What? A crowded marriage—what do you mean Lynette?"

"Well, you know what Princess Diana said. 'There were three of us in this marriage so it was a bit crowded'"

Oh my God, I thought. *Quotes—even at a time like this.* "Lynette," I repeated. "There will be a reasonable explanation."

With tears in her voice she said, "Well, Maggie, whatever he's up to, I'm definitely going to find out what it is. Both him and this Lena had better watch out."

Chapter Five

A couple of weeks crawled by as slowly as a tortoise in a race, with not one single word from Stephen, even though I'd been expecting to hear from him after the last message he had sent suggesting that we all meet up together again. I alternated between an "I don't care" attitude and an "Oh my God, why hasn't he been in touch with me?" stance.

I was very tempted to send a message to him instead of waiting for a text, and lost count of the number of times that my hand reached for my mobile phone. Every time though, my fingers poised over the keypad, I came to my senses and realized that I should leave well enough alone. He was obviously having second thoughts about our relationship after the disastrous evening with Jake and Vanessa.

In the meantime, I thought again about what Lynette had said about handing in my notice at Bloomers, and I did so to a very shocked Lilian, who asked what on earth she could do to make me stay—and, come to that, why didn't I want to stay?

I explained that I needed a change and that a job had come up in Cobby High School, which I had applied for and managed to get.

"I'm starting a new chapter in my life," I told her.

That very same day, I rang the school and accepted the job as Assistant to the Examinations Officer. My starting date would be in September, at the beginning of a new term, and after I had worked out my notice at Bloomers. For the first time since not hearing from Stephen, I felt quite excited about the future, even though, I thought with a sudden worried pang, taking the new job would mean I would see him on a very regular basis.

My worries vanished on a hot day in August—or so I thought. I'd just arrived home after a very busy shift at Bloomers. I was hot and sweaty, my thin skirt and T-shirt sticking to me like glue, so I opened the back door to let in what in the end only amounted to a tiny cooling breeze.

My old cat Arthur clawed at my legs, meowing for attention, and the kettle spat and bubbled to the boil as I got a mug from the cupboard. I was so longing to sit down with a restorative cup of coffee. There was a sudden ping and a text message popped up on my phone. Peering closely, I saw with a somewhat lighter heart that it was the text message that I had been waiting for—it was from Stephen.

Hi Maggie, sorry I haven't been in touch. Been so busy! Are you free for a drink at tea time? If you are, how about meeting in the Star in Cobby? About 4.00 p.m.? Good pub. Let me know S x

Hmm, I thought. *The Star Pub in Cobby? Isn't that where*

Johnny Emmerson used to go when he and his buddies were campaigning for the town council? I'm sure I remember reading that in his obituary. I decided that I would go. Good news or bad, it was time that Stephen and I met for a talk. I replied straight away. *Hi Stephen, yes would love to meet for a drink. C u in the Star in Cobby at 4.00 p.m. M x*

I looked at his message and read again the comment, "Been so busy!" *Not a good sign*, I thought to myself as I slowly went upstairs, my heart full of foreboding, to get ready for my date with Stephen.

~*~

As it was such a lovely evening, I decided to walk to the pub. It wasn't far, and as some of it was along the towpath, it was a pleasant stroll. I wore a simple green and white sleeveless summer dress and green open toed sandals. It was good to feel so cool after being trussed up, so to speak, in my Bloomers uniform for most of the day. I carried a light cardigan just in case it turned chilly later on.

The pub, quite dim after the glaring sunshine, was almost empty as, nervously, I made my way inside. A few old men stood at the bar nursing their drinks. The odor of yeast and hops hung in the air. I saw Stephen straight away, sitting at a small round table, a pint glass of foaming amber liquid in front of him.

My heels tip tapped across the stone flagged floor, and as he looked up a shaft of sunlight fell from the pub's tiny ancient windows, illuminating his sherry brown eyes. I didn't know it then, but this was the table where Kath Emmerson and Paul Timpson had fallen in love almost two years earlier.

"Maggie," he exclaimed as he stood up, leaned towards

me, and kissed me on the cheek. He smelt clean and soapy. There was a whirr and a click and Elton John and Kiki Dee began to sing, "Don't go breaking my heart…I couldn't if I tried…."

Oh my God, Lynette would think this a terrible coincidence. Please Stephen, don't go breaking my heart. That thought ran through my mind as I said, "Stephen, good to see you."

"What would you like to drink—red wine?"

Already, I thought, *He knows my drink.* "Yes please," I replied. I watched as he walked to the bar, such a familiar walk now that it made my stomach churn. I looked at the back of his head, at the way his hair still grew in tiny whorls, and I felt sad, the saddest I'd felt since Ray died.

"I was hoping we could sit outside in the beer garden," he commented as he came back from the bar and put my drink in front of me, "But it was packed when I arrived, no tables at all."

"Oh, that's OK," I said, "I like it in here. It's so old fashioned, like going back in time. I've not seen a jukebox like that for years—or heard this song for years, come to think of it!" I took a sip of the wine, which was fruity and smooth and very enjoyable.

"You've not been in here before?"

I shook my head. "No, Ray wasn't one for pubs so we didn't bother. I read that this is the pub where Johnny Emmerson and his pals set up Cobby Town Council."

"Yes, I believe it is. The notorious Band of Three, I think they were called. I remember seeing the article. I've always been interested in politics, so it made good reading. Did you know him?"

"No, but I know that his widow, Kath, is the town clerk now."

"Oh really. I didn't know that; good for her! Anyway, Maggie...." He leaned forward, his forearms on the table, "Have you handed in your notice at Bloomers yet?"

"Yes, I have," I replied. "And accepted the post at the school. I thought it was the right thing to do."

"Yes, it certainly is."

There was a tense awkward silence, then Stephen said, "Maggie, I don't know how to say this, but...." He took a deep draft of his pint.

There was a sudden commotion as a large party of people came through the door and milled around the bar, shouting their orders to the flustered bar maid.

"Yes, I know," I butted in over the hubbub. "I can guess what you're going to say—you don't want to see me anymore."

"Well, I wouldn't say that," he replied gently. "But the situation with Jake and Vanessa isn't helping, and I have to put them first. They lost their mother when I lost my wife, and I don't think they're ready for anybody to take her place."

"Take her place?" I exclaimed. "I've no intention of taking anybody's place. I'm Maggie—not Diana." I drew myself up straight and tall in my chair.

"Don't you think I know that that isn't your intention, Maggie? Why do you think it's taken me so long to contact you? I've been mulling over this situation every day since you met Jake and Vanessa, and every day it seems more and more...I don't know. What's the word?"

"Difficult?" I suggested, taking another sip of my drink.

"Yes," he agreed. "Yes Maggie, so difficult."

"You sent me a text suggesting another meeting. What happened to that idea?"

He looked shamefaced as he replied. "Yes, I wanted to have another meeting, go out for a drink or a meal, but they've both dug their heels in. Lauren wanted to, and privately she said that she would work on Jake. But…." He let the words hang in the air.

I gazed at him, at the alluring dimple in his chin and the sexy stubble that covered his cheeks, and wished and wished that he wasn't quite so attractive. I wished that he would put me before his children, I wished that he wasn't finishing our relationship, and I wished that I didn't care. But unfortunately I did. Close to tears, I stumbled to my feet, even leaving my wine, and said in what must have been a totally wretched voice, "Stephen, I have to go."

"Maggie…."

I felt rather than saw him stand up and put out his hand, but I brushed him away and fled out of the door, watched, I knew, by the old men that still loitered at the bar with their pints.

Once out on the street, the hot sun burning the top of my head, I made my way without hesitation to Cobby's ancient church, where I had been married so many years before, and to the tiny cemetery. I needed Ray, and the only way I could feel close to him now was to go to his grave. I felt strangely naked without the flowers that I usually took with me, but as this was an emergency visit, so to speak, I didn't think it would matter. I hurried along the rows and rows of headstones until I came to Ray's.

The stone angel that I had spent so long agonizing over

and finally choosing after Ray had died gazed sightlessly into the sky, reminding me of Lauren and her very pale, almost blind looking eyes. Distraught, I knelt in the dusty earth, my dress belling around me, and gazed at the wording etched into the stone. In Loving Memory, Raymond Anthony Sears. He'd always hated his middle name of Anthony.

Tears sprang into my eyes and coursed down my cheeks, so I had to fumble in my bag for a tissue. I sniffed hard and wiped my face, thinking how Ray would be laughing at me now, "What a softie you are," he had always said whenever I cried at anything sad on the telly. "What a softie you are, Maggie Sears."

I knew it seemed totally mad, and of course I didn't expect an answer, but looking at the grave, focusing on his name printed on the stone, I said, "Oh Ray, what am I going to do?" There was nothing of course; no response, no voice, nothing—no sound at all apart from the faint cooing of a dove and a warm breeze that whispered through the leaves of the trees.

Wearily I pulled myself to my feet, knowing without a doubt that the situation I was in was something I would have to deal with myself. Ray couldn't help me. How stupid I was to think that he could.

I wandered aimlessly around the little cemetery, peering at the stones and reading the inscriptions, when I noticed a headstone hidden like a little secret beneath a tree. It was an open book, the wording on one page strong and black, and as I bent down to read it, it didn't surprise me at all that the name Johnny Laurence Emmerson was clearly visible. One line of the epitaph caught my eye—May He be Lifted up into

Paradise.

As I repeated those lovely words to myself the air around me became charged as if with electricity, and a wind, playful as a child, gently fluttered the hem of my dress and teased the ends of my hair. The tree overhanging the grave bent and swayed and danced as if in a frenzy. Then suddenly everything was still and quiet, just as it had been before. Had I imagined it all?

With a heavy heart I began to walk home, totally unaware of the beautiful summer evening. I glanced around just in case Stephen was hurrying along behind me, his dear face creased in a frown, saying, "Maggie, where are you going? Come with me, I didn't mean a word I said." But there was nobody there, so I carried on walking until I came to a bench on the towpath.

I sank onto it, tired, weary, my head throbbing from the heat of the sun. I gazed at the canal, the water brown and sluggish and barely moving, dense clouds of gnats hovering over the surface. A runner jogged by, swaying to music that only he could hear, and an elegant swan, its beautiful white neck curved as a question mark, glided silently by.

My phone buzzed in my bag and, cupping my hand around the screen to block the glare of the sun, I saw a message from Stephen. *Maggie r u ok*? I literally threw the phone back into my bag, knowing straight away that I wouldn't reply. What was the point? What could I say? "No, actually, I'm not okay. I want you to change your mind. I want, I want, I want…."

"Would you mind very much if I shared your bench?" asked a voice, and looking up, squinting against the sun, I saw looming above me the unmistakable face of Kath Emmerson.

She was holding tightly to the lead of a cute curly haired dog, its tongue hanging out of its mouth as if in a smile, and a collar decorated with little pink hearts encircling its fluffy neck.

"No, of course not, please." I indicated the bench with an outstretched hand. She looked good, fit and healthy, wearing smart walking boots, black leggings, and a long red T-shirt with the words Cobby Fun Run emblazoned on the front in white letters.

"Thank you," she said, sitting down with a sigh. "Lay down, Honey." The dog carefully lowered itself to the ground and curled at Kath's feet, resting its long nose on outstretched paws. A few moments passed before she said tentatively, "Do I know you from somewhere?" As I turned to face her, the answer must have come to her because she said, "Yes, of course, you work in Bloomers, Maggie, isn't it?"

I nodded and replied, "Yes, and you're Kath Emmerson the town clerk, aren't you?"

"Yes I am. How nice to meet you." She held out a hand, so small and delicate, yet surprisingly strong as I found out when, heartily, she shook my hand. "This is Honey," she added, pointing to the dog.

"Hello Honey." I stroked the dog's soft curly fur and she nuzzled her warm wet nose into my hand. Looking at Kath, I said, "What sort of a dog is she?"

"A cross between a spaniel and a poodle," she replied. "A spoodle, I suppose you'd call her."

"She's gorgeous," I said as I stroked her soft fur.

"Thanks for letting me share your bench," said Kath, and then added, "It's a very special bench to me and my partner, and...," she turned slightly to look at the plaque affixed to it,

"Obviously to this couple as well."

"Oh yes," I said, reading the plaque. "Jack & Betty Lawrence, just because they loved this view of the canal." We smiled at each other. "How lovely."

A very smart blue and white barge, the wording Laura's Pleasure written on its side, sailed past, churning the water into tiny waves. Amidst much shouting and cheering the party on board waved to us and raised their glasses.

"Such a lovely evening," said one of the women as she sat on the stern in a red and white striped garden chair sipping elegantly from a glass of wine. The sun threw myriads of spangled light onto the water as we fluttered our fingers in a wave and the barge puttered away, leaving all the wildlife, the poor little ducks, geese, and swans, floundering in its wake.

"Have you worked at Bloomers for a long time?" asked Kath as she tucked a wayward strand of ash blonde hair behind her ear.

"Oh yes, many years. But actually, I'm leaving in a couple of weeks. I've got a job at Cobby High School."

"Oh, how wonderful," enthused Kath. "That's a bit of a change, isn't it?"

"It's a long story," I told her.

"I've got plenty of time for a chat," she said invitingly, and so I told her everything, from Ray's death, to Stephen turning up after so many years, to the disastrous meeting with his son and daughter, and to the disastrous meeting just this evening with Stephen in the Star Pub. I also told her all the good bits about the lovely Lauren and the eagerly awaited baby. Kath was very easy to talk to, and she gave a definite impression of not being a gossip.

"Oh, good God, Maggie, you have been in the wars," she exclaimed. "I can relate to some of it. I too lost my husband—in a car accident. It'll be two years in October."

"Yes, I'm so sorry. I read about it in the paper—Johnny Emmerson? He set up the town council, didn't he? With two other councilors?"

She nodded fondly. "Yes, the Band of Three as they called themselves—Johnny, Robert Holmes, and Peter Webster. Johnny was a good man, a very driven man. I still miss him so much."

Glancing at her from the tail of my eye I could see from the expression on her face that, yes, she did still miss Johnny. So where did the delectable Paul Timpson fit in with all this? Were they as in love as they seemed to be? I longed to ask, but felt far too shy, and was also well aware that I didn't know her well enough to ask such a personal question.

I told her that I'd gone to the cemetery to visit Ray's grave after my date with Stephen and had found Johnny's quite by accident. I didn't dare tell her about the wind that had come from nowhere, whipping everything into a fury, and the strange feeling that I'd had of a presence as I stood at the grave. But I needn't have worried about that, because the story that Kath told me next sent shivers like tiny cold hands running down my spine.

~*~

"Mum, sit down," I said. "You've only just gotten home, and you need to rest."

"I'm fine," she replied. "I suppose I'm just excited to be here. The home was lovely, such good people in there—I shall miss Winifred and Tracey—but I need to be here, back in my own place." She wandered around the sitting room, touching ornaments, moving them from place to place, running her fingers lightly, possessively, along her furniture as if she still couldn't quite believe she was there.

"I'm glad these are retirement housing flats, Mum," I said. "Just in case anything does happen and you feel poorly, all you have to do is press the buzzer."

"I know, I know," soothed Mum. "I'm fine though—I don't need a buzzer." When I started to protest, she held up her hand and said, "Although, Maggie, I do agree, it is better to be on the safe side."

I could hear the kettle sputtering and bubbling in the kitchen, along with the clinking of mugs, and the soft sucking clunk of the fridge door opening and closing.

"Coffee time," said Lynette as she came into the sitting room carrying a little round tray patterned with poppies. She put the tray on the coffee table and sat down, leaning forward in her chair to put milk and sugar into the mugs. I'd noticed earlier that Lynette looked quite pale and drawn, so I made a mental note to remember to ask her about Dave and his supposed affair when we were on our own. Quite frankly, she looked weighed down with troubles.

Mum, at long last sitting in her favorite armchair by the fireplace, took a hearty swallow of coffee, and looking around said, "Well, this is nice. Oh, I am glad to be home."

She looked well, her small frame encased in smart black trousers and a lovely beaded green top. She wore a shiny pink lipstick, and rosy blusher showed off her high cheekbones. Looking from her to Lynette, I came to the conclusion that anybody could easily mistake my sister as the one who had been ill and not Mum. The course of treatment that Mum was taking was obviously working as, totally on the ball, she suddenly turned her beady eye on me and asked, "How's things with Stephen then, Maggie?"

I hadn't had a chance as yet to tell Mum, or indeed, Lynette, anything about my meeting with Stephen and the decision that he had come to, but thought that I'd better get it over and done with. So I said, "Well, actually, Stephen has decided that he'd rather not see me at the moment."

"Not see you?" exclaimed Mum and Lynette in unison. Lynette, obviously in shock after my bombshell, kept quiet while Mum said, "Why ever not?"

"Well," I took a deep breath. "His two children, Jake and Vanessa, aren't very happy about their dad seeing anybody at the moment. I suppose they feel that it's too soon after their mother's death—it's only been a couple of years."

"Hmm," said Mum. "I don't know all the details, Maggie, but don't they want their dad to be happy?" Lynette nodded in agreement. "And as well as that," Mum went on, "Aren't they old enough to understand these things?"

"I don't know, Mum. All I know is that the only thing I can do is respect their wishes at the moment. I've got enough to think about just now with starting a new job."

I could tell from the look on Mum and Lynette's faces that they totally believed that I was okay with the situation with Stephen, when really and truly my heart was broken and I felt as though I was wallowing in a big black hole.

Lynette, seemingly recovered from the shock, chimed in with, "Yes, but you'll be seeing Stephen every day in the school, won't you?"

"Well, yes, I will, and I must admit that's been worrying me a bit, as I don't really want to be in such close proximity every day. But I'm sure I can cope."

"Yes, that's right," she replied. "Keep focused, Maggie," She took a tiny bird like sip of coffee, then said, "A mind troubled by doubt cannot focus on the course to victory." Mum and I exchanged a fleeting glance, but before I could say anything—not that I had a clue what to say to that—Lynette went on. "Oh, by the way, there's an opening for a councilor on Cobby Town Council, Maggie. I saw a notice in their glass case thingy by the cenotaph. I thought you might be interested. You're always on about all the good things the councilors do for Cobby. And anyway," she said, half to herself, "I can imagine you on the council."

I raised my mug to my lips and took a sip. "Yes, I know about it. Kath Emmerson told me, and—"

"Kath Emmerson, the town clerk?"

"Yes. I had quite a chat with her the other day, and she suggested that I apply. Apparently they need a councilor on their Events Committee." I recalled Kath's words. "The councilor that's standing down, Laura Miller, is on the Events Committee, so we need somebody to take her place really, to become involved with the Cobby Carnival and Music Festival that we set up last year. And other events of course, like the Fun Run and the market. It's a really good committee, Maggie. You'd love it, and I know you'd be just right as a councilor."

"Laura Miller?" I had asked. "That must be the same Laura Miller that's re-locating to Norbury?"

"Yes, it is," Kath agreed, frowning and looking a bit puzzled. "You know her then?"

"Well no, I don't know her. But that's the job I've got at the school—Laura Miller's old job!"

I related all this to Mum and Lynette, who said, "You see, Maggie, another co-incidence—"

She began another quote but I interrupted her, "Yes, Lynette, I know. 'If there was no such thing as coincidence, there would be no such word.'"

"Actually, no," she replied. "This is a different one. 'Coincidences mean you're on the right path.'" She sank back into the soft cushions of the settee, smugly folding her arms across her chest.

"Ah, so I'm on the right path taking the job in the school, even though it means I'll see Stephen every day."

"Yes, it's meant to be," said Mum quietly. "He'll come to his senses, Maggie—realize he misses you, and welcome you back with open arms."

"Hmm," I replied haughtily. "Well, maybe I won't want him back!" I put my mug down on the tray with a thump.

Mum and Lynette looked at each other and burst into great peals of laughter.

"What?" I said. "What are you two laughing at?" And when they still persisted in their high pitched, horsey neighing, I pleaded, "Let me in on the joke—please...."

~*~

Darkness was drawing in as I drove Lynette home from Mum's later that evening, and the street lamps slowly lighting up cast an eerie red glow on the paths and the roads. The beautiful Cobby countryside streamed past in silhouette as Lynette chattered on and on about Stephen. She didn't seem to be able to get enough of the subject. "Why would you want to go out with him anyway?" she said, wrinkling her nose as if in distaste. "He's going to be an old granddad soon."

Oh, here we go again, I thought. Soft rain drops pattered onto the car windshield and slid slowly down the glass like tears. I hadn't even thought of the baby as being Stephen's grandchild, but yes, Lynette was right—Stephen would soon be a granddad. I found that the thought didn't put me off him in the least; in fact, my stomach sank alarmingly at the thought that I might never see him again.

"Oh, I'm sick of talking about Stephen," I said flippantly. "Any news on Dave's supposed affair?"

"Supposed affair?" she said, glancing at me. "Only another sext. Listen to this." She scrabbled around in her bag for her phone. "Hi Lena, okay then c u on Tuesday…same place (Belmont Hotel Cobby)…same time, ie, 7 (haha) x."

"Something doesn't ring true," I said as I drove carefully around the tiny windy roads of Cobby to Lynette's house. "Not exactly the right wording for somebody in the midst of a passionate affair!"

"Wording? I don't think that wording has got anything to do with this situation," she said sarcastically.

"Well, I think it does, Lynette. The wording is convincing me that they're not the texts of a man having an affair—"

She cut me off in mid-sentence. "Well, whatever, I'm going to follow him on Tuesday night, and then I'll see exactly what he's up to."

"Oh, Lynette…."

With a set face she said, "Look out, Dave—look out Lena, whoever you are—here I come!"

Lynette's house, a modern semi-detached, was lit up in

an inviting yellow glow from a lamp in the hall window as I pulled up outside. A rosy light edged its way around the drawn curtains in the sitting room, casting dim shadows on the mature bushes and bright flowers in the sizeable garden. I peered closely from the car window, hoping to get a glimpse of Dave, the supposed adulterer.

"Will Dave be in?" I asked.

"Yes, he should be," she replied as she started to open the car door and edge her way out. "Probably sitting watching TV with a can of lager propped on his belly! Unless he's with Lena, of course."

I gave her a withering glance because of the Lena comment, then said, "Dave doesn't have a belly," thinking of how trim and fit he was from playing sports, particularly football.

All the same, I had to smile, and she grinned at me and said, "Look, Maggie, me and Mum know that you're pretty upset about all this business with Stephen...." I opened my mouth to speak, but she carried on and said, "What I'm saying is, you don't have to put on a brave face for us." Surprisingly she put out a hand and, reassuringly, squeezed my arm. Tears threatened, and I blinked my eyes to keep them at bay. "You just remember, Maggie." Then came the killer quote. "'Time waits for no man, and neither does a good woman....'"

She stood at the curb as I pulled away in my little Fiat, her arm raised in a wave. It was too dark by now to see the expression on her face.

Chapter Six

I started work in Cobby High School at the beginning of September, a hazy day, the sun just a muted gleam in a china blue sky speckled with long tendrils of clouds. Despite the warm sunshine the air smelled woody and dense as autumn. I drove nervously through the lovely Cobby countryside, my heart hammering and my palms slick and wet on the steering wheel. I took a deep calming breath. I'd been at Bloomers for so long that I'd forgotten what it was like to start a new job. Nerve wracking were the words that came to mind. I'd had good luck texts from both Mum and Lynette this morning, as well as, surprisingly, one from Stephen wishing me all the best.

Passing by the little church and cemetery, I thought of Ray and what he would have thought of me finally fulfilling my dream of working in a school. I fervently hoped that he could see me and approved of what I was doing. That thought led me to think of Kath Emmerson and the incredible story she had told me as we sat on her special bench on the tow path.

I recalled her words, "I still talk to him you know, Maggie—to Johnny."

"Yes," I replied, not understanding at first what she was trying to tell me. "I confide in Ray. It can be a comfort at times."

"No, not like that. Maggie, what I'm trying to say is that I talk to him, properly, about my council work and everyday things, and he talks back to me—we have conversations." I could feel her staring at my profile, trying to gauge my reaction. "He even told me a year after he died that it was time to for me to move on, and that I was free to pursue a relationship with Paul. I wouldn't have done that if it hadn't been right with Johnny."

I turned and looked her in the eye and said, "But isn't that—well…impossible?"

I noticed that she still wore her wedding ring and she fiddled with it a little as she smiled and said, "Well, yes, I always thought it was impossible. But it happens to me."

Arriving at Cobby High School, I pulled up in the parking lot, thoughts of Kath and Johnny Emmerson being replaced now by thoughts of Stephen and a feeling of dread at the thought of seeing him again. How should we be together in this situation? Should we be friendly, hostile, or just blatantly ignore each other? I suppose by sending me the text this morning he was hoping that we could remain friends, but how could I just be friends with him?

I found myself hoping that he wouldn't be in school today; that he'd had to go to a meeting or was away at a conference. But just as that thought ran through my mind, I saw him running energetically up the stairs to his office as, dodging around groups of students, I made my way to the reception desk. The bulldog barked at me to sit down, pointing to the row of hard chairs as before. Amidst the hubbub all around me, I found that I felt somewhat put out by Stephen running with such purpose. As if he was—what's the word? Happy? Shouldn't he be moping around, listless, upset and thinking of me? I shook my head at my stupid thoughts just as my name was called, and a small curvy woman that I recognized from the panel at my interview walked towards me, calling my name.

"Maggie Sears?" she asked. Once again she wore a suit—green this time—that clung just a little too closely to her curves, and a white blouse, the top buttons undone to display acres of a deep generous cleavage, putting mine to shame once and for all.

"Stella Atkins," She held out her hand, which was small and as soft and bendy as plasticine as I shook it. I followed her swaying bottom all the way up the stairs, along a wide airy corridor, and into a large bright office, where sunlight streamed through the tall windows and lay across the walls and floor in golden stripes. Several people bustled around carrying books and buff folders and fluttering pieces of paper in their hands.

I noticed that a small glass fronted office had been built into the corner of the room, its door bearing a plaque with the words, Stephen Gates, Headmaster, in thick gold lettering. Stephen was sitting at his desk, his back to me and, if I peered closely, I could clearly see his hair, which although streaked with grey now, I knew still grew in whorls like tiny mazes on his head. I saw that there was a desk and chair just outside Stephen's office, complete with a computer and filing cabinets, which I guessed belonged to Stephen's PA, whoever she was.

Stella Atkins led me across the room to where a pretty woman in her thirties sat gazing at the screen of her computer. She had long glossy black hair with a fringe that just scraped her eyebrows, and her eyes, dark as sloes, were framed by a pair of thick black framed glasses. She wore a bright red dress with a high neck and short sleeves that showed her thin tanned arms, and I noticed that she wore black court shoes with startlingly high heels.

"Jo," said Stella, "This is Maggie Sears, our new recruit. Maggie, this is Joanna Wheeler, the examinations officer. You two will be working closely together so, Jo, I'll leave Maggie in your capable hands."

I watched her as she walked away—such a tiny figure, childlike, but with the curves of a woman. I realized that apart from asking my name and introducing me to Jo, Stella Atkins hadn't spoken to me at all. I started to panic and my heart beat painfully against my ribs, and I longed for a cup of coffee and a cinnamon bun and to be on my break in the back room of Bloomers where I felt safe and—what's the word? Liked? What was wrong with me that I got the distinct impression, for no reason at all, after all we'd never met before the interview, that Stella Atkins didn't like me? Also, I hadn't expected the office to be open plan and for Stephen to be there right in front of me so that I could see him sitting in his fancy high backed leather executive chair day after day. I thought that because he was the headmaster his office would be hidden away somewhere down a long corridor away from all the classrooms and offices, in which case we wouldn't see each other or meet very often. It was bad enough to *think* of him on a daily basis, but seeing him—well, that was a different matter.

"Nice to meet you, Maggie, and welcome to Cobby High School," said Jo, her smile warm and inviting, making me feel a tiny bit better. Sincerely she shook my hand. "Come on, let's go and put the kettle on."

She stood up, towering over me in her heels just as Stella Atkins sat down at the desk outside the headmaster's office, revealing the identity of Stephen's PA. Ah, the mystery woman—now why wasn't I surprised? I took a sneaky glance as she busied herself shuffling papers on her desk yet, sensing something, she glanced up and returned my gaze with narrowed eyes.

"I think I've got some biscuits too," added Jo as she steered me into the kitchen, passing another couple of desks where glamorous, smartly dressed people sat either looking at their computer screens or talking loudly and purposefully into the phone. Thankfully, Jo put me at ease straight away, alleviating the feeling that I'd made a dreadful mistake in taking this job. I felt reassured by her friendliness, and hoped that we could work well together.

She chatted brightly as we waited for the kettle to boil, and then, taking our mugs and a plate of chocolate biscuits, she showed me to my desk, which was situated close to hers. We spent most of the day together. She showed me how to set out intricate seating plans for the examination rooms, and how to keep the student records up to date by collating all the student names and candidate numbers together. It was interesting work and the morning flew by, as did lunch time. Before I knew it, the day was almost over.

Just as I was shrugging into my jacket, Stephen came over to speak to me. "I wanted to come over and see you before, Maggie, but you looked so busy with Jo, I didn't want to disturb you. How's it gone today, okay?"

"Very well, thank you," I replied as I picked up my bag and prepared to leave.

"I'll walk you to your car," said Stephen. He looked remarkably dapper in a dark grey suit teamed with a white shirt, a faint silver stripe running through it, and a loosely knotted grey tie. Marring his whole smart look, he carried a scuffed brown briefcase which looked as if it had been his constant companion since school days.

Not really knowing what to say, I walked silently by his side, down the stairs and out to the parking lot. The day had warmed up considerably, and the heat hit me hard, making me gasp as if I'd just stepped from a plane into a foreign country.

"Well, here's my car," I said brightly as my little Fiat came into view.

"Maggie, I was hoping to hear from you after the text message I sent the other night—um—after you left the pub." I tried not to look at him but gazed slightly away, not wanting to meet his sherry brown eyes, not wanting to look at the dimple in his chin and the sexy stubble on his cheeks.

He was obviously referring to our meeting in the Star Pub when I had walked out on him in tears, even leaving my almost full glass of red wine. "Oh yes, sorry about that," I said airily. "I think I may have overreacted."

"Well, it's just that, Maggie. I've been thinking—"

Whatever Stephen had been thinking was lost in the ether as Stella Atkins came undulating towards us in her tight green suit, like a rather large curvy caterpillar.

"Oh, Stephen, thank heavens I caught you. You couldn't give me a lift, could you? My car's gone in for its MOT, and I'm quite lost without it." She did a remarkably fake double take when she saw me, and said, "Oh, sorry. I didn't realize you were with somebody."

"Well, actually Stella—" Stephen began to say.

I interrupted. "Oh, take no notice of me—I'm in a hurry. See you both later."

"Maybe we could talk tomorrow, Maggie," Stephen said as I walked briskly the rest of the way to my car, pretending that I couldn't hear him, my heels tip tapping on the concrete path. They were standing by Stephen's shiny black BMW as I drove out of the parking lot, Stella close to Stephen, a possessive hand over his arm like a hook. The odd yearning expression on her face as she looked up at him told me all that I needed to know.

~*~

I was at home laying full length on the settee, a glass of red wine on the little table beside me. Two days in and my new job had worn me out. The telly was droning on in the background, but I was not taking any notice of it. In fact, I thought as I woke myself enough to grab the remote, I was going to switch it off. My old cat Arthur was laid out fast asleep on the floor like a scraggy rug, and it wouldn't be long, I thought, before I was in the land of Nod myself. I always found Bloomers tiring with the constant queue of customers and din and chatter in the shop, but learning new things had left me brain dead.

Idly I wondered what Stephen was going to say to me yesterday before Stella Atkins turned up like a bad omen. I thought of her hand clutching his arm, and knew without a doubt that she wanted him and would probably fight for him to the bitter end. *Hmm,* I thought sadly. *I wish her more luck than me in capturing the cold hearts of Jake and Vanessa, for without them, Stephen won't want her either.* I was intrigued by Stephen's remark, "Maybe we could talk tomorrow, Maggie." What he wanted to talk to me about was still a mystery, because I'd seen very little of him today, just a glimpse in the morning, and then nothing until late afternoon through his office window, deep in conversation with two smartly dressed men. Stella Atkins, puffed up with importance, flitted in and out with sheaves of papers and trays bearing mugs of steaming coffee, before sitting at her desk and guarding Stephen's office like a formidable spider in a web.

I gazed at the empty chair next to me and thought of Ray, and wondered what he would make of this situation. If only he could speak to me as Johnny Emmerson spoke to Kath. I could imagine him saying, "If you want him, Maggie, then do something. Go and see Jake and Vanessa, talk to them, work things out. There's always a way." What about Stella Atkins though? Could I talk to her, work things out with her? The answer, I decided, was no.

My phone vibrated and I saw an email from Kath Emmerson enclosing all the relevant application papers to become a councilor in the Cobby Town Council. Interested, I scrolled through the details, noting that, as the closing date was in two weeks, I wouldn't necessarily have to look at them tonight. I'd suddenly realized that today was Tuesday, and tonight at seven, Dave, the supposed adulterer, was meeting Lena in a room in the Belmont Hotel, and Lynette was going to follow him.

In a panic, I looked at my watch and noted that it was well past eight o'clock, in which case Lynette might have caught Dave up to no good by now and the whole show could be over. Rousing myself, I decided that I would go to Lynette's house anyway, just in case she needed moral support. Or, with a giggle, I thought that it might be Dave that needed that and not Lynette.

There was no hint of a wind, just a dense warm darkness, as I drove to Lynette's, the moon like a great silver globe moving quickly across the sky. Parking outside and sitting for a moment or two, waiting for I don't know what, I caught sight of a slight figure dressed all in black like a cat burglar scurrying up the garden path and letting themselves in at the front door. The hallway light was suddenly snapped on, and seconds later a familiar rosy glow began to shine from between the drawn curtains in the sitting room.

I was just about to get out of the car and go in pursuit of Lynette—because the cat burglar figure was obviously her—to find out what had happened, when Dave's car pulled up with a jerk right in front of mine. Dave, unraveling himself slowly from the driver's seat and raising a hand, walked over to me, his face a pale oval in the gloom.

"Hey, Maggie, how are you doing?" Because of his long gangly frame, he had to bend almost double to look in the car window.

"Hello Dave, I'm fine. You?"

"Yeah, I'm okay thanks. Have a good evening with Lynette?"

Oh yes, of course. Dave thought that I was just leaving and not arriving. He didn't know that Lynette had been out dressed as a cat burglar intent on spying on him and someone called Lena in a hotel room.

"Oh yes," I told him. "We had a good chat."

"Hey, guess what?" he whispered, as he glanced over his shoulder towards the house, afraid, I think, that Lynette was going to creep up on him unawares and find out his dreadful secret. "Don't say anything, but I've just been to look at a room—well, a suite, I should say—in the Belmont Hotel so that I can treat Lynette to a couple of nights away. I wanted to see that the room was top class and make sure that the bed fits my rather large frame." He put a hand up above his head to emphasis his size, and burst into hearty laughter.

"Oh really," I said, thinking how much the sexts, as Lynette called them, now made sense. "That's lovely, Dave. Will the bed be okay then?"

"Yeah, it's a king king size, I think they call it. Whatever, my feet don't flop over the end like they usually do. Fabulous place—they do all that stuff that she likes; aromatherapy and massage, and there's a cracking swimming pool and a gym. What do you think, Maggie? Do you think she'll be pleased?"

"I think she'll be thrilled, Dave. Are you going to tell her tonight?"

"Yeah, course I am, I can't wait to tell her. My mate's girlfriend, Lena, she works at the hotel see, so she can arrange for the room to be spot on. And also…," he tapped the side of his nose, "A bit of discount, I hope."

As I drove home, I thought of Dave and his eagerness to please Lynette, and how she would feel at spying on him when she found out who the mysterious Lena really was, unless she had seen them tonight and already knew. I had been right that Dave wasn't the type to have an affair, and yet Lynette wouldn't listen to me. I decided that I would tease her unmercifully about this the next time I saw her, and it would be a good story to make Mum laugh too.

I heard the beep of a text message just as I parked in the driveway. My heart leapt, hoping that it might be Stephen, but I knew really that it wouldn't be; why would he text me?

My old cat Arthur was stalking through the bushes in the front garden, his eyes shining like gold in the car headlights, no doubt looking for a tasty field mouse for his supper. I found my phone in my bag and scrolled down to find the text message that I'd heard come through. I frowned when I saw it was from a number I didn't recognize, but read on with growing interest.

Hi Maggie, sorry to text you like this but I'd love to meet up with you for a coffee and a chat. I'm a bit worried about Stephen. Please let me know a good time and place. Oh btw It's Lauren x

I had to read it through a couple of times before it dawned on me that it was actually from Lauren. Where had she gotten my number? Worried about Stephen? What did she mean? Stephen was perfectly fine. I'd seen him today and he was fine—so what was the problem? Was he with Stella Atkins now, and had taken her home to meet Jake and Vanessa just as he had me? Hmm, I needed to think about this. What was going on?

There was only one thing for it, and that was to sleep on it. Yawning heavily, I put my phone back in my bag and, with my old cat Arthur mewing at my heels, let myself into the house where, after making a cup of hot chocolate, I climbed my weary way to bed.

Chapter Seven

I finally had all the councilor application papers ready to give to Kath Emmerson, but instead of posting them I decided that, as it wasn't a work day for me, I would call in at the council offices in the town hall to deliver them to her personally. It would give me the opportunity to see her; and also, to be perfectly honest, I was longing to see what her offices were like. I imagined the room to be rather grand and oak paneled, the town clerk sitting on a high wooden throne in solitary splendor, wearing a long dark robe and a tricorn hat—or was that the mayor?

It was another sunny September day, the sun a yellow glow overlaid with transparent skeins of clouds, and leaves already changing color shone bright red, orange, and yellow against the backdrop of a deep blue sky. Strolling the busy streets of Cobby I thought about my new job and how much I was enjoying it now. The only fly in the ointment was that I saw Stephen almost every day, and always alongside him the voluptuous figure of the dreaded Stella Atkins, who looked me up and down as if I was something not very nice to be scraped off her shoe.

It seemed that everywhere he went, she went. I'd seen them walking out of the school gates together at lunchtimes, and spied them eating together in the school café. She was often in his office, leaning over his shoulder, seemingly whispering in his ear, her ample cleavage firmly on display.

I was learning the job fast though, and Jo was great to work with. As an added bonus, many of the teachers came into the office now that we were preparing for the mock exams in November. They needed to check seating arrangements and candidate numbers and names, and to know in which rooms the exams would be taking place and give us inside tips, so to speak, on the behavior of certain students.

I got on well with Mrs. Speight, one of the English teachers, and Mr. Richards, who taught science. But mainly I recall Jo introducing me to the math teacher, James Jamieson, a straight-talking Londoner, slightly overweight, with twinkly blue eyes and a big personality.

"James Jamieson?" I remember saying as I held out my hand, which he shook in a surprisingly brisk manner.

"I know," he said. "I asked my mum and dad what they were thinking when they teamed James with Jamieson. 'Why didn't you call me Robert,' I asked them, 'or David?' David Jamieson sounds so much better, don't you think? It has a certain ring to it, whereas James Jamieson just sounds stupid!"

"What did your mum and dad say," I asked him, "When you questioned them about your name?"

He shrugged his shoulders and replied with a straight

face, "They said they liked the name James."

His visits to the office—particularly to my desk, I might add—were becoming more and more frequent and, much to the soaring of my stupid heart, I noticed Stephen giving him dirty black looks and behaving in a rather curt manner with him on more than one occasion. What did that mean? I tortured myself with wondering what those black looks meant. Surely now that he and Stella Atkins seemed to have become an item, he had no interest in me.

Maybe some light would be shed on all this when I saw Lauren. I'd replied to her text message and we'd arranged a meeting. But at the moment I was walking through the massive wooden doors of the town hall, holding tightly to a large brown envelope containing my councilor application papers.

The place was buzzing as usual and, as I went to the reception area, Paul Timpson came walking towards me, wearing a black suit and a white shirt, a silver chain visible around his neck, and carrying a black zipped case under his arm. He had very dark eyes and a stubbly chin, and as we passed he gave me a nod and such a cheeky grin that I couldn't help smiling back.

The receptionist buzzed me up, so I went through the big double doors and climbed the two flights of stairs to Kath's office.

I suspected that Kath was with someone when I arrived as, peering through the glass panel in the door, I saw her sitting at her desk gesticulating, and her mouth moving as if she were speaking.

"Yes, that's right," I heard her say, followed by a giggle,

and, "Well, okay, I knew you'd understand."

But the chair opposite her was clearly empty and I couldn't see anybody else in the room. I tapped the door lightly with my knuckles and saw her get up and walk towards me.

"Maggie!" she exclaimed. "How good to see you. Do come in."

She opened the door wide and I walked inside. She looked smart, as usual, dressed in a cream short sleeved dress, a gold chain belt encircling her slim waist. She wore tiny gold hoop earrings and a slim gold chain around her wrist.

"I hope I'm not disturbing you, Kath—I thought you were with somebody." I looked around the small room, at its sunny yellow painted walls and large window, through which I could see the village green and the imposing structure of the cenotaph.

But Kath gave another little giggle and said, "Oh, don't worry, it's only Johnny. But I think he's gone now." A somewhat delicious tremor ran up my spine at her words and I stared at her, open mouthed. But she was looking at the envelope that I held in my hand and said playfully, "Ah, Maggie, have you got your application papers?" Dumbstruck, I nodded and handed her the envelope. Sitting down, she laid the papers out on her desk, then said, "Please Maggie, do sit down. Would you like a drink? I can put the kettle on."

Eventually finding my voice, I said, "No, it's okay, Kath. I'm popping into Bloomers to see my old work colleagues after I've seen you, so I'm going to have a coffee in there."

"Excellent. How's the new job going?"

"Very well," I told her. Then, because I'd told her the whole sorry tale about Stephen, I added, "But unfortunately,

I do see Stephen every day." I then went on to tell her about Stella Atkins, and her, what I could only call obsession with Stephen.

Kath looked up from the papers. "Hmm. Well, she sounds like somebody you need to steer clear of, Maggie. Are you coping okay with this?"

"Yes, so so." I then told her about the text message from Lauren and that I had arranged to meet up with her.

"I hope you can sort things out, Maggie," she said sympathetically. "The meeting with Lauren sounds very promising." She glanced at her watch. "I have a meeting with the allotment officer in ten minutes, so I can only have a quick look at your application papers at the moment. I did tell you, didn't I, that a by-election hasn't been asked for, so we will definitely be co-opting."

"Yes, you did. Councilor Rawdon said that he will speak for me on the night—he's an old friend from Bloomers."

"Wonderful. I do so like Councilor Rawdon—he's a wonderful councilor and does a sterling job. The meeting is next week, Maggie, the sixth of October at 6:30 p.m. in the Council Chamber, here in the town hall. I hope that's okay."

"Oh yes," I replied. "I'll be there."

"I'll send you an agenda by email."

I stood up, gathering my bag and holding out my hand to meet Kath's, when I suddenly remembered Ray's hankering to move to Hampthwaite because Andrea and Les Dowling were selling up and he wanted to buy their house. "Kath," I asked, "Did Johnny's sister live in Hampthwaite?"

"Yes, she did, in rather a nice house with her husband Les. They sold up and moved around a year ago now—emigrated to New Zealand. Why do you ask?"

"Oh, so they moved only recently. My husband, Ray, wanted to buy their house quite a few years ago when it came up on the market."

"Ah, yes. They changed their minds then and decided to stay. Johnny and I used to go to Hampthwaite quite a lot—walking, you know. A lovely little village." Then, suddenly changing the subject, she said, "Actually, Maggie, I've got something to tell you." She paused and chewed on her lip. "I'll be at the meeting next week, but after that I've got a week's holiday. So if you're successful in becoming a councilor, I won't be here to settle you in."

"Oh, that's fine," I said. "I'm sure I'll be okay for the first week."

"Yes, a substitute will be coming in to cover for me. I'll be so glad when we can take on a deputy clerk. You see, the thing is, Maggie...." And here she hesitated and blushed such a deep red that I thought for a moment she might combust right there in the office, and only her black leather shoes would be found in a smoldering pile of ash. "I'm going on my honeymoon," she continued. "Paul—Paul Timpson, that is—and I are getting married."

"Oh Kath, that's wonderful! Congratulations."

"I can't quite believe it," she said quietly. "I never thought I'd marry again." She fiddled again with what I'd thought was her wedding ring when, clearly, it was an engagement ring, and a rather pretty one too. "That's what I was talking to Johnny about earlier, and thankfully, he's absolutely fine with it. Very encouraging, actually."

I nodded dumbly, then repeated, "Well, I think it's

wonderful. I hope you'll both be very happy. Where are you going on your honeymoon?"

"To the lakes," she replied. "Just for a few days. I need to be back for the twentieth of October." I must have looked at her questioningly. "It's Johnny's anniversary—two years."

~*~

The heat of the sun bit ferociously into my skin as, walking away from the town hall, I thought of Kath sitting in her office making plans for her wedding day to the gorgeous Paul Timpson, which no doubt would cause malicious gossip all around Cobby. True, she might still be having long, involved conversations with her dead husband, but even so, I still felt a sudden overwhelming sadness at Kath's happiness compared to my hopeless longing for Stephen. I vowed to myself that something must be done; but what?

Aimlessly I wandered the hot streets, breathing in the smell of meat pasties that hung in the air along with the greasy stench from Gallagher's fish and chip shop, thinking of my lonely life with only my old cat Arthur for company. A remark that the math teacher James Jamieson had said to me recently came to mind. "We'll have to go for a few beers one evening, Maggie. What do you say to that?"

I'd only mumbled a reply at the time, hoping that he wouldn't hear, feeling slightly disrespectful to Stephen. But good God, Kath Emmerson had grabbed her happiness when and where she could, so why shouldn't I? Next time he asked, if he asked, I would make sure I said yes.

Full of purpose, I strode down the street to Bloomers. After a catch up with Lilian and young Jeff, I would visit Mum with a box of those cream Bavarian slices that she liked. Maybe I should also call in at Bedrock & Rose to see if Lynette was free. We could have a girly afternoon together, which would give me a chance to talk to Lynette about her adventure the other night at the Belmont Hotel. Who needed men?

~*~

Oh my God, I felt as if my life was ending. I'd made a hash of my new job already, and felt as if everybody in the department was staring at me, pointing a finger and saying, "That's her, that's Maggie Sears. That's the idiot who has mistakenly deleted all the student examination records."

Jo's dark eyes behind her thick black framed glasses had looked troubled when it was ascertained that I was the last person to work on those particular records. I had been changing details such as telephone numbers and addresses, and setting up new spreadsheets for those all-important mock exam results in November. Examination results going back to God knows when were in there, and now all those records were gone and nobody could quite understand how it had happened.

Downhearted, I went again and again into the system looking for a backup document—surely there would be a backup—but there was nothing. No trace at all of all those crucial details. It would take hours and hours to input all that information. Work that I knew, if I still had a job in the school, would fall to me. Stephen came to talk to me as I sat at my desk, dabbing at my red rimmed eyes with a tissue. He spoke gently, kindly, making me want to cling to him, sobbing heartily into his clean, soapy smelling neck.

Stella Atkins, standing behind him like a fat slug in a tight black suit, gave me a smile of such victory that for a fleeing moment I thought she knew something—that it was her, that she had deleted the records, either by mistake or on purpose, and was letting me take the blame. Then suddenly the look was gone and I thought perhaps I'd imagined it.

Hopelessly I gazed around the room, looking at the bright white walls, the dust motes dancing in the sunshine that streamed through the windows, and all the now familiar people sitting at their desks looking at me with sympathetic faces—except for Stella Atkins, of course—and knew that I didn't want to leave. I wanted to be part of this school, so something had to be done, and quickly.

"IT," I blurted out. "I'll ring IT. I think they're based in Glasgow; maybe they'll have a backup document."

"Hmm. Good idea, Maggie," said Jo, sounding upbeat, as if I'd given her a lifeline. "It's worth a try." She gave me a small plastic card with all the relevant contact numbers on it.

The IT man on the other end of the phone had such a strong Scottish accent that I could barely understand him, but when he said the words, "I'm sure there will be a backup for those records," I could hear every lovely word he said. "I'll put you on hold for a moment." There was silence for a while and a few whirrs and clicks, then he came back on the line and said, "Go back into the system and bring up this document." He reeled off a long, complicated string of words and letters, which I typed slowly and carefully, my fingers clicking over the keyboard. There was a dense heavy atmosphere in the room, as if everybody was holding their breath in anticipation.

Stephen and Jo, Stella Atkins peering over their shoulders, a strange almost worried look on her face, watched every move I made, and when I pressed the return key and all the student examination records appeared on the screen as if by magic, I wept with joy.

"Well," said the Scottish voice into my ear. "Is it all there?" When I didn't reply straight away because I was sobbing my heart out and couldn't speak, he repeated, "Hey, is the document all there?"

"Yes," I said gratefully, sniffing heavily, with, no doubt, trails of mascara running down my face in little rivers. "Yes, it is. Thank you so much." The relief was such that I didn't care that I probably looked really unattractive in front of Stephen who, letting his guard down completely, encircled me in a hug.

At home that evening, going back over the day, my heart still hammering at the prospect of all that work being deleted forever, I thought again about Stella Atkins and the expression on her evil face, and knew without a doubt that it was her. She had done it; she had deleted those records and made it look as if I had. It was only then that I realized what a formidable opponent she was, and not only in the fight for Stephen. I wondered what, if anything, I could do about it.

Chapter Eight

I was early for the meeting with Lauren when I walked into Crumbs Coffee House, which was situated in Cobby on a back street next to an old run down vinyl shop called Rod's Retro Records. The weather had changed and raindrops dribbled down the glass fronted exterior, where the words, You Won't Leave a Crumb at Crumbs Coffee House were written in gold swirly letters. The interior had a cozy farmhouse theme, with a stone flagged floor dotted with round pine tables and hard chairs, the seats covered with lacey tie-on cushions. Primary colored framed pictures of farm animals adorned the plain misshapen walls, as well as a blackboard with the menu chalked on in neat capital letters. Knotty black beams crisscrossed the ceiling

I shook raindrops out of my umbrella as I sat down at a table by the window and then idly looked around. There was a general hubbub from people sitting at the tables; an elderly couple drinking cups of frothy coffee, and a young mum with a baby girl who grizzled incessantly while trying to escape from her plastic high chair. I noticed a small cold cabinet with a few tempting cakes on display, including cream slices similar to the ones I'd taken to Mum's only the other day—but they had been Bloomers' Just the Best Ever cakes. That led me to think of Lynette and her embarrassment when she told me what had happened when she had followed Dave, the supposed adulterer, to the Belmont Hotel.

"Well," she related. "I recognized that Lena straight away. We'd met up with her and Dave's mate one night in a pub in Cobby—not the Star, the other one."

"The Globe?" I asked.

"Yes, that's the one. Anyway, she's a nice girl. I watched through the window—they couldn't see me because I was dressed all in black."

"The cat burglar," I said.

Mum was in fits of laughter, and just about managed to stammer, "The milk tray man—do you remember that advert, Maggie?"

I nodded and said yes, I did remember that—he was dressed all in black too. And then I zoned back in to what Lynette was saying.

"I didn't know what I was going to see," she went on. "Dave lay on the bed—fully clothed," she hastened to add. "...And said it was okay because his feet didn't hang over the edge. And Lena said something about, yeah, it's a king king size bed, and he asked about aromatherapy and massage, and Lena said that yes, all that was included in the price. It was then I realized it was all a surprise for me. So I legged it quick as I could—I didn't want Dave to see me. I felt like such a fool."

I thought Mum was going to have a stroke, she was laughing so much.

"Sorry Maggie," Lynette said. "I should have listened to you. Dave's definitely not the type to have an affair."

Coming out of my reverie and back to Crumbs Coffee House, the door jangled open and Lauren walked in, her large belly leading the way. She wore a bright red coat with a hood, which she pushed back to reveal her lovely blonde hair, and then, spotting me straight away, raised her hand and hurried over to the table.

"Maggie," she said. "So good to see you."

I stood up and we exchanged hugs and kisses. She smelled of a flowery perfume and of the rain that was now slicing through the air in skinny silver rods. We ordered hot, fragrant cappuccinos that, when they arrived at the table, looked like ice creams with their white swirly tops decorated with chocolate chips. Lauren devoured a large slice of walnut cake, after which she gently patted her stomach and said that she didn't feel guilty because she was sharing with Rebecca. I laughed at that comment as I gazed at Lauren's pretty face with its high cheekbones and wide red smile.

"Where did you get my number, Lauren?" I asked as I took a sip of coffee. I leaned closer to her to hear better. Lauren was very softly spoken, and sometimes, very endearingly, I thought, lisped like a child.

"Well," she replied, swallowing hard, then wiping her mouth of any stray crumbs with a paper napkin. "I sneaked a look at Stephen's phone. He's always leaving it lying around—he's terrible with his phone." She glanced at me with her odd sightless blue eyes. "I suppose you think I'm awful for doing that."

"No, not at all," I replied. "You must have had a good reason to want to contact me. He's not ill, is he?"

She took a healthy slug of coffee before saying, "Ill? Well, only in the sense of love sick, I would say—moping around the house, barely speaking, barely eating. In fact, barely doing anything." She grinned wryly.

I frowned. "I don't think I quite get what you're saying, Lauren." My heart was beating hard now, and my hands felt clammy around the smooth sides of the coffee mug. What was happening to me? Was it the caffeine that was making my heart beat so erratically? What was Lauren trying to tell me? That Stephen missed me and was regretting our break up?

The café door jangled open again and a large party of young girls came whooping in, soaked to the skin and arguing in loud voices about which one of them had enough money to buy them all coffee and cakes. Lauren had to raise her voice above the din. "Moping around over you, Maggie."

"Oh, surely not," I said calmly, although my heart was still hammering, just the way Roger Taylor used to beat his drum when he played with Queen. "I think he's rather friendly with a lady called Stella Atkins now. Do you know her?"

"Her?" Lauren screwed up her face. "That woman from the school?" She made a curvy figure in the air with her hands. "Stephen's PA, the one that Diana put in a complaint about?" I must have looked suitably mystified, because Lauren said, "You don't know anything about this, do you?"

I shook my head and said, "No. The only thing I do

understand is the curvy figure thing you did." I then whispered behind my hand, "She does tend to wear very tight, revealing clothes."

I glanced at the party of young girls who were now sitting at the table next to us, thankfully quiet as mice, devouring cream cakes and drinking hot chocolate. They must have found the money from somewhere. The mum and grizzly baby were gone, and the waitress was busily rearranging the cold cabinet, which was virtually empty now.

"Well," Lauren said, leaning towards me, her elbows on the table. "Let me fill you in...."

She told me that Stephen had been the deputy head master of a school down south. "Highgate Priory, I think it was called," she told me. "His wife, Diana, Jake and Vanessa's mum, worked there on the admin team along with Stella Atkins. Apparently, Stella spent most of her time sucking up to Stephen and bullying Diana. Diana put in a formal complaint against Stella, but then suddenly dropped it and left the school. Apparently she'd had enough, couldn't take any more. Stella left too, but only because her job became redundant. She managed to get another job, in a local solicitor's office, I think. Obviously, a few years later Diana died and Stephen decided to sell up and move to Cobby. He applied for the job at Cobby High School, not knowing that Stella Atkins was the PA to the head mistress, Mrs. Faulkner, who was retiring."

"Oh my God," I said. "What a story! Did Jake tell you this, or Stephen?"

"Oh, Jake did. Stephen's not mentioned any of it to me. According to Jake, he's turned a blind eye to all that happened before with Diana, and is just trying to get along with Stella."

"Hmm. He certainly is trying to get along with her. I've seen them together on many occasions. In fact, most of the time they eat lunch together, and I've seen them in the parking lot after school."

"Oh, Maggie, he's just buttering her up. He's been so miserable since you two split, it's obvious he wants you back."

"Well, I'm not sure about that, Lauren. He hasn't been in touch with me at all apart from saying ages ago that he wanted to talk. And don't forget, it was his idea to end our relationship."

"How long ago did he mention a talk?" Lauren asked with interest.

"Oh, a few weeks ago when I first started working at the school." I then changed the subject. "So, he had no idea whatsoever that Stella was now living in Cobby and working at the school?"

"No. As I said before, she left Highgate Priory before Diana died, and as far as Stephen was aware, she still lived in that area. He had no idea that she'd moved to Cobby. Personally, I think she followed him here, and that she's a stalker."

Hmm. Coincidence or planned on Stella's part? I thought to myself. *I wonder what suitable quote Lynette would come up with in this situation.*

I then told Lauren the whole sorry tale about the examination records, and she agreed with me that Stella Atkins could very well be the culprit if her past bullying and intimidation of Diana was anything to go by. She then went on to say, "But that's not the main reason I asked you to meet me. Obviously, I wanted to tell you that Stephen is pining for you, but the thing is, Vanessa wants to meet with you—with Lucy—and I'm bringing Jake around to the idea. What do you think? Will you meet up with them all?"

~*~

I drove home through the damp streets of Cobby, the roads and paths glittering now beneath a weak sun that was struggling to come out from behind a dense bank of grey clouds. I passed Bloomers and, with a pang of nostalgia, saw one or two of the regulars sitting outside eating and drinking. Through the shop window I saw Lilian and Young Jeff, and another lady that I didn't recognize—my replacement?—busily serving a long queue of customers.

The conversation with Lauren kept going around and around in my head. I had questioned her as to why Stephen had taken the job when he realized that Stella Atkins would be his PA.

"Why shouldn't he?" Lauren had replied, vehemently. "He's worked hard for years to get where he is. He wanted to move on from being a deputy. Why should he allow Stella Atkins to ruin his life as she did Diana's?"

I had to admit that I agreed with her, and said, "You're right, Lauren. Stella Atkins can't be allowed to get away with this." I then added with a smile, "And yes, I'd love to meet up with Vanessa and Lucy, and Jake if you can arrange it. Just let me know when and where."

"I'll text you with all the details," she said as we stood together outside Crumbs Coffee House, Lauren carefully lowering the strap of her bag over her head so it hung around her bump like a school satchel.

"What's made them change their minds?" I asked. "Am I

a better bet than Stella Atkins, do you think?"

"Stella Atkins has got nothing to do with this. She doesn't stand a chance with Stephen because he wants you. And anyway, Jake and Vanessa owe you a proper meeting, Maggie—they treated you badly that night."

I watched her walk away, a slight figure in a red coat, the hood pulled up to shield her hair from the misty rain. She turned just once and, smiling brightly, raised her hand, wiggling her fingers in a little wave.

Chapter Nine

I'd had my head down all morning, busily updating the examination records yet again, carefully saving them and making sure that they were still there in the system, checking them time and time again. Yes, the school examination records had become my obsession. I had nightmares about coming in to work and finding that they were all gone again, and that the lovely Scottish IT man couldn't help me this time—that in fact, nobody could help and the records were gone for good. Stella Atkins was always there, like the wicked witch of the north, grinning in the background.

I rolled my head around on my shoulders, easing the stiffness in my neck as I peered across the room, where I could see the back of Stephen's head and the tempting whorls in his hair as he sat in his little glass office. Despite the meeting with Lauren and her assurance that Stephen was missing me, I'd still had no text message or phone call from him; only a curt good morning or good evening each time we met. So to tell the truth, I'd virtually given up on him and was more than ever ready to take James Jamieson up on his offer of a night out and "a few beers, Maggie" the next time he asked me.

Jo caught my eye and mouthed, "Don't forget the meeting with Ros and Giles in twenty minutes, Maggie." I nodded my head, remembering the meeting that had been arranged to discuss new health and safety rules and fire procedures within examinations. Glancing at the clock, a calendar tacked to the wall caught my eye, and I realized with a start that the date was the sixth of October, and that tonight was the meeting at the town hall where I hoped to become a councilor. I felt a sudden attack of nerves and began to wonder what nice things Councilor Rawdon could possibly find to say about me. Aware that the twenty minutes were quickly ticking by, I rushed to the ladies' room, passing Stella Atkins's neat and tidy desk which, for once, was empty. She was usually sitting there guarding Stephen like a large fat spider in its web.

The toilets were quiet with no queue for once. I noticed that they smelled good, of lemon and pine, as I stood at the mirror tidying my make-up—a touch of mascara, a slick of lip gloss. I was just about to leave when a cubicle door opened, and with a sinking heart I saw Stella Atkins wiggle out wearing a bright cerise figure-hugging suit—which I was sure I'd seen before—teamed with a white low necked blouse, the usual amount of sun tanned cleavage on display.

"Well," she said straight away. "Maggie Sears, I do believe." She began to titivate herself at the mirror, curling her fingers slowly around her blonde curls and watching them zing back into place. She applied a coat of lipstick then, after a little moue, pressed a tissue against her lips before applying more.

I smiled at her and nodded hello as I tried to slip unobtrusively out the door, when she brought me up short with the words, "I didn't realize you were so buddy buddy with Stephen's daughter-in-law, Maggie."

I frowned and said, "I know Lauren, yes."

"Yes, you certainly do. I saw you both air kissing outside Crumbs Coffee House." She made a little pouting motion with her lips. There was a split second of silence, which I was going to break with a suitable retort when she carried on in a tiny whispery voice. "If you think you're going to get Stephen by being nice to his family, then you'd better think again. Maybe another tactic?"

My blood boiled at her words and, moving away from the door and nearer to where she stood at the mirror, I said quite calmly, "I've been friends with Stephen for many years, Stella. I'm not out to get him." I then added quietly, "As you are...."

She laughed then, a scary laugh, making me jump, a bit like Vincent Price's manic chuckle in Michael Jackson's *Thriller*, and said, hands on her ample hips, "Oh, Maggie, you are a dear one. I'm not out to get him, because...," and she delivered this like a punch line, "I've already got him!"

I smiled thinly and said, "I know all about you, Stella. I know what you did to Stephen's wife Diana, I know that you seem to be following Stephen, and I also know that it was you that deleted the examination records and tried to put the blame on me."

I eyed her carefully, waiting for a reaction, wondering if I'd gone too far as we stood staring at each other, frozen into a sort of tableau. All of a sudden she came close to me, her face almost touching mine, and said in a cold, deadly voice, "Well, prove it then," before walking leisurely out the door.

Did that really happen? I thought as I looked in the mirror at my white, shocked face and hands that quivered as I smoothed my hair. *The bricks are down now*, I thought. *The bricks are well and truly down.* I remembered my mum saying that when she'd had a row with my dad over some silly trivial thing.

Glancing at my watch, I realized I'd be late for the meeting with Jo if I didn't hurry. Stella Atkins was sitting at her desk, seemingly without a care in the world, pushing papers around as she always did as I rushed past. She gave me an almost sneering look from under her lashes as I made my way over to Jo, where she was sitting at a table with Ros and Giles, ready for the meeting. I slid into my seat, my heart still thumping from the shock of the confrontation.

I suppose though, I thought as I tried to concentrate on what Jo was saying, *What happened today was inevitable – something that had to be brought into the open*. I dreaded what would happen next.

~*~

Stephen cornered me as I was leaving work that evening. I was on my way to the town hall for the councilor meeting, and was feeling a little jittery mainly because of that, but also because of what had happened earlier in the day with Stella Atkins. He looked smart as well as sexy, wearing a black suit with a faint silver stripe running through it and a cream shirt. His tie was knotted loosely, so I couldn't help but stare at the chest hairs that protruded from the slightly open neck.

He still carried the scuffed brown briefcase, which I couldn't resist commenting on as we walked down the steps and out into the parking lot. A chilly breeze blew and I hunched into my jacket. "Have you had that briefcase since school days, Stephen?"

"Yes, I have actually; I can't bear to part with it."

I glanced sideways at him. "Really? You've truly had it since you were at school?"

"Yes," he said with a mock frown. "I thought you'd remember it…." I shook my head, laughing, when Stephen said, "Ah Maggie, you've such a beautiful smile. It brightens my day."

A fiery blush, just like the October leaves that lit up the trees, suffused my face, making Stephen smile. He looked at the ground, then back at me and said ruefully, "Sorry, I think I've embarrassed you."

I turned away from the penetrating stare of his sherry brown eyes, and instead gazed at the blue sky and the brightness of the leaves as they rustled gently in the branches of the trees. I shook my head, not trusting myself to speak, tears welling in my throat. *Why*? I thought. *Why did Stephen telling me that I had a beautiful smile make me want to cry*?

"Are you free for a drink, Maggie?" he asked gently. "I really need to talk to you."

What does he want to talk to me about? I thought. *Is he going to tell me that he is with Stella now? After all, she said that she "already had him."* I didn't want to know that he was with her—I didn't want to hear those words just yet.

Glad that I had a previous appointment, I said, "I can't. I've a meeting at the town hall—with Cobby Town Council."

"Ah, yes. Well good luck, Maggie. I hope you get through to become a councilor. They need people like you. Maybe another evening?"

"Yes," I said. I had a sudden urge to tell him about the confrontation with Stella Atkins, but the cold wind made me shiver, and if I couldn't have the warmth of Stephen's arms then my car would have to do.

"Shall I text?" he asked, leaning over me as I climbed into the driver's seat.

I nodded yes and, as suddenly as it had come, the feeling to confide in him disappeared and I realized that no good would come of telling him about the row with Stella Atkins—not if she was his partner now as well as his PA. It seemed to me that she had caved in and given up the argument with the "Well, you'll have to prove it" remark. What a cop out that was! It should be written down and logged as "Stella's Surrender."

I drove away, glancing in my rearview mirror at Stephen as he stared after me, a strange hopeless expression on his face.

~*~

The Council Chamber was exactly as I'd imagined Kath's office to be, with its dark wood paneling and the high wooden seat which was reserved for the mayor or the chair of the council, and it was he or she that wore the long black cloak and the tricorn hat, and certainly not the town clerk.

I gazed around at the many framed black and white photographs of all the previous mayors, and the much larger painting of the first town clerk of Cobby Town Council, a very serious looking young man named Frederick Lancaster, who wore a wig very much like that of a court judge. I inhaled deeply of the chamber's musty odor, realizing how old the place was and thinking about the countless number of people that had sat in this seat before me.

Councilor Rawdon came over to speak to me where I sat with two other people with the same high hopes that I had of becoming a councilor. A rather large man with hands the size of shovels and a voice like the growl of a bear, he carried a few sheets of A4 lined paper with, I noticed, black scribbly writing on both sides. *Good God,* I thought. *What on earth has he found to say about me that covers so much paper?*

Kath gave me a discreet wave from her seat next to the mayor before several councilors surrounded her, waving copies of minutes and asking for agendas, and was there an addendum with it tonight regarding item number three? I could hear her speaking in a calm soothing voice when all at once the mayor banged the gavel and welcomed everybody to the October meeting of Cobby Town Council. Glancing at the agenda, I saw that myself and the two other hopefuls were at number six.

The room fell silent and then the mayor, Councilor Iqbal, began to read out the first item. There was a general air of discussion around the chamber, as this was concerning a very contentious planning application which Kath proceeded to outline for them, giving the pros and cons as she went along. I noticed that it was for the building of a Sparta Supermarket in Cobby, and people were up in arms about it, saying that this would definitely have a big impact on the smaller shops on Cobby High Street. Most residents felt that a large supermarket wasn't needed in Cobby because Yarrow's mini-market catered to all their needs. Hopefully the information that Kath was giving the councilors would help them in curtailing this massive project and, obviously, any advice received from Paul Timpson as the district council planning officer would be very useful too.

Councilor Webster, Chair of the Events & Leisure Committee, took the floor with a detailed report on the Cobby Carnival and Music Festival. Coming up to its second year now, the committee felt that the festival had been a great success and that next year even more top-class bands would be added to the lineup. I felt a great surge of excitement at the thought of being involved with this event and bringing forward ideas of bands that had been famous in the seventies and eighties that were still performing in some form, and could, perhaps, be persuaded to play for a minimum fee.

A small man with a shock of white hair and a raspy voice, who the mayor called Councilor Holmes when he asked him to please sit down and let Councilor Webster speak, made disparaging comments about the music festival, even saying that it was a waste of taxpayer's money.

"It's the taxpayers that pay for a ticket and attend this event," pointed out Councilor Webster, to which a resounding "Hear! Hear!" was heard from various councilors around the chamber.

A small dark-haired man, who I assumed was from the local paper as the word Press was clearly printed on his bench, took fast shorthand notes while avidly watching the proceedings.

"I've pressed that sign loads of times and nothing's happened," said Councilor Melrose with a grin while jiggling his glasses up and down his nose, just as Eric Morecambe used to.

Item six came around and before I knew it, the mayor was introducing myself and the two other hopefuls to the councilors, and one by one we each took the floor and told the council why we wanted to become a councilor.

My voice shook with nerves as I outlined my interest in Cobby Village, and told them that I had lived there all my life and that I had a great interest in the events that the town council organized, as I felt that they contributed towards the wellbeing of the people that lived in the village. I told them that I admired the councilors on the town council, and applauded all the good work that they were currently doing for Cobby and the surrounding areas.

Councilor Rawdon then pointed out that I had worked in the local Bloomers the Bakers for many years, and now worked in Cobby High School, where I supported the young people through their examinations to enable them to get good grades and go on to bigger and better things, whether they stayed in Cobby or moved to other areas. He rambled on and on, ending with the words, "I know that Maggie Sears will become a great councilor." I felt buoyed, lifted up, almost a paragon of virtue, and applause from nearly all the councilors rang out around the Council Chamber.

Huddled in my car with the heat turned up high, I drove home, the sound of councilors clapping their hands together still echoing in my brain. Councilor Rawdon had done me proud, as I had been co-opted on with a vast majority and was now Councilor Maggie Sears of Cobby Town Council. Kath, thrilled to bits, had produced all the relevant legal paperwork, which I signed with a shaky hand. I had committed myself now – I was a councilor, and determined to do the best I could for the local community.

The orange glow of street lights lit up the windy roads of Cobby as I drove slowly, my nose almost pressed against the dark windshield. Trees, their branches covered in an abundance of glowing red and yellow leaves, swayed in the breeze, and dirty grey clouds hung low in the dark sky like angel's pillows.

My phone beeped as, slumped on the settee, quite worn out after such a stressful day, I poured myself a welcome glass of wine. It was a text from Stephen.

Hi Maggie, congratulations on tonight, read in the early edition of the paper that you are now Councilor Maggie Sears – good one! Would you like to go for a drink soon, please let me know when you're free x

Several other texts came through too, from Mum and Lynette, and Lauren, even one from Jo, which I thought was kind. Reading Stephen's again, I felt a sudden surge of irritation at the fact that not so long ago Stephen didn't want me, and yet now it seemed that he did. Why? What had changed?

Had Jake and Vanessa accepted me, or didn't he care about that now? Did he want to meet up with me as a friend, or did he want to rekindle our romance? I felt that he was "messing with my head," which seemed to be the hip thing to say these days. That poor head, aching with so many thoughts, finally gave in and demanded sleep. Clutching my wine glass in my hand, I tottered unsteadily up the stairs, my old cat Arthur following close behind.

Chapter Ten

Kath Emmerson married Paul Timpson on a bright October day, just as Ray and I had when we tied the knot so many years before. The sun glowed from a porcelain blue sky as autumn leaves, vibrant orange, red, and yellow, pried themselves slowly from the trees and twirled softly through the air. I'd come along by chance, not realizing that they would be getting married in the town hall in Cobby, but oh, how glad I was that I was there to witness this lovely wedding.

Amongst the milling crowd on the village green, I spotted Kath's daughter, Lizzy, her spangled hair like a halo, with Martin and the two children, Layla clad in a long white dress that swept the floor as she walked. Also an older couple—a small man sporting a pencil thin moustache, and a larger woman, her eyes reminiscent of her brother's, Johnny Emmerson, but not so vivid, not so startlingly blue—who surely must be Andrea and Les Dowling.

Kath, wearing a cream tailored suit and unusual pink

high heeled shoes, held tightly to Paul Timpson's arm as they gazed into each other's eyes, hungrily searching each other's faces. She looked radiant, lit with an inner glow, like a candle flame burned and flickered within. Somebody threw tiny silver horseshoes of confetti that twinkled in the air like a fine mist. Martin snapped a picture with his phone as Joe, his tiny hand tugging at Kath's sleeve, piped up excitedly, "Nanny, Nanny, throw your flowers."

"Maggie," Kath mouthed as, catching sight of me, she raised her hand and, to the oohs and aahs of the crowd, the colorful bouquet soared through the air, and without a flicker of hesitation I reached up and caught it.

~*~

It was my first day at work since I was successful in becoming a councilor, and I walked into the office to what sounded like thunderous applause. Surrounded by such adulation, I begin to get an inkling of what it was like to be famous the way Elvis Presley was, or a member of a rock band, or even the royal family. With a jolt I realized that Princess Diana would have had to go through this almost every day!

I glance over towards Stephen's office and saw him standing at the door, a broad smile on his face, clapping just as hard as everybody else. There was no sign of Stella Atkins' curvy figure at his side. Some bright spark shouted, "Speech, speech, speech," until everybody joined in and I felt under pressure to say something. After a few nervous words about being a good councilor and doing my best for the people of Cobby, James Jamieson came over to my desk. He walked purposefully, his blue eyes sparkling. He was dressed down today in jeans, a white shirt tucked in, and a pale blue tie, slightly askew, that matched his eyes.

"Hey, good speech, Maggie—congratulations." He shook my hand hard, pumping my arm vigorously up and down as if he was drawing water from a well. "What do you say we have a celebration and go out for a few beers?"

"Yes," I agreed straight away, remembering the decision I'd made to grab my happiness wherever I could. "That sounds like a good idea to me."

"Friday night? I could pick you up in a taxi from your place."

After I gave him my address and we agreed on a time, he wandered off, frequently glancing over his shoulder and giving me the thumbs up sign. I gave him a little wave of my fingers, then settled down at my desk and fired up my computer.

Looking through my emails, I immediately saw a message from Kath, sent the day before her wedding, welcoming me to Cobby Town Council as a councilor and an integral part of the team. She had attached a little booklet she thought I would find useful, entitled, *Everything You Need to Know to be a Successful Councilor*. Flicking through the pages, I saw that it contained all sorts of good advice that would certainly be of help to me.

She went on to say that I wasn't to be nervous at the prospect of my first Events & Leisure Committee meeting. *The committee is very nice and friendly*, she said. *And Mrs. Stead, my fill-in, and of course Councilor Webster, the chair, will look after you*. She then went on to say that she would see me as soon as she returned from her holiday. I smiled to myself as I thought of Kath on her honeymoon at the lakes with the delectable

Paul Timpson.

Kath's bouquet that I had so successfully caught came to mind, and once again I inhaled the sweetness of the roses and the woodiness of the dahlias. What was said about the person that caught the bridal bouquet? That they would be the next to marry? Glancing towards Stephen's office, where I could clearly see the back of his head and the tiny whorls in his hair, I had an awful sinking feeling in the pit of my stomach that that definitely wouldn't be happening to me any time soon—perhaps never.

Jo's voice brought me out of my reverie. "Maggie, Stella Atkins has rung in sick, and Stephen needs some work done urgently. Is there any chance you could give him a hand for a couple of hours?"

"Of course," I replied, while thinking, *Stella Atkins off sick? Well, that's a turn up for the books*!

"We're fairly quiet today as all our records are up to date and in the system—thankfully," Jo said, giving me a wry smile. "So I can spare you for a while."

"Oh, what's wrong with Stella?" I enquired.

"Some sort of tummy bug, I think," she replied with a slight twist to her mouth.

Shafts of lemon sunlight fell through the office windows, dazzling me as I went across to Stephen's office. He was on the phone talking quickly, busily, so I hovered uncertainly in the doorway until he had finished.

"Maggie," he said, standing up. "Sorry about the wait. Please, come in."

"Um, Jo said you needed some help?"

Looking faintly harassed and, unfortunately for my

madly beating heart, sexily tousled, he replied, "Yes I do. I've a number of letters that need to go out today, and a couple of reports that I'd like typed up. Could you help with that?"

"Yes, no problem at all."

Then, fixing his sherry brown gaze directly on me, he whispered urgently, "Maggie—did you get my text asking if you're free for a drink? I was thinking maybe Friday night?"

Friday night? I thought with a jolt. *That's the night I've made plans to go out with James Jamieson*. What a predicament—now what did I do? Did I let James down and go out with Stephen, or say no to Stephen—which, after the way he'd treated me would serve him right—and go "for a few beers" with James?

I returned his gaze with mine, mulling over the situation, trying to think of the best thing to do, then I came to a decision.

~*~

I recognized some of the councilors entering the town hall as I parked my little Fiat in the parking lot at the front of the building. Although Kath had told me not to be, I felt just a little bit nervous, because tonight was my first Events & Leisure Committee meeting as a councilor on Cobby Town Council. It was a beautiful evening and the sun, hanging low on the horizon, was a burning orange disc shining through the fiery leaves of the trees on the village green. Even the imposing structure of the cenotaph was bathed in an eerie orange glow. The air smelled woody and damp.

I spied the large bulk of Councilor Rawdon disappearing through the massive town hall doors, as well as the chair, Councilor Webster, and a tiny grey-haired lady who I assumed was Kath's fill-in, Mrs. Stead. Another very small elderly lady with hair like cotton candy also went in, chattering nonstop to a pretty young girl who seemed to be struggling under the weight of a black shiny briefcase and a laptop.

I really had to rouse myself so, taking a deep breath to try and slow down the erratic beating of my heart, I gathered my jacket and bag from the passenger seat. I was just about to get out of the car when my mobile beeped and, peering at the screen, I saw that it was a message from Lauren.

Hi Maggie, hope u ok. At last I've managed to get Vanessa and Lucy together. Can you meet next Sat in Cobby at around 3.00 p.m.? Either in Crumbs again or Bloomers? Not sure about Jake yet cos of work. Let me know, looking forward to seeing u x

I was pleased to hear from Lauren, and felt quite excited at the thought of meeting up with Vanessa and Lucy, which could well be interesting. Thoughts of what they might say to me ran through my mind, but for now I had a meeting to attend, so quickly, I made my way into the town hall. The committee members, chatting idly together, were sitting around a large polished oval table set in the middle of the room when I entered the Council Chamber. Councilor Webster, deep in conversation with Mrs. Stead, stood up straight away and said, "Ah, Councilor Sears, welcome to your first meeting of the Events & Leisure Committee. Please, do sit down."

Introductions were made formally around the table, after which Councilor Rawdon growled, "There's no need for all that councilor business on this committee." Pointing at me with a stubby finger, he said, "Her name's Maggie." Short and to the point—that was Councilor Rawdon.

The two-hour meeting passed in a fun filled hive of

activity. Several members of the public attended to advertise their own events, and to ask if it would be possible for the committee to help with funding. A few people wanted to take part in our events and be, for example, a runner in the Fun Run, while others wanted to play at the music festival to get much needed promotion for their band.

I put forward an idea that I would like to pursue of a band that hailed from Cobby who might play for a cheaper rate at a local event. Councilor Webster said I should go ahead with that and report back at the next meeting. I also suggested that the Hale & Hearty gym in Skelmanthorpe might be interested in joining in with our Christmas Fun Run, and perhaps that could be looked at as well. "After all," I pointed out. "We're in October now and Christmas is looming!" A few murmurs of agreement were heard around the table. I then carried on to say, "Perhaps the runners might want to dress as Father Christmas."

"Or Mother Christmas," piped up the cotton candy hair lady, who I'd found out was Councilor Brearley.

"Or a Christmas fairy," said Councilor Webster with a grin.

"How about a Christmas bauble?" growled Councilor Rawdon. There was laughter and general murmurs of agreement to all of the proposals, and I was given the go ahead to contact Hale & Hearty in Skelmanthorpe to put forward our ideas.

I thought about the meeting when I got home that night, my old cat Arthur curled in a tight ball on my knee, which was most unusual for him. I felt excited at the prospect of being a councilor, and was so glad that I'd taken on the role.

Kath had been right when she'd said that the Events & Leisure Committee would be just right for me. I was also thinking of attending other committee meetings—the Planning maybe, or the Police & Transport. Even the General Purposes Committee sounded interesting.

With a jolt I realized that I hadn't replied to Lauren's message, so I texted her back saying next Saturday was fine and that I looked forward to meeting up with her, Vanessa, and Lucy—and Jake, of course, if he could make it. Satisfied with that, I pressed send and then thought back over my conversation that morning with Lynette.

She'd rung to wish me luck for the meeting at the town hall that evening, just an excuse really, I think, to find out the current situation with Stephen. I told her everything about the confrontation with Stella Atkins and the nasty words that we had exchanged in the ladies' toilets, and also my predicament regarding Stephen and James Jamieson and who to go out with on Friday night.

"Well," she said. "Your head or your heart. It's a no brainer, isn't it?"

"Not necessarily," I replied. "James Jamieson seems like a bit of fun, and I think I need that at the moment. Maybe Stella Atkins can have Stephen if she wants him. I don't think he wants me anyway."

"Hmm," she replied in a rather disappointed tone. "The heart has reasons that reason does not understand."

"Oh, Lynette," I remember saying. "I'm only going for a drink with him. My heart has nothing to do with this."

It was only after I'd hung up that I thought that maybe it did. But in this case the decision I'd come to was made following my head—and definitely not my heart.

Chapter Eleven

Loud rock music sounded from the open taxi windows as I picked my way carefully down the garden path in my heels. The driver—questionable, with heavily tattooed arms, a nose ring and something silver on his lip—nodded his head to the beat, eyeing me suspiciously as I got into the car. He chewed gum, pulling it over his tongue like a pink gauzy bubble until it burst with a resounding pop. It was a balmy evening, the sky just beginning to darken, and the sun blood red on the horizon.

James, sitting in the back seat, grabbed hold of my hand, saying, "Hey Maggie, Maggie May, you look great." He wore a black and white striped granddad collar shirt over a pair of smart black trousers. The top few buttons of the shirt were open, showing an expanse of hairy—I have to say graying—chest hair, which was as thick and unruly as my garden was beginning to look without Ray's expert hand.

"Hi, James," I said. "Thank you. But I'm not called Maggie

May. Just Maggie will do." I gave what sounded very much like a high pitched titter, letting him know it was okay though, I was up for it and determined to have a good time.

In reply he burst into a poor rendition of Rod Stewart's "Maggie May" which, luckily, was drowned out by the heavy beat of the taxi drivers' rock music. *Good God*, I thought. *The evening has barely begun, and already he sounds – and smells – as if he's drunk the entire contents of a bottle of Jack Daniels all by himself.*

"Thought we'd go to Skelmanthorpe," he told me with a wink. Then to the driver, in an upper class accent reminiscent of Roger Moore as Bond, he said, "First stop, my good man – cocktails in the Star & Garter." My stomach plummeted as if I was on a very fast fairground ride; I'd never tasted a cocktail in my entire life!

The only word I could use to describe my night out with James Jamieson was mayhem. Cocktails in the Star and Garter, curry in Skelly Spicy Hut, more drinks in a local hotspot The Drink's Shed. This was all followed by dancing in a night club called Frenzy that boasted a strobe lit pink, blue, yellow. and orange dance floor and a silver rotating ball that spun wildly above our heads as, amidst the gyrating crowd, we threw our arms and legs to all four corners of the tiny dark pulsating room.

The taxi home was a blur; the only thing I remembered was James's manic laughter echoing around Cobby as I wound my weary way indoors and somehow up the stairs to bed, my old cat Arthur following me and wrinkling his whiskery nose in disgust.

~*~

The ringing of my mobile awoke me the following morning, a persistent ringing that went on and on, however much I tried to ignore it. My head was throbbing, which was a completely new experience for me, as in all my fifty-four years I'd never suffered from the after effects of alcohol. Loud disco music still pounded through my head as, blearily, I answered the phone. "Hello?"

"Maggie, it's Mum. What time are you coming for me?"

"Coming for you—what?"

"We're going shopping, aren't we? To Cobby. I need to go to Yarrows, and we said we could have a snack in Bloomers or that other place, Coffee Aroma."

Coffee Aroma? I thought. *Just what I need.* I almost giggled out loud when with an awful thud, as if I'd hit earth, Mum's words sank into my brain and I remembered with startling clarity making the arrangements—and looking forward to it, too. But shopping in Cobby—today—with this head? Impossible!

"Okay, Mum, of course. Sorry, still half asleep. I'll pick you up in an hour. See you then."

Mum was ready and standing at the door when I arrived. She looked good in tailored black trousers with a red V necked top, the whole look spoiled slightly by a fleecy black marl jacket adorned with pictures of snarling wolves—oh well, each to his own. She wore tiny gold hoop earrings, and her face was made up with a smudge of eye shadow and a slick of pink lipstick.

"Mum." I kissed her papery cheek, and she smiled at me and gripped my arm tightly as we set off on the short walk into Cobby Village. It was a dazzling October day with a fresh nip in the air that stung my face. I shivered, hunching my shoulders as we shuffled through the leaves that lay in crispy golden heaps on the paths.

We talked first of all about how much better Mum was feeling since being treated at the hospital, and how we hoped that the medication would keep any infections at bay. We then went on to discuss Stella Atkins and Stephen, and then moved on to my night out with James Jamieson.

"What's this James like?" asked Mum.

"He's a fun guy, but that's as far as it goes. To tell you the truth, Mum," I confessed, "I think I've got a hangover, and I'm in dire need of coffee."

She gave a short bark of laughter and said, "Well, let's try that Coffee Aroma place first then, Maggie. I've never known you to have a hangover."

Coffee Aroma was packed, most of the square yellow and orange tables full. The cheery chatter of so many people pounded through my sore head like a jackhammer, and the odor of coffee beans, frying bacon, and burnt toast made my stomach roll and twist as if on a choppy sea. Thank God the background music was muted.

A far too chirpy waitress dressed in tight black clothes and a white frilly apron found us a table by the window where, once I'd consumed a large coffee with a mountain of cream and a currant toasted teacake slathered in butter, I began to feel almost human.

Glancing around, I noticed a couple of women at the next table. They were having a deep discussion, heads close together but talking in rather loud voices so we could hear every word they said. They were both dressed in long sleeved

T-shirts topped with a padded body warmer, which made them both look as large and bloated as Michelin Men. My ears pricked up considerably when I realized who they were gossiping about.

"Have you heard the latest on Kath Emmerson?"

"You mean that woman whose husband died—Johnny Emmerson? Town clerk now, isn't she?" She took a rather generous bite from an enormous slice of coffee cake.

"Yes. He was a very attractive man." She gave the other woman a sideways glance and a flutter of her eyelashes. "And yes, town clerk now. Well, she's only gone and married that planning officer that she took up with so soon after he died."

"Married him? Never."

"Oh, she has. Didn't muck about, did she?" She took a hearty sip of coffee.

Then Mum said in a very loud voice, "How did your first meeting with the council go, Maggie?"

The two women looked around and fixed Mum with a hard stare and, smiling to myself, even though it made my head thump even harder, I replied, "Really good. It was the Events & Leisure Committee, which is good fun. Kath is responsible for the organization of most of the events—she's a brilliant town clerk."

The two women had gone very quiet, not even bothering with their coffee and cakes, and not even trying to hide the fact that they were listening to our conversation.

"Oh, she is," agreed Mum. "A lovely person."

"We've got some brilliant events coming up, including a Christmas Fun Run."

"You're not running?" asked Mum, mouth agape, currant

teacake halfway there.

"No—not running, Mum." I had to laugh, even though it made me wince and my head thumped dangerously. "Just helping to organize it." Then, remembering a familiar face in the Council Chamber that night, I asked, "Do you remember Ron Wooler?"

The two women were talking quietly together now, giving us furtive glances while munching away on their cream cakes, obviously realizing that we weren't talking about the notorious Kath Emmerson anymore. Mum frowned at my question, thinking hard for a minute or two. Then, like a light going on, her brow cleared and she said, "Oh yes—Ron and his wife Marjorie and the two boys? We lived next door years ago; you were only in your early twenties."

I nodded. "That's right. Well, he's a councilor on the Events Committee."

"Well I never," replied Mum. "How is he? The boys must be grown up now."

"He's fine, very enthusiastic. He said he'd bring his lads along to the events so they can help set up, which I'm sure will be really useful. He said to send his regards to you."

"That's lovely. When you see him again, say hello for me."

I nodded and then, changing the subject, asked, "Did you know that plans have gone in for a Sparta Supermarket to be built in Cobby?"

"Whatever for?" she said, taking a huge bite of teacake and chewing rapidly. "We've got Yarrows here—we don't need one of those big places. To tell you the truth, Maggie...." Mum glanced over one shoulder, then the other.

"What?" I asked, taking another big gulp of coffee and licking the cream from my lips. I couldn't seem to get enough of it. This must be what they call the "hangover from hell."

She leaned forward and whispered, "I'm a bit scared of those big supermarkets."

"Scared?" Holding tightly to my mug, I scraped out the last of the cream with a long handled spoon.

"Yes. A person can get lost so easily you know, Maggie. I know where everything is in Yarrows, but those big places—well...."

"Yes," I agreed, a smile tugging at my lips. "All those little aisles. I know what you mean, Mum—like little mazes." And of course, that put me in mind of Stephen and the way his hair grew in tiny whorls on the back of his head.

Arm in arm we meandered slowly along High Street, passing Bedrock & Rose, where I knew Lynette would be bossily selling properties to would be owners. We glanced in the window as we walked past, Mum standing on her tiptoes, but apart from a bored looking woman sitting at a computer, there was no sign of anybody, let alone Lynette. I wondered how things were with her and Dave now that she knew he wasn't having secret liaisons in a hotel room with Lena, and whether they'd been on their weekend away yet.

I noticed that Cobby was busy with plenty of people out and about, enjoying the autumn sunshine. Groups of teenagers stood idly around the doors of the shopping precinct. Most of the boys wore jeans that hung low, well past their hips, cheekily showing their underpants to all of Cobby. Others had the hoods of their sweatshirts up over their heads, hiding their faces and making them look faintly sinister and surly.

"Who's Calvin Klein?" asked Mum, puzzled, standing stock still in the middle of the pavement. "Oh, it must be his name. Look Maggie, he's got his name on his underpants." She pointed at one of the boys with the low jeans.

The group laughed raucously. "Hey Grandma," they shouted.

I pulled at her arm, shaking my head at the teenagers. "Come on, Mum."

Now that the hangover had subsided a little, I felt good and marveled at the fact that I was out with Mum, who walked along beside me as if she'd never been so ill that she couldn't remember her own daughters. Looking sideways at her, I said, "It's great that we're out together, Mum."

She gave me a little smile and squeezed my arm. "I'm so relieved to be back in the land of the living, Maggie."

We strolled on, jostling for space with busy shoppers until we came within sight of Bloomers. I held back a bit and said, "I feel guilty for not having our snack in Bloomers."

"Well, they won't know, will they? Let's go to Yarrows first; then we can come back and get some of those lovely creamy cakes you got the other day. You can say your hellos then."

I nodded and glanced into the shop as we walked past. Lilian was there, and young Jeff and Marta, the polish girl with the thick legs. There was a long queue snaking out of the door as usual, and I noticed that there was a couple in the café, a man and a woman, sitting opposite each other, cups and paper bags all in a mess between them

I thought at first that I was hallucinating, and that perhaps it was all part of the hangover experience. But the more I looked, the more I realized, with an awful tight knot in my stomach, that the man was definitely Stephen, and that, leaning in close with ample cleavage on display even on a Saturday afternoon, was the curvaceous Stella Atkins.

~*~

"What a cracker of a night eh, Mags?"

James Jamieson had suddenly appeared at my side, making me jump. He leaned forward, his hands on my desk, thick fingers splayed. He was dressed smartly in a black suit teamed with a white shirt, even a black tie knotted tightly around his bulging neck. His voice was a decibel or two louder than usual, and I noticed a few people turning around to look at us.

I put a finger to my lips and glanced around as I replied quietly, "Yes. I have to say, James, that I had a very interesting time."

He smiled happily, as if I'd told him I'd had the best night of my life. "Bit of a hangover?" he stage whispered, leaning even closer. A shaft of sunlight fell through the tall office windows, highlighting the glint in his sparkly blue eyes.

"You could say that," I whispered back.

"Up for another one then, are you?"

"Hmm—maybe," I replied. Jo, a pained smile on her pretty face, looked over at us, giving me a very clear message. "Look James, I'm really busy at the moment. I'll text you."

"Oh sure, Mags, no probs. I'm off to a meeting anyway." He gave me a rather lewd wink before strutting away.

I watched his retreating back, shaking my head, a smile hovering around my lips, when, looking up, I caught sight of Stephen standing in his office watching me, hands on hips, an expression on his face that I'd never seen before. Lowering my gaze, I turned my attention back to the computer screen, trying desperately to concentrate. It was mid-October and getting nearer and nearer to those all-important mock exams in November.

Stella Atkins was still off sick. How strange it was to see her desk so bare and clutter free, and for her not to be there guarding Stephen's office like a painted predator. Jo had explained that they couldn't spare me now to give Stephen a helping hand, so an agency worker was being sought. That meant that Stella Atkins was possibly going to be off long term—so how come she was sitting in Bloomers as bold as brass only two days ago? Some tummy bug!

I had a sudden flashback to Saturday when I'd seen the two of them in Bloomers. How I hoped they hadn't seen us as I dragged Mum away from the massive plate glass window, almost running in my haste to put some distance between us.

Mum had no idea what was going on—she hadn't seen Stephen for years, so definitely wouldn't recognize him, and she'd certainly never had contact with Stella Atkins. But even so she protested heavily as we fled along High Street, past Ye Old Wineo, past Cromer's the Chemist, and had almost reached the Village Green when a familiar, albeit breathless voice brought us to an abrupt halt.

"Maggie, for God's sake...."

Slowly I turned to see Stephen, gasping heavily, slightly bent over; his hands on his thighs.

"Well, I never," said Mum straight away. "It's Stephen Gates." So much for thinking that Mum wouldn't recognize him.

~*~

The beeping of my mobile brought me out of my reverie, and looking at the screen I saw it was a message from Stephen.

Hi Maggie, I'm sorry to text you on such an important matter, but please could you come and see me in my office. I met with Stella Atkins the other day. She has made some very serious allegations against you. I need to hear your side before it goes any further. S

What trouble is Stella Atkins hoping to cause now, I thought. *And why didn't Stephen mention this when he caught up with me and Mum on Saturday? We had time for a chat*. I had a quick word with Jo, making up a story about having to see Stephen about some work that I had done for him. Then, with butterflies fluttering madly in my stomach, I walked what seemed a mile-long trek across the room to his office.

Chapter Twelve

It was with heavy dragging footsteps that I walked along the tow path that evening. It was damp and misty and I should have been at home snuggling in front of the fire, but I needed to be outside, and even the company of my old cat Arthur couldn't make me stay in at the moment. I felt stifled and short of breath, as if all four walls were closing in on me, and if I stayed, I would be crushed between them. Above me the sun was a muted yellow glow floating behind shredded grey clouds. Not a sliver of blue sky in sight.

Taking a deep breath and pushing my gloved hands deep inside the pockets of my raincoat, I walked along, halfheartedly admiring the view of the canal, its sluggish water festooned with ducks and the irritable geese that hissed and pecked and fluttered as people walked past. Barges of all sizes and colors sailed slowly by, regal swans following in their wake, and leaves like little flames swirled softly from the overhanging branches of the trees.

A beautiful red barge, the name Hey Jude depicted in white cursive letters on its side, chugged by, and the large black and white dog snoozing on the deck watched me from one lazy half open eye. Raindrops pattered on my face, so I pulled up my hood and carried on walking, feeling even more down and depressed as the events of the day ran through my mind. I recalled Stephen's bewildered face as he told me that Stella Atkins had said that I had shouted and sworn at her in the ladies' toilet, that I had accused her of stalking Stephen and driving Diana to an early death.

"It's all been pulled out of context," I told him. "I would never say those things or behave like that. Let me explain what really happened."

"The truth," Stephen told me. "That's all I want, Maggie, the truth."

I gazed at his sherry brown eyes, at the alluring dimple in his chin and the sexy stubble on his cheeks, and wished that he believed me, that he didn't have to ask for the truth, but that he knew without a doubt that I would never tell him a lie.

"She started it," I remember telling him, knowing full well that I sounded like a child, like a school girl. "She made a comment about Lauren."

"Lauren?" asked Stephen.

"Yes," I said. "She saw us together outside Crumbs Coffee House, and accused me of trying to get closer to you by becoming friendly with your family."

"You've met up with Lauren?" said Stephen helplessly. "You should have told me, Maggie."

"Stella also said," I told him, "That she 'already had you.' What does that mean, Stephen?"

At least I knew now why he was with Stella Atkins in Bloomers on a Saturday afternoon, and it certainly wasn't because they were having a love affair.

"I'm not in a relationship with Stella," Stephen said. "She texted me and asked to meet in Bloomers as she had something to tell me—something about Maggie Sears, she said."

After telling him what now appeared to be an exaggerated version of the confrontation between us in the ladies' toilet, Stella had said that unless this matter could be sorted out "in house," so to speak—she meant by Stephen—she would be getting "expert advice," and wouldn't be returning to work from sick leave until "all this business was dealt with." Ah, so there was no tummy bug then. Stella Atkins was skiving off work and trying to blame me for that as well.

I stopped walking and gazed across the water at the row of tiny houses opposite. One had a small paved yard dotted with large pots of colorful flowers, a small green wrought iron table and chairs, and the address 17 Spinkwell written in deep black letters on a rectangular golden sign attached to the fence. A woman came out the door carrying a large bouquet of flowers. She wore jeans and a pale blue coat belted tightly at the waist, the hood of which had slipped low over her face. She looked familiar, but it wasn't until she moved her head so the hood fell back that I realized who it was, and my heart leaped at the very welcome sight of Kath Emmerson—or should I say Kath Timpson now? For some strange reason tears formed like a tight knot in my throat, so I could barely speak, let alone call out to her. Luckily she saw me and raised a hand as she hurried across the little stone bridge that spanned the canal.

"Maggie, how wonderful to see you." She frowned when

she came close enough to see my face. "Are you all right?" When I burst into tears, she exclaimed, "Whatever's the matter?" She put a comforting arm around my shoulder; the bouquet lodged precariously in the crook of her other arm. The flowers, deep orange and umber, autumnal and earthy, brushed our faces with woody stems.

We sat on Kath's special bench, the beautiful bouquet resting on the ground at our feet, and I told her all that had happened that day, the accusations that Stella Atkins had made and the look on Stephen's face. As the tears still fell, I scrubbed at my face hard with a paper tissue.

"I can't imagine that the accusations are true," she said.

"Well, I did say that she was stalking Stephen, but only because I was told that by Lauren, his daughter-in-law. And she also told me about the bullying that Diana, Stephen's wife, had put up with from Stella." I also told Kath about the mysterious disappearance of the school examination records, and that I had accused Stella Atkins of deleting them on purpose and letting me take the blame.

"Oh Kath, I know I shouldn't have said that, but...."

Kath looked me straight in the eye. "Well, Maggie, I don't blame you. It seems that she's exactly the sort of person who would do a thing like that. I fully support you in this, and Stephen should too. What's his reaction so far?"

"That's exactly what Lauren said," I told her. "As for Stephen, I think he understands the comments I made about the stalking and the bullying of Diana, but I'm not sure if he supports me in the matter concerning the school records being deleted by her. After all, what proof do I have? I think he suspects that I did it by accident. He said he'd have to have to look into it, and then he would contact me for a further meeting." My voice trailed away sadly.

"I hope you told him that you wanted it sorted out quickly, Maggie."

"Yes, I did," I replied. "I told him that I didn't want the worry of it hanging over me."

There was a brief silence as we watched a woman, arms outstretched, legs almost a blur, being pulled along the towpath by a very large black fluffy dog, then a couple running, their high viz gear shining brightly in the impending gloom. Idly I wondered where Kath's dog was, but before I could ask, she said, "Honey's at my daughter's today."

"I was just about to ask you that," I said.

Kath smiled and said, "She loves to be with Layla and Joe. They play hide and seek, you know."

I grinned at the thought of the three of them playing together, which in some odd way reminded me that I hadn't told Kath about my wild night out with James Jamieson and the subsequent hangover.

"I haven't had a night out like that for years." Kath was laughing hard now at my story, holding her stomach and gasping for air.

"But do you know what?" I said, glancing at her from the corner of my eye. "Throughout the whole time I was with James Jamieson, there was only one place I wanted to be, and that was in the Star pub in Cobby—with Stephen. What an old saddo I am."

"No, you're not at all," she replied, hiccupping now, but still laughing. Then, pulling herself together, she said, "Actually, that's where Paul and I used to meet. I bet you even sat at the same table as us—the little round one, opposite the bar?"

I nodded, "Yes, we did sit there."

Smiling, she picked up the bouquet and said, "I was just about to take these to Johnny's grave. Come with me, Maggie?"

"Oh, is it the two-year anniversary?"

"No, that was last week, the twentieth. I don't know why, but I had an urge to visit him again today."

"Well, yes," I said, standing up. "I'd love to go with you. I can visit Ray."

We talked of other things as we strolled along. Kath asked how I'd been getting on with the council meetings since she'd been away. I asked her about her honeymoon, to which she said it had been lovely, and that she was finding it hard to believe that she was a married woman again.

"I didn't think I would ever marry for a second time."

"Well," I said, "It must have felt right."

She nodded and said, "Yes, I'm very lucky. Paul is a good man." Then she added, "As Johnny was."

Together we walked through the ornate cemetery gates and picked our way delicately in between the gravestones. The air was peaceful and still as I stood at Ray's stone looking at the angel, its sightless eyes raised towards the sky. I wondered what he would make of this business with Stella Atkins. I could imagine him saying, "She's poison, Maggie, sheer poison. Tell Stephen everything—he'll believe you against her any day."

Kath, hunkered down beside Johnny's stone, was putting the beautiful bouquet of flowers into vases wedged deeply into the damp earth. I felt the familiar tensing in the air around the grave, a vibration, and thought I heard a whispery voice. Or was it the wind as it blew through the leaves on the trees?

Glancing at Kath, I wondered if she sensed it too, but she didn't say anything and I didn't like to ask. We stood there for a while, Kath and I, until the sun sank in a fiery red ball; until, cold and shivery in the twilight, we linked arms like a chain and slowly walked away from the cemetery and toward home.

~*~

In my capacity as Councilor Maggie Sears of Cobby Town Council I arrived at Hale & Hearty, Skelmanthorpe, just before my two o'clock appointment. Pulling up in the parking lot in my little Fiat, I could see quite clearly into the extension that had been built on to the original building, and the lovely blue pool inside. It was busy with a lot of people thrashing up and down, the water choppy and white with foam, like the sea. Children shrieked as they played, throwing soft balls and bashing each other over the head with long bendy pool noodles. Yes, they were having fun!

People milled about in the reception area, some carrying massive unwieldy sports bags, struggling through the turnstile as they entered the club. I noticed that music with no apparent melody, or even words, was playing in the background, and I wondered if they'd be interested in listening to my Spotify playlist that had a lot of seventies and eighties tunes on it, which were very popular nowadays.

Wafts of chlorine came from the pool area as I approached the circular reception desk, reminding me of childhood swimming with Lynette at the tiny pool in Cobby Village.

All gone now of course, and as far as I was aware, Yarrows, Mum's favorite mini-market, was actually built on the old pool footprint.

I told the receptionist my name—she was an attractive girl, all long dark hair with a fringe cut well above her eyebrows—and that I had an appointment with Shelley, the manager, at two o'clock. The girl looked familiar, and when I saw her badge, the name "Melanie" clearly displayed, I realized she was one half of the couple that Stephen had pointed out to me on the day of our first meeting when we had gone to Ziggi's Pizza Parlor, and Stephen had kissed me until I thought I would faint with pleasure. All I felt now was considerably downhearted, and sadly convinced that kisses like that would never happen again.

A pretty girl with honey blonde hair tied into a neat ponytail, and dressed smartly in the Hale & Hearty uniform of black trouser suit and white shirt, appeared, her hand outstretched, where I stood watching the activities in the pool and looking out at the beautiful lake and gardens beyond.

"Hi, I'm Shelley. You must be Councilor Sears?"

I nodded and shook her hand, saying, "Yes, but please call me Maggie." Gesturing at the extension, I said, "I heard you had a fire here not long ago."

"Yes," she replied. "You should have seen it—total devastation. But the builders have done a fantastic job—it looks exactly as it looked before the fire."

"Well, I certainly would never have known. Have you any idea how it happened?"

Shelley glanced around, and then said in a low voice, "An unfortunate incident with a member of staff." She then hastened to add, "They're not here now, of course."

I nodded as she led me into a tiny office, posters of very fit looking tanned muscular men and women dripping in sweat tacked to its cream painted walls. The room was mostly dominated by a large wooden desk heaped with papers, and an enormous cheese plant that lurked in a corner like a triffid.

Shelley listened intently to my suggestions for a Christmas Fun Run, and said that Hale & Hearty would be really happy to support the event in any way they could, with funding and with runners and a presence on the day. "Robert Bryce leads our running club," Shelly informed me. "So if I know Rob, he'll be really interested in being there, as well as organizing a team for the day. What do you think?"

"I think that would be fantastic," I said. "Far more than I was hoping for."

"Well," she replied briskly, looking at me with her big baby blue eyes. "I do think that businesses flourish even more if they work with their local councils, and you're doing such great things in Cobby."

I nodded, pleased with what she was saying. "I've only just become a councilor," I told her. "But I really hope that I can make a difference too."

She smiled and said, "I'll introduce you to Rob before you go. He's on pool duty at the moment, so while we're waiting, would you like a tour of the club—and a coffee, perhaps?"

After a tour of the very impressive club facilities and an excellent coffee in the club's café, followed by a meeting with Rob, who was a very charming and attractive man with his muscular arms and chest and glossy black hair tied in a ponytail, I said that I would email an agenda for the next Events

& Leisure Committee meeting to Shelley and Rob and any other interested parties. "It would be good if somebody could attend it," I said. "Then we can get on with the organization."

As I was leaving the club, feeling more than pleased with my councilor work that afternoon, my phone vibrated in my bag. Peering intently, I saw that it was a call coming through—from Stephen. I answered it immediately.

"Maggie?" I was in Hale & Hearty's parking lot, and there was a lot of background noise—cars revving and loud music pumping from open windows, sirens wailing from the busy Skelmanthorpe High Street—so I had to press my mobile to my ear to hear him properly.

"Hello, yes, it's Maggie."

"Are you free to come to a meeting regarding Stella Atkins on Monday at ten o'clock in my office?"

"Yes, of course," I replied. "Will Stella be there?"

There was a strange clicking noise on the line, then a loud beep, beep, beep and then nothing. Any words that Stephen may have said to me were lost forever, gone, never to be recovered. I could almost see them fading away right in front of me like smoke. "Will Stella Atkins be there? Yes? No? I don't know!"

I felt an awful clenching in the pit of my stomach at the thought of Monday morning, but before then I had another meeting; tomorrow afternoon, with Lauren, Vanessa, and Lucy—and maybe Jake. I was looking forward to that, which made all the difference.

Chapter Thirteen

A dreary November day, I thought as I peered from between my bedroom curtains. The sky was one big mass of grey cloud, only the vibrant leaves on the almost bare branches of the trees brightening an otherwise dour view. The familiar odor of fireworks hung in the air, along with the smell of earth and decay, and the loud fizzing and banging I'd heard the evening before had left my old cat Arthur cowering in a corner, quivering from head to paw.

I dressed carefully for my meeting with Lauren, Vanessa, and Lucy, putting on a pair of new smart jeans and a warm fleecy jumper. I blow dried my hair and made up my face carefully with discreet eye shadow, mascara, and a slick of pink lipstick. I still didn't know whether Jake would be there, but I was keeping my fingers crossed that he would be and that this time he would talk to me as Maggie, and not somebody who was trying to muscle in and take his mum's place. I wanted to explain to him and Vanessa that I wasn't there to replace her, but only to try to make their dad happy after all he had been through.

Saying that, whether or not this meeting would result in Stephen and I getting back together, I had no idea. Maybe not; after all, there was the business of Stella Atkins to clear up as well, and I had the feeling that Stephen thought badly of me because of that. Hopefully the whys and wherefores of that situation would be cleared up on Monday morning at ten o'clock in Stephen's office.

Before I left the house, I texted Lynette, telling her about the impending meeting on Monday and assuring her that I would let her know what happened. She wished me luck and said, "Bullying is a terrible, terrible thing." I assumed it was a quote.

I was just about to put my phone in my bag when a text message popped up from James Jamieson. *Hey Mags, haven't heard from you about our next nite out. How about next Friday? Let me know, we can go wild – again!!!!! Jx* I shook my head, smiled, and dropped my phone into my bag, thinking, *I'll have to deal with James Jamieson later.*

The sun bravely showed its face from behind dark clouds as I drove into Cobby and parked in the small parking lot behind the village green. The market had been set up again and was bustling, a victory for Cobby Town Council, I had to say, and all thanks to Kath, who'd had the idea in the first place—against much opposition from Cobbydale District Council, I might add. I thought of Lynette and what she would have quoted in this case—maybe this one? "It is the fight alone that pleases us, not the victory."

Checking my watch, I saw that I was very early, as usual,

but made my way along to Bloomers anyway so I could have a chat with Lilian while I was waiting. I strolled along North Street, glancing in the shop windows, enjoying the unexpected sunshine that touched my face with its gentle fingers.

Bumps a Daisy, the maternity shop, had some beautiful little baby things displayed in the window. Such tiny clothes embroidered with the little daisy logo in pastel blue, pink, lemon, and white, reminding me of the flying saucer sherbet sweets that Lynette and I used to fight over when we were children. She always took all the pink and left me with the boring white ones.

I thought of Lauren's unborn baby, Rebecca, and how cute she would look in one of those little outfits, and that I would certainly buy a couple for her when she made an appearance, which I calculated would be in about three weeks' time. I was sure Lauren had a date for the end of November. I felt a sudden surge of happiness at the thought of Stephen's first grandchild, but was also aware that the arrival of this baby might make Jake and Vanessa feel their mother's death even more, which certainly wouldn't be doing me any favors.

Bloomers was fairly quiet for once, the lunch time rush being over, and Lilian and Marta, the Polish girl with thick legs, were standing chatting behind the counter. Lilian, very enthusiastic in her welcome, said that as it was quiet at the moment she'd have a quick cuppa with me.

The shop smelled familiar and comforting, of cream cakes and coffee beans, breakfast bacon and sausage. Sitting in the little café, thoughts of Stephen came rushing back, and I wished that I had chosen somewhere else for our meeting, somewhere more neutral. But it was too late now, as all three of them, or maybe four, would be here soon. As I sipped my coffee and chatted with Lilian, asking after Young Jeff, telling her about the current situation and who I was meeting, I watched the door keenly for their arrival.

Lauren came in first, opening her arms wide for a hug, followed closely by Vanessa and then Lucy, a tall slim girl with blonde highlighted hair that fell in luxurious waves past her shoulders. Vanessa and Lucy wore trendy leather jackets and jeans, while Lauren looked lovely in a long black coat adorned with large red buttons that she'd left open, hanging over her baby bump. Her bump looked far larger today, and low, as if Rebecca was anxious to get out and make her mark in the world.

Hmm, not just yet, baby Rebecca, I remember thinking to myself as I helped Lauren to sit down on a comfortable seat with a back rest. She sat down stiffly, like an old woman, one hand on her lower back, and even though she'd given me her lovely wide red smile when she came into Bloomers, she looked tired, or a bit peaky, as Mum used to say.

"Maggie," said Vanessa, "This is Lucy, my girlfriend."

"Hello, Lucy. It's so good to meet you."

"And you," she said in a small soft voice as she and Vanessa did little moue moue kisses on both of my cheeks.

"There's no Jake I'm afraid, Maggie," said Lauren, "He's caught up at work, all because of this new supermarket that's planned for Cobby." I knew that Jake was a trainee architect and worked for a small firm in Skelmanthorpe called Wrightsons & Wright, and that they were preparing the plans for the much maligned Sparta Supermarket that I'd been talking to Mum about.

"Never mind," I replied. "Maybe next time?"

"Oh, I hope so," Lauren carried on. "He did say that he would have liked to come today, Maggie. He is prepared to meet you again." She squeezed my hand and gave me a kind look from her strange light blue eyes.

I nodded and said, "Well, that's progress anyway."

"Yes, it definitely is, I can promise you that. Anyway, I thought you'd know all about this new supermarket in Cobby, seeing as you're a councilor now. Congratulations."

"Thank you, Lauren. I'm really pleased I got in. Yes, I do know about the new supermarket development and all the opposition to it. Even my mum says we don't need it!" I rolled my eyes and Lauren laughed, and said Jake had told her that there had been lots of objections.

"Wow, a councilor," said Vanessa. "Well done. That's brilliant. Does Dad know?"

"Yes, he does. I see him at the school, you see."

"Yes, I know you see him at work, Maggie. Look, I—"

Vanessa started to try to apologize for her behavior on the night of the dinner party, but I interrupted her and said, "There's no need to apologize, Vanessa. So, first things first, let me buy the coffees—and cakes, I hope. I doubt any of you are watching your waistlines."

Lauren giggled at that remark. "Particularly not me," she said, patting her bump. "This little baby loves cake."

"Oh, definitely cake for us two," said Lucy, exchanging a glance with Vanessa, who nodded her head in agreement.

I stood up to go to the counter, but Lilian bustled over to the table and said, "Now you sit down, Maggie love. Let me take your order for you while you have a good chat."

"Lilian, you are a star," I said. I introduced her to all three girls as "my old boss," which made her laugh as she brought our order of hot frothy cappuccinos and Bavarian slices and cream doughnuts, and then rushed back behind the counter to help Marta, the Polish girl with thick legs, serve a long straggly queue of hungry people.

An elderly couple smiled shyly at us as they sat down carefully at the adjoining table, propping their walking sticks over the backs of their chairs. The lady fussed over the man, putting extra sugar and milk into his tea and leaning forward to dab at his mouth with a serviette. They smiled at each other as they ate and drank. A group of chattering children scampered to the sweet counter, drooling and pointing at their favorite cakes, leaving sticky fingerprints on the glass.

Vanessa, her upper lip coated in froth from the cappuccino, said, "I do need to apologize, Maggie, Jake and I were very rude to you that evening at Dad's. We've realized since that you care for each other, and—well...." She lowered her eyes as a hot red blush suffused her face.

"What I think Vanessa is trying to say," butted in Lucy, "Is that neither Jake nor Vanessa would stand in the way of you and Stephen being together." She licked cream from her fingers and took a deep gulp of coffee.

And then Lauren said, "Yes. Maggie and Stephen being together doesn't mean that Stephen didn't love Diana or that Maggie didn't love her husband, Ray. Both Diana and Ray will never be forgotten."

I swallowed hard, touched by their words and desperately trying to keep at bay the tears that had welled up like a tight knot in my throat. I rubbed away a stray tear with a fingertip, and then, sniffing hard, put my hand palm up on the table. Within seconds Lauren, then Vanessa and then Lucy, each put their hand into mine. Looking intently at Vanessa, I said, "All I want is for your dad to be happy. I would never try to take your mum's place."

"I realize that now," she replied. "And I think Jake does too. He was particularly rude to you about your new job at the school. I know that he feels bad about that, but that's for him to talk to you about." She took a deep breath and sat back in her chair, crossing her arms over her chest. "To be quite honest, Maggie, I just want to see Dad smile again. Since he's not been seeing you he's as miserable as sin!"

I must admit that that comment chased the tears away and made me smile too. I felt light again, light as air, as if a heavy burden had been lifted from my shoulders. We talked then of the incident with Stella Atkins, and the up and coming Monday morning meeting. Vanessa, angry now, said, "I remember her, that Stella Atkins, and how upset she used to make my mum. If you—"

Lauren, who I noticed had been unusually quiet, suddenly interrupted. "Sorry to butt in, Vanessa, but.... Maggie, is there a ladies' room here?"

"Well, not a public one, but I'm sure Lilian would let you use it. What's wrong, Lauren?"

"I'm not sure," she said, her face white and pinched, both hands cupping her huge stomach. "I've got a pain...."

We all stood up in a panic, our chairs scraping against the floor, causing the elderly couple to stare at us in surprise. I looked over at Lilian and mouthed, "Can we use the ladies'?"

Summing up the situation immediately, she rushed

forward and opened the little half door leading to the back room. With my arm carefully around Lauren's waist, I escorted her through, my heart thumping hard as I wondered what on earth was going to happen now.

Chapter Fourteen

Knots of students stood idly around the gates as I made my way in to the school on Monday morning. They all seemed to look at me, their gaze appraising, as if they knew all about my situation and feared the worst. Thinking about it though, how could they possibly know anything? I was being paranoid.

A fine misty rain fell from heavy pewter clouds which, illuminated in a sudden shaft of sunlight, magically became a rainbow arched across the sky. Groups of boys played catch with wet leaves rolled into balls, throwing them hard through the air like ammunition.

I felt slightly queasy and butterflies fluttered madly in my stomach at the thought of the meeting with Stephen, and possibly the dreaded Stella Atkins. I hadn't even been able to eat any breakfast. The thought of her curvy figure and ample cleavage in a far too tight suit wasn't something I wanted to see at the moment—if at all. Yet really, having the meeting without her would be pointless.

The office was quiet, just one of the junior girls, Lorraine, staring at her computer screen. Languidly, in a typical Monday morning fashion, she raised her hand as I walked past. Jo's bag was on her desk, so I assumed she was in the kitchen making an early morning coffee. I wrinkled my nose at the smell of burned toast.

Glancing over at Stephen's office I saw that it was still in darkness, his computer, desk, and chair shrouded in gloom, the blinds pulled halfway across the windows. I wondered where he was. It was most unusual for him not to be here at this time. Perhaps he wouldn't come in today. Perhaps he was too busy with family matters, and the meeting would have to be cancelled.

I was feeling considerably lighthearted at that thought when the double doors swung open and he walked in, smartly dressed as always in a dark grey suit brightened by a pale pink shirt and a grey tie. As usual he carried the brown scuffed briefcase, which he put on the floor beside his desk as he pulled the blinds fully around before switching on the lights. I watched his silhouette as he took off his jacket and settled in his chair.

Gradually the office filled up. James Jamieson, looking a touch disheveled—obviously a fun filled weekend—sauntered in. Glaring hard at me, he made a point of looking at his phone and shrugging, as if to say, "What? Still no text about our night out?" I smiled sweetly, then turned my gaze back to the computer screen and the spreadsheets that I was working on. Jo sat down next to me and asked about my weekend. She sipped at her coffee and the phones began to ring, and so the working week began.

My heart racing, I watched from the corner of my eye the long black hands of the clock as they swept slowly around its large white face, and at ten o'clock on the dot Stephen came out of his office and, barely keeping a broad smile from his face, called my name. Jo nodded to me as I stood up and walked across the room.

"Good morning," I greeted him. "Is Stella here?" I peered cautiously around the door, but there was no sign of Stella Atkins posing on a chair like a poor man's Marilyn Monroe.

"Come in," said Stephen as he closed the door with a firm click and gestured with his head towards a chair. "Please, Maggie, take a seat." I sat down as he went behind his desk to sit opposite me in his leather executive chair. Then, leaning forward, his elbows on the desk, he said, "Stella isn't coming—there's really no need for her to be here. We need to discuss her allegations and get the true story from you."

"But she needs to be here," I said. "How can I speak against her allegations if she's not here to confirm them?"

"I have a statement from Stella, and I'll take a statement from you today. But Maggie, there is a far more important thing to discuss first, don't you think? And I really don't know how to thank you."

"Oh Stephen," I replied carelessly, as if it was nothing; as if I brought babies into the world every day. "I just did what I had to do in the circumstances."

"She's beautiful though, isn't she, Maggie? Rebecca. Such an early baby too, but such a good weight—eight pounds."

"Yes," I said. "She looked to be a very pretty baby, and yes, three weeks early but eight pounds, that's really good. I've got to say it was a bit of a shock when Lauren went into labor, and in Bloomers, of all places. I wasn't sure if Jake would be very happy about that—he doesn't seem to think much of Bloomers."

Flashbacks of Saturday afternoon raced through my mind; Lauren's groans as she tossed and turned on her bed of Bloomers uniforms, Vanessa's panicked voice when she said the ambulance couldn't get through because of road works.

"Road works?" I remembered saying in horror.

"The phone's ringing and ringing," said Lucy, "but we can't get Jake."

The baby was lying so still after slipping quietly from the womb, then there were raucous cheers from Bloomers' customers as they heard her first cries, and I saw Rebecca's scrunched red face as she lay at last in Lauren's arms.

Suddenly realizing the enormity of what had happened, of what I had had to do, I began to tremble, and cupping my shaking fingers around my face, I burst into noisy sobs. Stephen jumped up and hunkered down at my side, his strong arms encircling my shoulders and his hands stroking the back of my neck.

"Maggie.... Oh, Maggie," he said into my hair.

"I'm sorry," I said, pulling away slightly. "I don't know what came over me. I shouldn't have made that comment about Jake." I pulled a tissue from my pocket and dabbed at my face. He stood up and handed me a cup of water from the dispenser, which I gulped thankfully.

"Jake is thankful that his daughter was born safely," said Stephen. "You're shaking—it must be the shock of it all. My God, Maggie, you brought my first grandchild into the world! It's all in the paper today—look...." He pulled a copy of the

Cobby News from his scuffed briefcase and laid it on the desk between us. The headlines, in large black letters, screamed out at me. Councilor Delivers Baby in Bakery!

I noticed that the local reporter was Sam Beck, the small dark man that had been taking notes at one of the Cobby Town Council meetings, and had also been in Bloomers on Saturday asking me questions when I came out of the back room, with Lauren and baby Rebecca carried on a stretcher by the long awaited paramedics.

I remembered talking to him, but what I had said was a mystery, my words lost in the chaos and panic of the afternoon. I glanced at the write up in the paper, where short sharp sentences jumped out at me; the much repeated, "I did what I had to do in the circumstances," "Only trying to help," Lauren and the baby mean a lot to me," "It all happened so quickly." Oh my God, reporters should never interview at the scene like that. People didn't always know what they were saying when they were in a stressful situation.

Peering carefully through the blinds into the main office, I looked at my colleagues, heads down, busily working, and wondered if anybody had seen the paper this morning. Surely if they had, somebody would have said something. There would certainly have been a comment from James Jamieson.

"Don't say anything about this to anybody yet, will you, Stephen?" I said to him.

"No, of course not. But—well, I'm afraid, Maggie, they'll find out from this anyway," he pointed at the paper. "Have you seen the baby since?"

"No," I replied, shaking my head, still looking at the paper and yet barely reading the words, not wanting to meet

Stephen's eyes.

"Lauren was expecting you at the hospital yesterday. Well, we all were."

"No, I felt that it was a family day," I said.

"But Maggie," said Stephen as he hunkered down beside me again, then put his index finger under my chin, lifting my face up to look at him. "You are part of the family. I want you to be there—with me. Lauren has told me everything."

I glanced at him questioningly and frowned.

"Yes, about you two meeting up and the fact that she told you that I was miserable without you. It's all true, Maggie. I've been trying to tell you that I want to be with you, even without the blessing of Jake and Vanessa. Why do you think I ran after you the day you saw me with Stella Atkins in Bloomers? I wanted to speak to you about it then, but you brushed me off."

"I didn't realize," I said. "But even so, Stephen, I can't be with you at the moment. I don't want everything to be fine now just because of this."

"I don't understand, Maggie. What do you mean? Are you seeing James Jamieson now?"

"Good heavens, no!" I said in horror. Stephen looked relieved, but his face darkened again as I said, "I don't want you to bring me into the family now because you have to, because of what I had to do on Saturday afternoon—just because I helped to deliver Rebecca."

"But Maggie...."

Stephen looked tired and worried as he pleaded with me, but I couldn't think of that at the moment. I had to turn away from him, from his sherry brown eyes and the dimple in his chin, and the overwhelming attraction that I felt for him.

I had to think of myself, and knew that I had to take a step back, and whether it was a small step or a giant step wasn't clear to me yet. My gut instinct was telling me to retreat or surrender, just as Stella Atkins had on the day of the confrontation between us, and that was exactly what I was going to do.

I spoke up firmly. "No, Stephen. Please, can we just get on with my statement regarding Stella Atkins? I need to get that cleared up before I think of anything else. It's hanging over my head."

"Yes, of course," he replied, business-like now, moving to sit behind his desk, pulling a notebook in front of him, taking hold of a pen. "In your own words then, Maggie, tell me what happened on the day of the confrontation between yourself and Stella Atkins."

I took a deep breath and began to tell him everything.

~*~

"Good God, Maggie," said Mum. "What's all this in the paper?" She waved a scraggy looking, much thumbed Cobby News in the air. "Sit down, you must tell us all about it."

I'd called in at Mum's on the way home from work. Lynette had texted earlier to say that she would be there and wanted the "low down"—where did she get these expressions?—on exactly what had happened in the back of Bloomers the Bakers on Saturday afternoon.

"Who do you think you are now?" she exclaimed. "Not content with being an assistant examinations officer and a councilor, you want to be a midwife too?" She cackled like a witch over a cauldron, sending shivers down my spine.

A real fire, bright orange and yellow, roared like a lion in Mum's little sitting room, and deep red curtains shrouded the windows cozily against the rainy blackness. Lamplight shone in pools on the carpet. Lynette appeared from the kitchen with steaming hot coffees on a tray. I took a tentative warming sip and sank back into the deep cushions on the settee, closing my eyes, my bones at last feeling soft and relaxed.

My phone beeped and picking it up, hoping that it wasn't a text from Stephen—I didn't think I could deal with him at the moment—I saw it was from Kath, asking if I was okay after my ordeal over the weekend. She was concerned after what she'd read in the paper, and as I was a councilor now, the town clerk needed to know what had happened. There were very strict rules about what councilors were able to say to the local press. *Oh dear,* I thought. *I'll text her later, or better still, call in at the town hall tomorrow to give her the "low down" too.*

I opened my eyes to see both Mum and Lynette staring at me expectantly. I took another sip of coffee, sat forward, and said yet again, "I just did what I had to do in the circumstances,"

"What happened though, Maggie? Why didn't the ambulance arrive straight away?"

"It got caught up in the road works, on the main road coming into Cobby. The sirens were wailing—we could hear them—but the ambulance couldn't get through and the baby starting coming so fast. Vanessa and Lucy tried to contact Jake as well, but he didn't get the messages until Lauren had been taken to the hospital."

"Oh my," said Mum. "What did Lilian say about all this happening in her shop?"

"Oh, she was marvelous," I told them. "We had no towels, you see, so she made a bed for Lauren from Bloomers uniforms—the trousers and the tops and the aprons—and she brought boiling water. It only took a few minutes, though, before the baby's head appeared."

"What were Vanessa and Lucy doing?" asked Lynette as she took a sip of her drink. She leaned forward even further in her chair, so close that her nose almost touched mine.

"They were outside trying to contact Jake, and also speaking to the paramedics, who were trying to get to us as a matter of urgency—and giving instructions, too, about the birth. They were concerned because the baby was so early." I stopped and took a breath.

"Go on, go on—don't stop," said Mum. "What happened next?" I hadn't seen Mum so excited since she used to scream at the wrestling on a Saturday afternoon.

"Well, I told Lauren to take deep breaths because I could see the head. I told her it was just a question of getting the shoulders out, and when the time was right, I would tell her to push."

"Oh, my God, you are so brave," breathed Mum and Lynette at the same time, then looked at each other—astonished, I thought, that they'd said exactly the same thing at exactly the same time.

"Well, Lauren pushed and pushed, groaning and screaming and wriggling about. I could hear Bloomers' customers shouting out words of encouragement, and Marta, the Polish girl with the thick legs, telling them that 'due to a state of emergency there will be no sausage rolls this afternoon' in her strange halting accent. Oh my God, it was mayhem, you wouldn't believe it. Then all of a sudden, after an almighty push, the shoulders were out, and then another push and Rebecca, the baby, just sort of—slid out."

Mum and Lynette gazed at me open mouthed, their faces red and shimmery in the glow of the crackling fire. "Go on, don't stop," said Mum, waving her hand at me.

"Well, the baby just lay there—I was really worried."

Thinking about it made my hands shake again, so very carefully I put my coffee mug back on the tray, being careful not to spill. Lauren had been trying to sit up, trying to get a look at her, at Rebecca, but I told her to lie back down and not to worry.

"Why is she quiet?" I remember Lauren saying. "Why is she so quiet, Maggie?"

"Shh, don't worry," I told her. Poor Lauren, who looked worn out with her strange light blue eyes sunk into black sockets, and her hair spread out all lank against the Bloomers uniforms.

I looked at Mum and Lynette. "And then, carefully—I didn't want to hurt her—I picked up the baby, and with my fingertips massaged her back and her chest. All of a sudden she gave a little jerk, a tremor I suppose you'd call it, and screamed so loud I almost dropped her. Oh my God, the place erupted with cheers."

"Well done, Maggie." Mum clapped her hands like a child.

"I laid her on Lauren's chest, and then the paramedics rushed in and sort of took over. They cut the cord, not me."

I remembered the rush of relief that surged through me as, with capable hands, they wrapped Lauren and the baby in warm blankets, smiling at me as they squeezed past with the stretcher.

I stood there when they'd gone, taking deep, calming breaths, listening to the wail of the siren as it got fainter and fainter. I remember looking at my hands and being surprised that they were all sticky and covered in blood, and without thinking I wiped them down my jeans—my lovely new jeans. I started to cry then, holding on tight to Lilian, my tears soaking right through her Bloomers apron.

"What did she weigh, Maggie?" asked Mum.

"Eight pounds," I said. "That's good for an early baby, isn't it?"

"That's excellent," agreed Mum.

"Oh my God," exclaimed Lynette. "It's a good thing she didn't go for another three weeks then, isn't it?" She laughed heartily. Lynette leaned forward and put her mug on the tray, while asking, "Did you go to the hospital with them?"

"Oh no," I replied. "Vanessa and Lucy went with Lauren and the baby in the ambulance."

"Why didn't you go?" she asked. She frowned, making the hated crease between her eyebrows deeper than ever. "Lauren must have wanted you with her!"

"I was worn out, Lynette—I just wanted to get home. God knows how real midwives cope with it—it's a traumatic experience. Lauren had both Vanessa and Lucy with her, and Jake arrived when she got to the hospital—and Stephen. She didn't need me then."

"Are you going to visit the baby though, Maggie?"

"Oh yes," I told them. "Of course I will. I just feel as if I should keep a bit of a low profile at the moment."

They both nodded in agreement. “You do what you think is right, Maggie,” said Mum gently.

“Yes,” I told them. “I really think I’m doing just that.”

Chapter Fifteen

"Well really, Councilor Webster," said Kath playfully. "I don't know why you think I could be a runner in the Christmas Fun Run!"

"I've seen you wearing a Fun Run T-shirt," he replied. "So I thought—"

"No." She shook her head and laughed. "That's just for show. That's why these people have come here tonight for the meeting." She indicated across the table to where Rob and Melanie from Hale & Hearty gym sat. "These are the brave people that will be doing the running." Kath looked good in a black shift dress offset by tiny gold hoops in her ears and a gold chain with a little heart hanging from it that I suspected might have been a present from the delectable Paul Timpson.

Rob and Melanie laughed and said that they certainly would be running, and were looking forward to it. They'd already had a lot of interest from Hale & Hearty members, and would be bringing a team of people on the day. "All dressed up in Christmas outfits too," added Rob.

"We've got Councilor Sears to thank for this as well," said Councilor Webster, pointing towards me, "For her persuasive tactics with Melanie and Rob. And I have to add, for her skills not only as a councilor, but as a midwife too."

I felt a hot blush suffuse my face as all of the committee members looked at me and varying comments were made around the table. I took a deep breath, but instead of the fresh air that I needed, I inhaled the old musty odor of the Council Chamber.

"All that happened a couple of weeks ago now," I pointed out. "It's an old story."

"Well, yes," said Councilor Brearley. "But a truly brave story that will never be forgotten."

"Yes, a councilor to make us proud," said Kath, beaming at me from her seat next to the chair.

Kath and I had met earlier in her office, just before the start of the Events & Leisure Committee meeting, to have a chat about exactly what had happened on that Saturday afternoon at the back of Bloomers, and the subsequent article in the Cobby News. I explained that I certainly hadn't had an official meeting with Sam Beck, the reporter, but he had asked me questions when it was all over and Lauren and the baby had been taken to the hospital.

"To tell you the truth, Kath," I told her, "I didn't even know it was him at the time—I've only seen him once in a meeting. I didn't realize that his interested questions were for the benefit of the paper!"

"Yes, reporters are a pretty wily bunch," replied Kath. "Oh, don't worry, Maggie, I don't hold you responsible at all. No doubt you were in a bit of a state after all you'd been through."

I had to agree with her there, and admitted that yes, I had shed a few tears after realizing that I'd actually brought a baby into the world—and an early baby at that. "It was a very tense experience," I said.

"That little girl will always be special to you, Maggie," Kath said, and with a guilty pang I realized that it had been a couple of weeks and I hadn't even gone to visit her yet. I still had a very strong feeling that I should keep my distance from the family at the present time.

Kath went back to the matter in hand. "I was only worried about it because as a rule, it's only the mayor and the clerk that can talk to the press. But I think you were hoodwinked into it anyway. Just forget all about it."

Then, as she gathered all her papers together for the meeting and as we were leaving the office, she turned and gave the empty room a little wiggly wave of her fingers. I had a weird feeling that she was saying goodbye to Johnny and that he had been in the room with us all the time. Where had he been, I wondered? Standing over by the window admiring the view of the village green and the cenotaph? Lurking in a corner, or even perhaps standing right behind my chair? A tremor ran down my spine at that thought.

The Events & Leisure Committee was very productive, with all the arrangements for the Fun Run being put in place and many thanks given to Rob and Melanie for their input. I lingered for a while outside the town hall afterwards, chatting with Kath and Councilor Webster. We talked of other up and coming events, including a councilor and staff Christmas party at a local restaurant called Cobby Cuisine—which boasted a very nice bar and a small dance floor—which we were all looking forward to. It was a fine evening, clear and bright, the sky inky black studded with tiny silver stars. The paths glittered white and felt quite slippery beneath the soles of my shoes as I walked carefully to the parking lot, where my little yellow Fiat waited patiently for me.

At home my old cat Arthur greeted me at the door with a husky meow, and began to wind sinuously in and out of my legs purring loudly all the time. I gave him Droolies, his favorite treats as, softly, I fondled his ears, thinking of Ray and how close he and old Arthur had been. My lap was never good enough when Ray was around.

Kicking off my shoes, I sat on the settee sipping from a glass of red wine, wondering when I was going to hear from Stephen about Stella Atkins. The whole horrible business was still hanging over my head, and I wanted it sorted as soon as possible. Stephen, in his capacity as headmaster, had been away at a conference for a few days, so I was hoping that I would hear from him when he returned. I loved my new job, and definitely didn't want this business with Stella Atkins to put it at risk.

My thoughts turned to Lauren and the fact that I hadn't seen her since Rebecca was born. The situation weighed heavily on me, and I had been tempted to text her on many occasions, particularly as I'd received another message from her only yesterday thanking me for everything that I had done, and looking forward to meeting up soon. Perhaps I should text her tomorrow and explain how I felt, and that it wasn't her that I was avoiding, but Stephen. Would she understand though? After all she'd done to try to get us together?

I gave a great frustrated sigh at the intricacies of relationships and, relieved that I wasn't working the following day, drained my wine glass of every last little drop, and closely followed by my old cat Arthur, made my way upstairs to bed.

~*~

I awoke the next morning feeling quite groggy, my head so deeply entrenched in the lovely soft pillows that I had difficulty lifting it. I had already decided—maybe I had dreamt it—that today I would go into Cobby and to the maternity shop Bumps a Daisy, and buy a couple of those beautiful little pastel colored outfits that I had seen in the window and then visit Lauren and the new baby. I wouldn't text beforehand, I would just show up. I had a good idea of where she lived. It wasn't Lauren's fault that I'd decided against a relationship with Stephen at the moment. I wasn't being fair to her, and actually not to Vanessa, Jake, or even Lucy for that matter.

I peered from the kitchen window at the garden that, even to my untrained eye, was looking a mess. Ray would be horrified if he could see it. Making yet another decision—and it wasn't even nine o'clock yet—I thought that I would make an effort later this afternoon and go out there and tidy it up. Even though it was late November, the day looked fine enough for gardening, with no rain in sight, a wide blue sky, and large fluffy clouds that looked like my big puffed up pillows.

If Ray was going to be anywhere up there inspecting his garden, then I was pretty sure he would be lounging around on one of those pillows, a clay pipe in hand, as if in an opium den. I fed my old cat Arthur who, crouched at his bowl now, had earlier been climbing my legs in his eagerness to tell me that he was hungry and wanted his breakfast.

I had just put on my jacket and was checking my bag for purse, phone, and car keys, all ready for my trip to Cobby, when the doorbell rang. I frowned, wondering who it could be, and as I walked to the door several thoughts ran through my head. Could it be the postman with a special delivery? Had I ordered something online? Some more books? Some more clothes? Shoes—to go with the many pairs I already had? I couldn't think of a thing.

I swung the door open and there stood Lauren, one hand gripped tightly around the handle of a stroller, her face mutinous and her strange, almost sightless looking eyes screwed up against a sudden shaft of sunlight that fell across her pretty face. Her lovely blonde hair fell in waves across the shoulders of a vivid pink coat. Needless to say, she didn't give me her wide red smile.

"Well," she said as she stood there, her whole stance angry and frustrated. "If the mountain won't come to Mohammed, then Mohammed will come to the mountain." The quote reminded me so much of Lynette that, even though I tried not to, I began to smile. "Oh, smiling are you?" she said. "What is it with you, Maggie? You're all friendly with me, I try to help you get back with Stephen, Vanessa, and Jake—you even help me to have my baby—and then suddenly you dump me. What are you playing at?"

"Oh Lauren," I said helplessly. "I haven't dumped you. I—"

Sensing something behind her, a whisper, a movement, Lauren turned around to see a couple of nosey parkers standing in the garden opposite, arms folded, glancing from the sides of their eyes, obviously taking a great interest in the drama that seemed to be unfolding right in front of them. At Lauren's light blue sightless glare, they all looked away. Turning back to me, she hissed quietly, "Aren't you going to let me in, Maggie?"

"Of course, of course," I said, ushering her in, helping her maneuver the stroller up the two small steps and into the hallway. I caught a glimpse of dark springy hair and a cute turned up nose as she wheeled her in. I shut the front door with a firm click while Lauren, bending down, unstrapped the baby and, lifting her up, placed her in my arms.

"There you go, Maggie," she said briskly. "There's the child that you brought into the world nearly three weeks ago. Yet you haven't even bothered to visit her once." Her voice sounded choked then, as if she couldn't say anything else.

I looked down at Rebecca, at the dark springy hair and the cute turned up nose, and then at her eyes, the color of blackberries in September, that stared at me as if she knew me, that she knew who I was and knew everything about me. I felt the weight and the warmth of her against my body, and the milky smell that wafted from her skin and her clothes.

"Oh my God," I said. "I'm so sorry. Come in here, Lauren."

She followed me into the sitting room where we sat on the settee, Rebecca now laid out in a star on my lap. I tried to explain how I felt about Stephen, and how he hadn't wanted me to be a part of his family, and that I didn't want him to change his mind and make me a part of that family just because of what had happened with the baby. I then told her about the decision that I'd made that very morning to go into

Cobby to buy Rebecca a present, and after that the plan to visit them.

Thankfully, she nodded as if she understood everything, and I went into the kitchen to make us a drink while Lauren fed the baby. I put the mugs of hot coffee and a plate of biscuits on a tray and went back into the sitting room where Lauren, Rebecca at her breast, sat in the wing chair that had always been Ray's.

"Vanessa and Lucy wanted to come with me today, you know," she said as I sipped my coffee and took a bite of a digestive biscuit. "But I wanted to come on my own. I wanted you all to myself. I've missed you, Maggie."

"I've missed you too, Lauren," I said. "I'm so glad that you're here – and Rebecca. She's a beautiful little girl, and I am sorry, Lauren. I know I should have contacted you sooner."

"You're forgiven," she said. "In a strange way I understand exactly what you're saying."

"Good," I said. "I thought that you would."

She took Rebecca away from her breast and, laying her across her shoulder, gently rubbed her back. The baby looked dozy and sated, her pretty mouth wide open. "Stephen does want you though. He has for a long time, and it's not just because of what happened the day Rebecca was born. He misses you and wants you."

My heart leapt at those words, but I still, for some strange reason, had reservations. "Perhaps I'll feel differently when this business with Stella Atkins is cleared up," I told her. "I'm hoping to see Stephen about it tomorrow."

Lauren looked at me and frowned. "But I thought that was all finished with. Hasn't Stella Atkins dropped those stupid accusations against you?" I must have looked suitably confused, because Lauren then said, "Oh dear, maybe I wasn't supposed to say anything. Maybe Stephen wants to tell you himself."

My phone beeped, indicating that a text was coming through, and we both jumped. I looked at the screen, narrowing my eyes, trying to read the message even though I wasn't wearing my reading glasses.

"Is it from Stephen?" asked Lauren with a giggle. "If it is, I bet his ears have been burning." She rocked Rebecca in her arms backwards and forwards, backwards and forwards. The baby was whimpering a little, a bit cranky, a thin stream of milk encircling her rosebud mouth that, with a fingertip, Lauren wiped away.

The message, unfortunately, wasn't from Stephen, but from James Jamieson.

Hey Mags, any thoughts on nite out yet? If you have, give em to me baby!

Chapter Sixteen

A large white banner, Cobby Fun Run emblazoned in thick black letters with the Hale & Hearty logo of the orange running man and woman alongside it, was strung tightly between the trees on the village green. It was a bright December morning, the sky blue and the sun a muted yellow glow behind clouds that resembled skeins of white cotton. Festive decorations sparkled along High Street, and small twinkling Christmas trees adorned each shop front. Cobby was beautifully dressed for the Fun Run. Clad in fluorescent jackets, Kath and I, and all the volunteer councilors, darted about amongst the runners, giving out hearty words of encouragement.

Little groups of Lycra clad runners jogged up and down on the spot, rubbing their hands together and puffing freezing cold air from their mouths as they spoke. I noticed a lot of Father and Mother Christmases, their bright suits standing out like red stains against the frosty whiteness. Silver clad fairies fluttered their wands, and there were plenty of roly poly Christmas puddings, their faces white ovals against deep brown, brightened by sprigs of holly and mistletoe.

I'd already spoken to Rob and Melanie who, true to their word, had brought a massive group of runners from Hale & Hearty gym. Melanie had introduced me to several people, including Kate and Sue and Jaz, who she had walked the Dalesway with, and the Three Peaks, and even the Pennine Way, which she said had been a very enjoyable challenge. Lauren and Vanessa had come to watch Lucy run—I didn't even know she was a runner—and Rebecca was sleeping soundly in her stroller, which was decorated for the occasion with red and silver tinsel twined around the handle like a barber shop pole, and brightly colored baubles that swung gaily from the hood.

Even Mum, wearing her strange snarling wolves jacket, was there, holding on to Lynette who, head swiveling like the girl in *The Exorcist*, watched her grandchildren running around like mini tornados and asking so many questions. "Why are you wearing a bright yellow coat, Aunty Maggie?" "Why aren't you running, Aunty Maggie?" "Are they running soon, Aunty Maggie?" "Why are other people wearing yellow coats, Aunty Maggie?"

A sudden hush descended over the village green as the mayor, Councilor Iqbal, resplendent in his mayoral chains and finery, ascended to the little makeshift stage He raised a hand and the crowd went wild. There was a short silence, then a deafening squeal from the microphone before the mayor launched into his speech.

"Thank you all for attending the COBBY FUN RUN!" There was another wild cheer from the crowd. "Remember, runners—you have a choice. You can throw in the towel—or use it to wipe your face! GOOD LUCK EVERYBODY!"

I thought about the event that evening as I sat in front of the fire, sipping from a glass of wine, my old cat Arthur curled up in a tight ball next to me. I remembered the general good luck shouts from the crowd as the runners set off at a steady jog, the ungainly gait of the Mother and Father Christmases totally at odds with the delicate steps of the fairies and pointy eared elves, and the gentle roll of the Christmas puddings.

What a great day it had been. I felt proud to be a councilor, and glad too that we had joined forces with Hale & Hearty Gym. Both Rob and Melanie had suggested that we put on another Fun Run, as everybody seemed to enjoy it so much—maybe an Easter one, which would give us plenty of time to organize it.

I checked my phone yet again for messages. It was becoming an obsession, but all I wanted was a reply from Stephen to the text that I had sent him that morning asking if it was true that Stella Atkins had dropped all the accusations against me. There had been no reply, just a blank screen desperately waiting to be filled with comforting words of reassurance. I kept imagining the little envelope icon appearing as if by magic, and all my worries dissolving into the air like the smoke from Mum's fire that wound its mysterious way up the chimney.

I glanced at the fireplace, where a real paper envelope and not a little icon on a screen was propped up against a black cat ornament that Ray had bought me for our twentieth wedding anniversary. It was an invitation to Rebecca's christening, which was to take place the following week in the little church in Cobby. The tiny ancient church where I had said my goodbyes to Ray almost four years before, and where Kath had bade farewell to her Johnny.

My old cat Arthur twitched in his sleep as my phone beeped, bringing me out of my reverie. I grabbed it straight away and, looking at the screen intently, saw that it was at last a text message from Stephen. It read, *Hi Maggie sorry for the delay in replying, but....*

~*~

It had been snowing and the path leading to the massive oak door of Cobby's tiny church was covered in a blinding white layer, unmarked except for the tiny fork like footprints of birds. The sun shone glaringly white in a deep blue sky yet the air was cold, bitingly cold, and stung my face as I walked through the graveyard, my boots creaking on the ice and snow. I felt sure that there had never been such beautiful snowy weather as this in time for Christmas.

A workman, his spade harshly scraping the ground, was clearing the path, the bird prints disappearing as he worked. A lone robin, its red breast startling against the misty white, hopped among the branches of the trees, dislodging tiny flakes that drifted down to settle softly on the workman's cap.

I shivered, hunching into the collar of my long black coat and fleecy red scarf. I wore a hat that looked, said Lynette, like a big fluffy black cat curled upon my head. "And yet it suits you, Maggie, it really does." Compliment or insult? Whatever, I'd have to tell Lynette this one. "We are prepared for insults, but compliments leave us baffled."

People stood in a huddle at the church door and, looking closely, I saw the tall figure of Jake, his arm around Lauren's waist, who held Rebecca, a tightly wrapped pink bundle. I saw Vanessa and Lucy, but where was Stephen? I couldn't see Stephen. He had to be there; surely he wouldn't miss his first grandchild's christening. There were people that I didn't recognize—friends of Jake and Lauren's? Other family members? Aunty Violet, Uncle Ted, Cousin Rose? Who knows!

Nervous about seeing Stephen, but Jake in particular, I lingered at Ray's stone, putting off the time of our meeting. The angel rose above me, her eyes looking up to Heaven, always looking to Heaven, always and forever. I tried to wipe away the snow that was packed into her empty sockets, but it clung stubbornly like tiny particles of sugar. The sweet voices of children singing carols echoed from the church, bringing a sudden spurt of tears to my eyes that somehow became lodged in my throat, making it difficult to breathe.

I walked on through the graveyard, past the great yew with its massive centuries old trunk, stopping just for a moment to look at the initials entwined within a heart shape that Mum and Dad had carved into the bark in their heady courting days. With a pang of nostalgia I thought of Mum, and of all the years that she'd had to endure without Dad, and the fact that she'd never met anyone else, "Well, nobody worth bothering about," she had often said.

Glancing up, I could see Stephen now standing with the rest of the party at the church door. He wore his long black overcoat and black leather gloves. I watched him as he bent over Rebecca, tickling her chin, kissing her cheek. I imagined his sherry brown eyes shining in the hazy light and the alluring dimple in his chin. My need for him was so great, so consuming, that if I closed my eyes, I could almost feel his lips against mine.

I watched them file into the church, Stephen going in last, glancing over his shoulder, his gaze searching, as if he was looking for somebody. Silently I went in, seating myself in a pew at the back. Organ music played softly and I could see the children singing in the choir, their long white robes fluted around their necks like chocolates in a box. Sunlight fell softly through the tall arched windows, throwing lozenges of color all around the rough white painted walls, and a real Christmas tree, feathery green and aromatic, glittered in a corner.

Making sure that my phone was switched off, I pulled it from my bag, hesitating just for a moment with the urge to re-read Stephen's text message from last night.

Hi Maggie, sorry for the delay in replying but I've only just got home from conference and phone wasn't charged! No worries now, Stella Atkins has dropped all accusations against you, she didn't have a leg to stand on! She handed in notice at work too. Will tell you all details on Sunday. Please be there. I'd love to see you S x

I felt as if a weight had been lifted, as if the whole world had been balancing on my shoulders and now it was gone. Thank God! Stella Atkins had dropped the accusations, and as a wonderful bonus she had handed in her notice at work. No longer would I have to endure her wiggling about the office like a predatory snake, or guarding Stephen's office like a loathsome spider in a web.

I felt a gentle tap on my shoulder, making me jump and, looking up in surprise, came face to face with Jake. He looked so much like the Stephen from years ago that I felt as if I'd gone back in time and was sitting in a math class in Cobby High School, totally besotted with the back of somebody's head. As he smiled at me, he held out his hand and said, "Please Maggie, come and join the family."

My hand grasped his and I held on tight, as if it were a lifeline, as he led me tip tapping across the stone flagged floor to sit thigh to thigh next to Stephen.

~*~

"We'd love you to be Rebecca's godmother," said Lauren as we sat chatting in the Star Pub after the ceremony in the church. The pub was festive and cozy, a real fire crackling in the fireplace. We sat at a table in the large bay window so we could see all of Cobby going about their daily business. I glanced at Rebecca, who lay in Lauren's arms, and thought of her face, all red and scrunched as she slipped so quietly onto the bed of Bloomers uniforms.

"Yes," agreed Jake. "There's nobody else that could possibly do the job."

I sipped my wine, a hot blush suffusing my face, but this time with pleasure and not embarrassment or shame. "I don't know what to say," I said. "Except thank you, of course, and yes, I'd like that very much."

Stephen raised his pint and said simply, "To Maggie." He drank his Landlord bitter heartily, foam coating his upper lip, which he immediately licked off, making my heart beat just that little bit faster. "I dread to think what would have happened if you hadn't been with Lauren on the day that Rebecca was born."

"Yes, what a day," said Vanessa. "But Maggie kept a cool

head throughout."

"Well," I replied. "Maybe not that cool. But can I just say…." I looked around at their eager expectant faces, all of them hanging on to my every word, wondering what I was going to say. "I don't want you to welcome me into the family just because of what happened on the day Rebecca was born. I need you all to want me for myself." My voice trailed away and I blushed again, a blush so hot and red I swear they could have fried eggs on my cheeks.

"Of course I want you for yourself, Maggie," said Lauren, putting a comforting arm around my shoulders. "You're my friend."

"And mine," piped up Vanessa and Lucy.

Jake, placing his hand on my shoulder, said, "Maggie, truly, I couldn't wish for anyone better to be with my dad. I behaved badly on the night of the dinner party, and I'm sorry. I have been for some time, a long time before Rebecca was born. I just didn't know how to say it."

There was a sudden whirr and a click as the old-fashioned jukebox sprang to life and a familiar tune began to play. "Oh," I said. "I haven't heard this for ages. It's 'The Love Affair.'" Stephen and I looked at each other and smiled.

"Bringing on back the good times…," he said to me.

~*~

Later, heading home, we walked along Cobby High Street, slipping a little on the icy paths. My hand was holding tightly to Stephen's arm, reminding me of the day that I saw him with Stella Atkins in the school parking lot, her hand hooked over his arm like a claw—the day that I thought they were a couple and that Stephen didn't want me anymore.

The afternoon had turned into evening and the sky arched above us, black and glittering with stars, and the moon hanging like a great silver disc illuminated the snow covered bushes and boney trees. I felt a warm glow inside me radiating outwards from my chest, along my arms and my fingers, and then spreading like the branches of a tree down into my stomach and my legs and to the very tips of my toes. I was hoping that the feeling was happiness, but I had my suspicions that it could also be the effect of the two glasses of red wine that I had drunk earlier in the Star Pub.

I thought of all the good things that were new in my life; my job in the school, becoming a councilor, Kath, Lauren and Jake and baby Rebecca, Vanessa and Lucy, Rob and Melanie—James Jamieson?—and of course, Stephen. And then I remembered the good things that I'd had already; Mum, memories of Dad, Lynette and Dave and all my nieces and nephews, Bloomers the Bakers, and of course my old cat Arthur and my memories of Ray that would never die. Yes, life was good and, glancing sideways at Stephen, I suspected that it might get even better.

Hand in hand we meandered past Bumps a Daisy, where I'd recently bought Rebecca's tiny outfits, past the old-fashioned shop fronts of Sweet Things, Ye Old Wineo, and Lynette's workplace, Bedrock & Rose. Cobby's tiny ancient church squatted low in the gloom like a pouncing cat, and in the graveyard headstones gleamed like very white teeth. A group of people dressed up for a night out slithered along the pavement.

My garden glimmered in the moonlight that lit up the weed free borders, tightly clipped hedging, and the lawn covered with a layer of snow as white as the icing on Rebecca's christening cake. How glad I was that I'd made an effort to tidy it. I stopped at the garden gate, a curly wrought iron affair that Ray had always liked, and said, "Well, this is me. Would you like to come in for a coffee?"

Stephen followed me along the snowy path, our boot prints marring its perfect smoothness, when suddenly he stopped and, snaking his arm around my waist, pulled me close. "Maggie, have you ever had the irresistible urge to become a headmaster's wife?" Tiny white flakes of snow swirled through the air.

I gazed up at him, at his sherry brown eyes and at the lovely dimple in his chin. "Hmm. Well...." I frowned, pretending to think about his question, remembering the day that I caught Kath's bouquet and what it was supposed to mean, before saying with a little smile, "I think it could be quite an education."

I felt his breath hot against my cheek, his mouth so deliciously close to mine. "Ah. Well, in that case, I could soon be having lots of fun educating Maggie." His mouth, coming ever closer and closer, finally found mine.

THE END

About the Author

Debbie Chase (married name Debbie Spink) was born in Emsworth in Hampshire in 1959, although she has lived in West Yorkshire since 1979. She is the eldest of five children (two sisters and two brothers) and has many nieces and nephews, great nieces and nephews, aunties, uncles and cousins, having come from a very large family. She has been married since 1984 and has one daughter, Lara and two cats Ruby and Teddy.

She has always been a reader and has enjoyed writing since school. Her proudest moment being when she achieved an A+ for an essay! She has had many short stories and poems for adults and children published in books and magazines. She has written four books, the first being part fact/part fiction and called "You to Me Are Everything." The second book based on a real life pet sitting job is called "The Confessions of a Pet Sitter (from the Pet's Point of View) and the third, the sequel to that book, "What A Catastrophe (Teddy's Tale). The fourth book is a book of poems. All four books are available to buy on Amazon as a paperback or kindle. She has also had two pocket novels ("Planning on Love" and "Romance on the Run") published with My Weekly magazine.

Her other hobbies are running, walking, swimming, yoga, pilates and Tai Chi. After many years of office work she is now partially retired and works part time in a baker's shop and is also an Examination Invigilator in a local school!

Printed in Dunstable, United Kingdom

77913698R00109